W9-CEI-814

Advance Praise for *Multichannel Marketing*

If the past decade has been marked by widespread adoption of online marketing channels, the future must surely witness better integration of online and offline interactions. Customers want complete flexibility to use the channels that suit them best. Multichannel Marketing *provides excellent down-to-earth insights on how to move from theory to practice, enabling customer-centric engagement while delivering a solid marketing ROI.*
  —BOB THOMPSON, Founder and CEO, CustomerThink Corp.

In your pursuit to measure and manage the TRUE *impact of marketing, you must read* Multichannel Marketing *and put its good advice to practice. Akin Arikan provides excellent insight into the terminology, measurement techniques, and best practices necessary to get online and offline marketing managers aligned and working collaboratively toward improving marketing profitability.*
  —JIM LENSKOLD, President of Lenskold Group and author of *Marketing ROI*

With multichannel marketing emerging as the next big challenge for today's enterprise, Multichannel Marketing: Metrics and Methods for On and Offline Success *provides the in-depth knowledge needed for building a successful multichannel marketing program. Akin's straightforward approach to a complex topic will bring many actionable insights to the student of multichannel marketing.*
  —JOSH MANION, CEO, web analytics consultancy Stratigent

"Integrated marketing" has become a buzz phrase that marketers set as an ideal but struggle to act upon beyond a single campaign with multiple components. This book seeks to change that by introducing marketers from disparate disciplines to one another, making a clear and compelling case around why it makes sense for them to pool their efforts, and providing realistic approaches and practical tools to help them get beyond campaign and channel-centric approaches and move towards multichannel and customer-centric approaches. Way to go, Akin!
  —ELANA ANDERSON, Marketing Strategy Consultant, NxtERA Marketing

If you operate your company online (web, e-mail, etc.), you are multichannel. If your company has both on- and off-line touchpoints (store, website, catalog, call center, etc.), you are a multichannel company. If you are a multichannel company, you need to read this book. Whether you are just starting to create and analyze multichannel metrics, or have been doing it for years, this book codifies best practices in multichannel analytics.
  —JACK AARONSON, Multichannel Marketing Expert and
    CEO of The Aaronson Group

i ■ INTRODUCTION

As my good friend David Hughes says, we live in a "nonline" world—move over offline and online!! There is little you do with your offline efforts that won't impact your online presence—vice versa, anything you do online will have an offline impact. We have all struggled to measure the holistic impact of our marketing efforts in this nonline world. But we are lucky to have someone of Akin's intellect and experience to show us how. This book will erase a lot of your headaches!

—AVINASH KAUSHIK, author of *Web Analytics: An Hour A Day* and the *Occam's Razor* blog

Multichannel Marketing

Multichannel Marketing

Metrics and Methods for On and Offline Success

AKIN ARIKAN

Wiley Publishing, Inc.

Acquisitions Editor: WILLEM KNIBBE
Development Editor: PETE GAUGHAN
Production Editor: ELIZABETH GINNS BRITTEN
Copy Editor: KATHY GRIDER CARLYLE
Production Manager: TIM TATE
Vice President and Executive Group Publisher: RICHARD SWADLEY
Vice President and Executive Publisher: JOSEPH B. WIKERT
Vice President and Publisher: NEIL EDDE
Compositor: KATE KAMINSKI, HAPPENSTANCE TYPE-O-RAMA
Proofreader: RACHEL GUNN
Indexer: NANCY GUENTHER
Cover Designer: RYAN SNEED
Cover Image: ©TOM NULENS/ISTOCKPHOTO

Copyright © 2008 by Wiley Publishing, Inc., Indianapolis, Indiana

Published simultaneously in Canada

ISBN-13: 978-0-470-23959-9

ISBN-10: 0-470-23959-X

No part of this publication may be reproduced, stored in a retrieval system or transmitted in any form or by any means, electronic, mechanical, photocopying, recording, scanning or otherwise, except as permitted under Sections 107 or 108 of the 1976 United States Copyright Act, without either the prior written permission of the Publisher, or authorization through payment of the appropriate per-copy fee to the Copyright Clearance Center, 222 Rosewood Drive, Danvers, MA 01923, (978) 750-8400, fax (978) 646-8600. Requests to the Publisher for permission should be addressed to the Legal Department, Wiley Publishing, Inc., 10475 Crosspoint Blvd., Indianapolis, IN 46256, (317) 572-3447, fax (317) 572-4355, or online at http://www.wiley.com/go/permissions.

Limit of Liability/Disclaimer of Warranty: The publisher and the author make no representations or warranties with respect to the accuracy or completeness of the contents of this work and specifically disclaim all warranties, including without limitation warranties of fitness for a particular purpose. No warranty may be created or extended by sales or promotional materials. The advice and strategies contained herein may not be suitable for every situation. This work is sold with the understanding that the publisher is not engaged in rendering legal, accounting, or other professional services. If professional assistance is required, the services of a competent professional person should be sought. Neither the publisher nor the author shall be liable for damages arising herefrom. The fact that an organization or website is referred to in this work as a citation and/or a potential source of further information does not mean that the author or the publisher endorses the information the organization or website may provide or recommendations it may make. Further, readers should be aware that Internet websites listed in this work may have changed or disappeared between when this work was written and when it is read.

For general information on our other products and services or to obtain technical support, please contact our Customer Care Department within the U.S. at (800) 762-2974, outside the U.S. at (317) 572-3993 or fax (317) 572-4002.

Wiley also publishes its books in a variety of electronic formats. Some content that appears in print may not be available in electronic books.

Library of Congress Cataloging-in-Publication Data:

Arikan, Akin, 1969-

  Multichannel marketing : metrics and methods for on and offline success / Akin Arikan. — 1st ed.

    p. cm.

  ISBN 978-0-470-23959-9 (paper/website)

  1. Internet marketing. 2. Multilevel marketing. I. Title.

  HF5415.1265.A75 2008

  658.8'72—dc22

                                    2008008356

TRADEMARKS: Wiley, the Wiley logo, and the Sybex logo are trademarks or registered trademarks of John Wiley & Sons, Inc. and/or its affiliates, in the United States and other countries, and may not be used without written permission. All other trademarks are the property of their respective owners. Wiley Publishing, Inc., is not associated with any product or vendor mentioned in this book.

10 9 8 7 6 5 4 3 2 1

Dear Reader,

Thank you for choosing *Multichannel Marketing: Metrics and Methods for On and Offline Success*. This book is part of a family of premium quality Sybex books, all written by outstanding authors who combine practical experience with a gift for teaching.

Sybex was founded in 1976. More than thirty years later, we're still committed to producing consistently exceptional books. With each of our titles we're working hard to set a new standard for the industry. From the authors we work with, to the paper we print on, our goal is to bring you the best books available.

I hope you see all that reflected in these pages. I'd be very interested to hear your comments and get your feedback on how we're doing. Feel free to let me know what you think about this or any other Sybex book by sending me an e-mail at nedde@wiley.com, or if you think you've found a technical error in this book, please visit http://sybex.custhelp.com. Customer feedback is critical to our efforts at Sybex.

Best regards,

Neil Edde
Vice President and Publisher
Sybex, an Imprint of Wiley

May the better marketer win

 # Acknowledgments

When you stand at the rim of the Grand Canyon in Arizona, it merely looks *somewhat* grand at first. Only after you have had a chance to make the pilgrimage down into the canyon and back out do you realize just how grand it really is. Well, it has been a similar experience working with the many editors and contributors to the book in your hands. I have come to appreciate marketers' brilliance so much more in the process of learning from these folks. I wish I could build them a Mount Rushmore–sized "thank you!" for their mentoring, hand holding, and tutoring.

The first thank-you must go to our customers at Unica Corporation who have worked with us over the years and many of whom have shared their experiences for this book. Without them I would know nothing useful to report.

Judah Philips, director of Web Analytics at Reed Business, has been one of the technical editors for this project. Many in the industry know Judah as one of the nation's sharpest web analysts. He also is an ardent blogger (judah.webanalyticsdemystified.com) and writes a column on the MediaPost. We expect many more great things to come from his pen in future years. For this book, he deserves the Oscar for attention to detail and for calling me back to the carpet many times over.

Entrepreneur Frank Faubert has been the second technical editor. He is best known for his decade-long work as co-founder of web analytics software company Sane Solutions. I received my Internet-marketing education while working at his company. Anyone who has worked with Frank cannot help but be amazed at the amount of productivity coming out of this one person. When Frank is in high gear he radiates so much energy that I am convinced the Earth's gravitational field bends around him. For this book, Frank deserves the Golden Eagle for his precision edits during the technical-editing process.

Kevin Cavanaugh is a colleague at Unica and a veteran in the marketing industry. He has one leg firmly in the online space and another in the relationship marketing world. That is why I think of Kevin as *the* Mr. Multichannel—i.e., a prototype for multichannel marketers of the future. He has been my teacher and mentor in all things regarding direct and relationship marketing.

Pat LaPointe is the author of *Marketing by the Dashboard Light* and managing partner at MarketingNPV, a specialist firm focused on determining the financial returns from marketing investments for their clients. Their website MarketingNPV.com is an amazing resource for insights into marketing measurement. Thank you, Pat, specifically for your guidance on brand marketing measurement. The same thank-you also goes to two more of my colleagues at Unica, Jay Henderson and Bill Phelan. I am amazed at their multidisciplinary resourcefulness. Without their tutoring I would not even have known what I did not know.

Many more colleagues at Unica have volunteered their time to help during various stages of the project, especially Amartya Bhattacharjya, Andrew Hally, BJ Morgan, Brian Perry, Karen Hudgins, and Kerry Reilly. In fact I owe the entire idea for this book to the fertile grounds that I found working among the marketing enthusiasts who are my colleagues.

The Wiley book team deserves the greatest appreciation for turning what used to be a vague dream into a real book fit for human consumption. Most notably, thanks go to Willem Knibbe, Pete Gaughan, Liz Britten, and their many behind-the-scenes helpers.

Finally, I did not come here alone but was propelled by the support of my wife and family throughout the years. Thank you for bearing with the inevitable toll on family life during the six months of writing. I love you very much!

About the Author

Akin Arikan lives in San Francisco and is a fan of multi-channel metrics and an evangelist for the use of intelligent software solutions for creating more successful businesses with more satisfied customers. Currently, Akin is senior segment manager for internet marketing at Unica, a provider of Enterprise Marketing Management software. He is responsible for ensuring customer satisfaction with Unica's web analytics and internet marketing solutions.

Akin has been working with web analytics practitioners since 1999, serving clients across insurance, banking, retail, telecommunications, and travel industries. Akin also frequently writes magazine articles and is a highly praised speaker and panelist at such trade shows as Search Engine Strategies, eMetrics Marketing Optimization Summit, net.finance, and Web 2.0 Expo.

Previously, Akin developed analytical enterprise applications at business intelligence software vendor MicroStrategy. It was through the great people of MicroStrategy that Akin received his professional introduction to business intelligence and data warehousing practices. Akin has a degree in computer science and business administration from the University of Hamburg, Germany.

Foreword

By Don Peppers and Martha Rogers, Ph.D.

The single most important step in becoming a more customer-centric firm—with a stronger brand franchise, a more loyal and valuable customer base, more resilient and innovative policies, and better prospects for future growth—is to put yourself in the customer's own shoes and try to experience doing business with your company the way the customer does. In other words, rather than seeing your business from the inside-out perspective of the products and services you sell, you need to see it from the outside-in perspective of the customers whose needs you're trying to meet.

This axiomatic principle, that success requires taking the customer's point of view, underlies nearly every best practice in modern marketing.

Customers are the source of all value for a business. No business can create shareholder value without a customer being involved, in one form or another. Customers are an indispensable element of the very definition of the word "business." And leading-edge companies realize that customers are not as plentiful as they may once have been thought to be. When you lose a customer, or an opportunity to acquire a customer, you can't simply replace that customer with the next one. There is no secondary market for customers. You can't go to a bank, borrow some customers, and then pay them back with interest. Whatever value your business creates, you have to create it by using the customers and prospective customers available to you. So a smart company will try to create as much value as possible from each customer.

There are two ways that customers can create value for a business. The most obvious and immediately measurable way a customer creates value is by buying things in the current period. This is how sales and earnings are tabulated and reported.

But in addition, a customer can change his intent or likelihood to buy in the future, based on his current experience. This is a value-creating event that many firms simply overlook. Suppose, for example, that a customer calls your firm to complain, but for some reason the complaint isn't resolved, and the customer hangs up the phone angry. In that event, the customer's lifetime value will decline *immediately*, because the amount of future cash flow you predicted from that customer, prior to the call, must now be adjusted downward. You won't see the cash effect of that decline in value until some time in the future, but the actual value destruction occurred with the customer's phone call.

Initiatives designed to generate current-period earnings from a customer can often conflict with increasing the long-term business that the customer might also generate—including not only repeat purchases, but additional product lines, reduced service costs, and (more important than ever these days) referrals of other customers. Market too aggressively, in order to pump your current sales up and you may cannibalize future business, or—even worse—you may irritate your customers into not wanting to listen to any more of your solicitations. On the other hand, if you invest too heavily in providing great service today, in order to improve your customer's loyalty (and lifetime value), how do you know whether you'll be able to recover these costs fully with future business?

As a result, if you want your business to be successful over the long term, then you have to balance your marketing and sales efforts carefully, always seeking to "optimize" the mix of immediate sales and future value.

Because customers are scarce, the most critical productive resource any business has is its base of customers and prospects. The most direct way for a firm to maximize the overall value it creates for shareholders is to optimize the short-term and long-term value each customer creates for the business.

Of course, customers make their own decisions with respect to whether and how much to buy from you. The value any individual customer creates for your business will be determined by the overall experience the customer has with your brand, including all the various marketing messages received, offers considered, interactions undertaken, and purchases made. And if you stop and think about how each customer experiences your brand, along with all the marketing efforts you engage in to affect this experience, you'll realize that the customer doesn't categorize the various marketing channels you use into different brand experiences. Rather, each individual customer will categorize these messages and interactions into the *same* experience, the customer's individual, overall experience of your brand.

In other words, it makes no difference to your customer whether you are an effective multichannel marketer or not. The customer—every customer—is still going to be a multichannel consumer.

For this reason, if you just consider what it takes to manage your business rationally, the case for coordinating, measuring, and managing all the various channels through which you touch and interact with an individual customer is as obvious as the nose on your CMO's face. There simply is no more direct way for your business to generate profit and create shareholder value, than by managing each customer's individual experience of your brand, across all the various channels of interaction.

But this isn't a book about the *what, when,* or *why* of multichannel marketing. This is a *how to* book. And what a "how to" it is, too. There's more "how to" in this book than you may realize you need. But if you work in any kind of modern marketing environment today, then within these pages are the answers to a great many of the questions you've probably asked yourself within just the last few weeks, as you've tried to allocate resources and make rational choices with respect to your own company's marketing efforts:

- How should you reconcile the costs and benefits of both a keyword search initiative and a comparison-shopping engine?

- How can you best use a website to capture responses to a print ad or a television commercial?

- How do you calculate the amount of spot television spending you should reallocate to fund your online initiatives? Or should you perhaps slim down your online budget to beef up your spot TV purchases?

- How can you determine which print, radio, or television promotion stimulated a customer to visit your website? And what's the best method for determining where your online visitor is coming from, geographically?

- What tried and true methods of batch-processed direct marketing should (or should not) be applied to the interactive or e-mail marketing program you're trying to launch?

- How can you use e-mail marketing, or any other channel, to boost the retention rate for visitors to your website?

- How should you ensure that your direct mail campaign and your online marketing initiative reinforce each other?

Face it: Multichannel marketing is steadily becoming more and more "multi." Every day, it seems, someone invents a new way to communicate or interact with customers, whether it's location-specific mobile phone messaging, or one-to-one messaging based on the flight reservations you just made, or variable point-of-sale offers, or viral messaging within social networks, or video monitors in bars, airports, gas stations, taxi cabs, and even restrooms.

The marketing task is getting steadily more complex. If you want to continue with a career in marketing, you're just going to have to deal with it. And you can start by reading the rest of this book to learn *how* to deal with it.

Don Peppers and Martha Rogers founded Peppers & Rogers Group, and have written eight books on customer strategy that have collectively sold more than 1 million copies in 17 languages. Their most recent book is Rules to Break and Laws to Follow: How Your Business Can Beat the Crisis of Short-Termism *(Wiley, 2008).*

Contents

CONTENTS ■

Introduction

My aim with *Multichannel Marketing* is to provide a missing key for unlocking the most anticipated marketing strategies of our days. Namely, the rise of "customer-centric marketing" (where the customer, not the product or marketing campaign, is the focus) places a premium on marketers having a deep understanding of their customers. Yet, just as companies were beginning to figure out how to turn "customer-centricity" into reality, the goal posts for achieving it have been moved further away. For crying out loud! As if it had been easy earlier! What is to blame for the new hurdle? It is the multichannel revolution—i.e., the constant birth of new avenues for interacting with companies and their marketing messages, especially online.

While many marketers are still stunned with the plethora of new channels that have sprung up in recent years, customers have long since integrated them into their relationships. Therefore, customer-centricity now asks marketers to understand customer relationships that span online and offline channels. However, weaving together disparate customer insights and marketing metrics from multiple channels is something that few marketers have tried and even fewer mastered. Worse than that, most marketing organizations continue to be split across online and offline channels as if their customers were still from the 1990s.

Without overcoming the chasm between multiple channels, marketers cannot understand true ROI of their marketing initiatives, will miss opportunities for improving their results, and will certainly fail to achieve customer-centricity. This book aims to provide the key for overcoming the chasm, namely practical methods for integrating marketing metrics and actions across online and offline channels.

Who Should Read This Book

The book is intended for marketers who are down in the trenches, responsible for creating marketing programs and assessing their outcomes. It is especially for marketers who have had enough of the artificial divide between online and offline channels and who seek practical advice for bringing together what belongs together.

For some of these marketers, the goal will simply be to better understand the outcomes of marketing programs by measuring results across all channels. For others, the goal will be to contribute to a better customer experience by basing marketing communications on a more complete understanding of customers. The marketers may be from any of the disciplines within marketing teams, namely:

- Online marketers who realize that many of the visitors to their websites come there because of impulses from offline interactions with their companies. The same online marketers may also recognize that the fruits of their work will often only be harvested in the form of purchases that customers complete offline following their online research.

- Direct marketers who comprehend that the response to their campaigns increasingly often occurs online through the website. The success of direct marketing efforts directly hinges on these customers' experiences while online. The same direct marketers will also appreciate that analytics on customers' behavior on the website provides a rich lather of behavioral data for targeting marketing efforts.
- Brand marketers who see that their target audiences are spending an increasing amount of their time on online channels. For them, it would be a crime not to translate that observation into advertising campaigns that are integrated across online and offline channels. These brand marketers may also observe that advertising online is different from traditional advertising channels. Namely, the direct response nature and better measurability of the medium bears hope for refining advertising programs by drawing on online and direct marketing principles.

What You Will Learn

Readers coming from any of these corners within their marketing teams can extend their knowledge as to:

- How online, direct, and brand marketers have been practicing multichannel marketing analytics each within their own disciplines.
- How the multiple multichannel methods from these three marketing disciplines can be amalgamated for an integrated view of marketing success and customer insights across on and offline channels.
- How integrated multichannel metrics and customer insights can then be employed for greater marketing success across on and offline channels.

The metric that will tell whether this book has been successful in achieving its purpose will be the number of earmarks that you may make for recipes that you wish to apply to your own marketing campaigns. If I can have the pleasure of meeting you one day, I very much hope to find your book full of page markers, flags, arrows, and with torn-out pages that you may have pinned up by the water cooler.

What Is Covered in This Book

Multichannel Marketing: Metrics and Methods for On and Offline Success is organized in three parts to address exactly the three learning goals stated above.

Part I: Building Blocks for Multichannel Metrics will look over the shoulders of web analysts, direct marketers, and brand advertisers as they solve multichannel measurements and metrics problems within their own confines. But first, we will begin by exploring today's marketing landscape to discuss the role and importance of multichannel metrics.

Chapter 1: With Great Opportunity Come Great Challenges will describe the opportunities for the marketer who can master multichannel marketing metrics and methods.

Chapter 2: The Web Analyst Tackles Multichannel Metrics Online provides an overview of web analytics methods for connecting the dots from online marketing channels of all kinds to the website and over multiple site sessions all the way to the sales events that ultimately ensue.

Chapter 3: The Offline Marketer's Bag of Tricks compares the viewpoints of online and offline marketers to highlight how they differ from each other and why that may be.

Chapter 4: The Direct Marketer Digs into Multichannel Analytics studies the direct marketer's approach to multichannel metrics that was originally developed for offline channels.

Chapter 5: The Brand Marketer's Take on Multichannel Analytics reviews how traditional brand marketers have gone about measurement so that we can borrow suitable methods to apply across online and offline.

Part II: Measurement and Metrics is the heart of the book. It provides methods for fusing the multiple multichannel analytics methods from Part I into a bridge across channels. This is the section of the book where I hope to see the most page markers flagged by readers.

Chapter 6: Measure Lift Between Online and Offline provides recipes for measuring the outcomes of marketing initiatives across channels. The methods in this chapter are for measurement at the aggregate level which is in many cases sufficient for assessing marketing ROI (return on investment).

Chapter 7: Measure 1:1 Interactions Between Online and Offline takes measurement a level deeper down to the individual customer level. These are the multichannel methods that customer-centric marketers want to put in place for providing a better experience thanks to a more complete understanding of individuals.

Chapter 8: Measure Multi-Touch Conversions addresses what is probably the most difficult problem in marketing measurement, namely multi-touch conversions. This refers to methods for sharing the credit for customers' business between multiple preceding marketing touch points.

Part III: Multichannel Marketing Methods reaps the rewards of the work that we have done in Part II. Namely, the three final chapters showcase how to conduct integrated marketing across online and offline channels with the help of the metrics that we have developed.

Chapter 9: Attract and Acquire explores several ways in which integrated marketing goes to work for raising awareness and acquiring new customers.

Chapter 10: Engage and Convert provides hints for upgrading many staple marketing methods, such as funnel reporting and cross-selling, to today's multichannel world.

Chapter 11: Grow Lifetime Value completes our journey with recipes for extending typical customer-centric marketing endeavors across online and offline channels by drawing on every marketing discipline and metric in the book.

About the Screenshots

Throughout the book, screenshots have been used for illustration purposes. Following the precedence set by other recent books on analytics, the screenshots were created using the applications that were most-easily accessible and familiar to me. Therefore, unless marked otherwise, the screenshots are from Unica's Affinium NetInsight, Affinium Campaign, and Affinium Model solutions. In no way, however, was this to suggest that similar reports could not be created with other, comparable solutions.

How to Contact the Author

I welcome feedback from you about this book or about books you'd like to see in the future. You can reach me by writing to AArikan@Unica.com or Akin@MultiChannelMetrics.com. For more information about multichannel metrics and to join ongoing discussions, please visit the accompanying website at www.MultiChannelMetrics.com.

Sybex strives to keep you supplied with the latest tools and information you need for your work. Please check their website at www.sybex.com, where we'll post additional content and updates that supplement this book if the need arises. Enter **multichannel** in the Search box (or type the book's ISBN: 9780470239599), and click Go to get to the book's update page.

Building Blocks for Multichannel Metrics

Online, direct, and brand marketers have been facing multichannel measurement challenges and crafting solutions for years. Unfortunately, many of these solutions haven't been shared across marketing disciplines. The online has remained separate from the offline.

Let the sharing begin now! In Part I, we will explore today's marketing landscape and discuss the importance of multichannel metrics. Then we'll look over the shoulders of web analysts, direct marketers, and brand advertisers as they solve multichannel measurements and metrics problems within their own confines to discover many building blocks for bridging marketing metrics across online and offline.

With Great Opportunity Come Great Challenges

1

Has marketing become more challenging today or is it easier than ever? Both! On the one hand, there is formidable competition for the attention of today's over-messaged, out-of-time, and in-control buyers. On the other hand, new channels for connecting with buyers are springing up left and right. The marketer who is able to ride on the coattails of the multichannel revolution has the opportunity to connect with always-on consumers anywhere, any time. Doing so, however, requires a new set of know-how. Let's picture the opportunities for the marketer who can acknowledge and overcome the challenges ahead.

Chapter Contents

Multichannel, Schmultichannel!
Just What Kind of Trouble Are Marketers In?
Chicken Soup for the Troubled Marketer
Multichannel Metrics, the Missing
  Puzzle Piece

Multichannel, Schmultichannel!

Mobile devices are in every hand. Television and the Internet are converging. The *online* and the *offline* are fusing into two sides of the same coin. When marketers take stock of all the channels through which they are interacting with their customers today, the count quickly reaches 10 to 15 different avenues. So, most marketers feel like multichannel artists already. What is there left to talk about?

Well, it is one thing to interact through multiple channels in parallel. It is quite another to fuse those activities together in an intelligent way to maximize response and conversion rates. That is the mark of multichannel marketing as a science, and few marketers claim to have embraced it to date.

The channels in question include the traditional brand advertising outlets, as shown in Table 1.1. What the traditional outlets have in common is that they are *nonaddressable*—i.e., the message is delivered to whoever happens to be listening or watching, and those individuals are not identifiable. Marketers align their advertisements on these media based on their target audiences' affinities and passions, say around soccer.

▶ **Table 1.1** Overview of Brand Advertising and Direct Response Channels

Brand Advertising Channels (Not Addressable)	Direct Response Channels (Addressable)
TV/radio/print	Store (purchases)
Out-of-home	Call center
Marketing events	Direct mail
Product placement	Sales and service teams
In-store displays	Mobile devices
	E-mail
	Web display ads
	Search engines
	Website

In contrast, the addressable channels speak to individual prospects. Therefore, they have the opportunity to tailor the message to each individual, prompt for a purchase or inquiry, and measure the response. Typical direct response channels are listed in Table 1.1 also.

As online and offline converge, more and more channels are becoming addressable. For example, display ads on the Internet used to be nonaddressable but now they can be targeted to individuals, as we will review in later chapters.

Technological advances are making it easier to measure marketing success within individual channels. Yet, the proliferation of channels is making it harder to gauge the real picture of success because any marketing impulse has repercussions across multiple response channels. The complete business results attributable to a marketing initiative need to be added across all the online and offline channels where activity increased. At the same time, the marketing initiative can cause activity to decrease on some channels due to "cannibalization," i.e. buyers switching to other channels; that needs to be taken into account as well.

Not by coincidence, this channel fragmentation has been taking place in conjunction with two other tidal shifts in marketing. Namely, consumers are increasingly in charge of the dialog with companies. As a consequence, marketers are working to change from a product centric to a customer centric way of running their businesses. Let's examine the implications with which marketers wrestle.

Just What Kind of Trouble Are Marketers In?

Let's use a recent first-hand experience that my family and I lived through to illustrate the kinds of trouble that today's marketers face when reaching their audience. It all began after we changed houses. Moving is one of those major life events that attentive marketers rightfully watch out for as an opportunity to capitalize.

Interruption Marketers, Not Welcome Anymore!

It barely took 24 hours at our new home before we were abruptly stopped in our tracks and reminded why this is the right time for this book. Namely, the telemarketing squadrons began attacking our new phone number with no less than ten calls a day. A side effect of the U.S. National Do-Not-Call Registry (www.donotcall.gov) is apparently that unregistered phone numbers receive maybe ten times the volume of telemarketing calls that we had deemed annoying a few years ago.

Have those marketers ever heard of a customer-centric approach to marketing? Yes, to a certain degree, actually. You might be surprised. Their databases flagged our family as having moved recently and predicted correctly that we would be making a plethora of purchases for setting up our new home. So, some of them prioritized us for phone offers for lower credit interest rates and called us multiple times per day to deliver the offers. Not a bad bet, if you put yourself in that marketer's shoes. Some recipients should find this interruption to be a valuable service. But for the rest, what a nuisance!

Yet, we can assume that the person allocating the marketing budget did their Return On Investment (ROI) analysis and concluded that they would get their money's worth of orders. However, had they used a balanced-scorecard approach for evaluating their campaign ROI instead of just looking at the monetary results, surely they would have noticed that they would be in the red in terms of being cursed out many times by annoyed prospects!

Equipped with caller ID and a short temper, my family became very fast at swatting out the unwelcome phone offers. It is not that telemarketers are unpleasant people; they tend to be very friendly actually. However, our willingness to spend our precious time on a telemarketer's inquiry has been greatly diminished for many reasons. Every day we see more advertising messages than we can possibly act on. Estimates frequently range from a couple hundred to a couple thousand messages per day for the average person in the U.S. The Internet has given us confidence that we can find almost anything we want, whenever we want. We also know we can find independent reviews and peer recommendations whose advice we have come to trust more than a vendor's pitch. Finally, for most of us, our past experiences with telemarketing do not instill us with hope that we'll be surprised with a particularly relevant offer.

The plight of the telemarketer is singled out here as an obvious telltale for the increasing challenges that interruption marketing is facing in all its forms. What a comic battle between marketers and prospective buyers! Whenever marketers find a new avenue for interrupting buyers to shove ads down their throats, buyers gear up and find a new way around them. In just the minute or two that it may have taken you to read the previous paragraphs, your e-mail filters probably stopped another batch of spam from reaching your inbox. DVRs (digital video recorders) such as TiVo enable us to dodge the umpteenth repetition of the same commercial interruption. Satellite radio and iPods enable commercial-free listening. The only difficult thing about filtering untargeted direct mail offers from your mail box is not the minute that it takes every day, but the bad feeling that you get about all that wasted paper and energy.

 Note: Although rumors of interruption marketing's death have been greatly exaggerated, it is clearly suffering from increasing inefficiencies.

Competition among companies has become less about competition between products and more about competition between marketing communications seeking buyers' attention, writes Prof. Manfred Bruhn in the German-language book *Guide to Integrated Communication (Leitfaden Integrierte Kommunikation),* published in 2006 by Marketing Börse (www.marketing-boerse.de). This point of view places an enormous amount of responsibility on the marketer's shoulders. Namely, the marketer's role is seen to grow beyond creating a market for their products toward becoming more of a part of the offering itself. Likewise, under this view, a business's failure cannot be blamed on the product's competitiveness alone; the marketer's competitiveness is also part of the equation.

Buyers Want to Be in Charge

Funny though, our family really did make a plethora of purchases within two weeks of moving into our new home! Yet, in our case, the telemarketers missed out on the opportunity. As soon as our Internet connection became live, we went researching online to make our buying decisions. At that point, the dialog was in our hands and any ads that we saw, if we noticed them at all, were relevant to our search. Earlier we were swatting out the telemarketers as "too much info." However, during our research, no amount of information seemed to be enough to satisfy our appetites. After all, we wanted to make good decisions. This was true especially when it came to the biggest buying decision that we had to make, namely the car. We happily clicked on all sorts of relevant advertising messages. Ironically for the telemarketers, we even thoroughly studied offers for financing with low interest rates.

As long as we believed that it was our own idea to do so, we were highly motivated to examine financing options. Earlier, when the marketers were interrupting us and asking us to check on the same idea we were stubborn.

Note: Although buyers are not listening when you talk, paradoxically they have become more information-hungry than ever in their research for buying decisions.

This constitutes a great opportunity for those marketers who know how to be at the ready with the right information at the right time.

Buyers Are Multichannel Beings

After all the product research we did online for our shopping spree, my family and I dropped off from most of these websites without completing a purchase. For example, after narrowing down our choice of car make and model, the exact car and financing option that we picked was still sold to us the old-fashioned way—namely offline, and by a friendly sales person at the dealership. Of course, the opposite happened too. When we found products of interest in stores, we used comparison-shopping engines to find better prices online. Sometimes after a shipment arrived, we returned the purchase to the local store if it wasn't what we expected.

As typical buyers, we did not think in terms of channels. We just sought the most convenient way of accomplishing our goal. From the *multichannel* marketer's point of view, we exhibited *cross-channel* behavior. Let's define these terms for the purposes of the book.

Note: A *multichannel business* is one that interacts with its customers through multiple media—for example, through a telephone, store, and website. Short of an ice cream vendor on the beach, there must be very few businesses left today that are not multichannel. *Multichannel marketing* refers to marketing communications delivered on multiple media in parallel and, hopefully, in a coordinated fashion. The term also implies that responses to marketing initiatives are accepted from multiple channels.

 Note: The term *cross-channel* is often used interchangeably with multichannel. However, a more precise definition of the term differs from multichannel. Namely, cross-channel refers to the act of beginning a communication, or buying cycle, on one channel and crossing into another channel to continue it there. This is the meaning that we will assume for this book.

Cross-Channel Behavior Patterns

My colleagues at Unica Corporation use the wiggly line chart in Figure 1.1 to describe the seemingly random paths that customers may take across channels during the life cycle of their relationships with vendors. Sales cycles that may be triggered on one channel may cross to another channel for consideration and to yet other channels for the transaction and post-purchase relationship. For instance, a TV commercial by Crate & Barrel may make one customer aware that they also carry home office furniture. Considering a replacement of her ratty office chair, she may check models and prices on the website. Then she may call the call center to inquire about available colors and delivery options. Yet, ultimately she may go to the nearest store to try a few choices and pick the one she finds most comfortable.

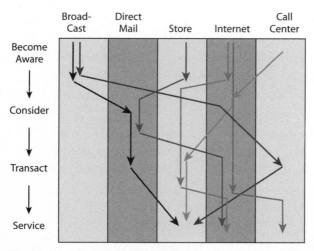

Figure 1.1 Sample wiggly line paths of buyers through the buying cycle (Source: Unica Corporation)

At first it may seem as if there is no pattern here that marketers can pick up. When we look at an individual's buying cycle, this may be true—so much depends on circumstance, let alone the individual's preferences. All of us have wiggled our ways through almost any possible path on the chart. However, when we aggregate the behavior of groups of buyers, it becomes clear that certain channels are more typically frequented during certain stages of the customer life cycle. My colleagues at Unica lay this out in the form of the Harvey Ball chart in Table 1.2. A full Harvey Ball indicates that a particular channel is very typically used in a particular stage of the relationship. A half-full Harvey Ball means that a channel can be used with certain limitations, whereas an empty Harvey Ball suggests that a channel is ill-suited for a particular stage in the buying cycle.

▶ **Table 1.2** Channels Most Typically Used in Each Stage of the Buying Cycle. (Source: Unica Corporation)

	Channel \ Stage	Awareness	Perception	Consideration	Trial	Initial Purchase	Retention	Cross-Sell, Up-Sell
Offline	TV / radio / print	●	●	◐	○	○	○	○
	Out-of-home	●	◐	◐	○	○	○	○
	Events	◐	●	●	●	○	○	○
	Product placement	◐	◐	●	○	○	○	○
Online	Web ads	●	◐	●	○	○	○	○
	Blogs	◐	●	●	○	○	◐	○
	Search	◐	◐	●	○	○	○	○
	Website	○	◐	◐	●	●	●	●
	E-mail	○	○	○	◐	◐	●	●
	Mobile	?	?	?	?	?	?	?
Offline	Direct mail	○	○	○	◐	◐	●	●
	Call center	○	○	○	◐	◐	●	●
	Store / sales	◐	◐	◐	◐	●	●	●
	Service team	○	○	○	○	○	●	●

One could argue whether some of the Harvey Balls should be more or less full. But for most of the channels, it makes intuitive sense that they are better suited for specific goals than others. For example, TV can raise awareness for a product, but until the TV and Internet truly converge, it is still necessary to go to another channel for learning more and purchasing. Direct mail can sometimes raise awareness. However, raising awareness is not typically thought to be its best application. Due to consumers' short temper at the mail box, direct mail is much more likely to get attention from recipients once their brand awareness and acceptance has already been raised through other channels.

Then, there is mobile commerce. Ever-smarter mobile devices are now like multi-channel microcosms themselves, namely across voice, SMS, MMS, e-mail, WWW, audio, video, and other channels. Acceptance levels for receiving marketing communications are, however, still difficult to judge. They have reached different levels in different countries with users in Asia and Europe being much more tolerant currently than U.S. consumers. For instance, most in the U.S. would still say "No!" to receiving unwelcome advertising on their mobiles. Yet, when your mobile is equipped with GPS (i.e., geo location and local search capabilities), wouldn't you want it to make you aware of nearby cheap gas stations? I would. There is no doubt that as marketers increase the relevance of their messages, their acceptance will increase as well.

When you step back and look at Table 1.2 from a distance, it becomes obvious that the channels in the first seven rows of the figure are best at attracting potential buyers but not so apt at converting them to customers and maintaining an ongoing relationship. The latter purposes are better achieved through the channels in the bottom seven rows of the figure. This suggests why cross-channel behavior is pretty much a given for most customer relationships. For example the "research-shopper" is a phenomenon coined in an article published by Verhoef, Neslin, and Vroomen in May 2007 in the *International Journal of Research in Marketing:* "The research-shopper phenomenon is the tendency of customers to use one channel for search and another for purchase" (shortcut via multichannelmetrics.com/ResearchShopper).

Note: Marketers should expect prospects to cross channels from those media that are good at raising their awareness and facilitating their research to other media that are better suited for product evaluation, purchase, and service.

Good Morning! This is Your Wake-Up Call

The marketer who is stretched thin across many responsibilities may still be asking: "Is cross-channel behavior from online to offline (and vice versa) a significant enough phenomenon that it should be prioritized for attention now? Or is it a marginal occurrence that can be neglected?" The answer could not be more loud and clear. Multiple independent studies over the last years have confirmed that the greater portion of sales that resulted after online research is not completed online but offline. For example, see the chart in Figure 1.2 from JupiterResearch's *US Online Retail Sales Forecast, 2006 to 2011,* published in January 2007. The chart shows total U.S. online sales per year in relation to the far greater amount of offline sales that were influenced by preceding online activity. The chart also projects that the portion of online plus online-influenced offline sales in comparison to total U.S. retail sales is expected to grow further from 36 percent in 2007 to 47 percent by 2011. In other words, 47 cents of the average dollar spent in retail is projected to be spent either online or influenced by preceding online activity. Researching online before buying offline is becoming the norm.

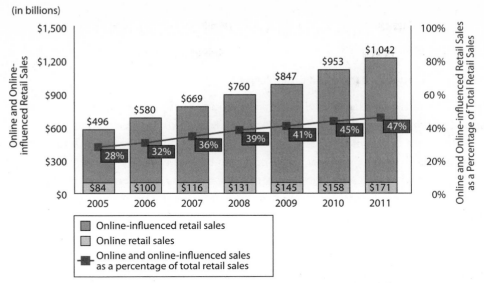

(in billions)

Figure 1.2 Online and online-influenced retail sales, 2005 to 2011. (Source: *JupiterResearch Internet Shopping Model*, 11/06 (US only))

The biggest wake-up call for marketers here is the following: Even the most beautifully designed and optimized websites unfortunately may still not convert online shoppers into offline buyers from the same company's stores or call center. Shoppers often leak from the sales funnel just at the moment when their buying process switches from one channel to another. In fact, Brandweek, citing research by Forrester, reported something that many of us already knew intuitively from our own experience:

Forty-three percent of consumers purchased a product from a different retailer than the one whose Web site they used to research the item.
—Study: Web Research Nets In-Store Sales, *Brandweek,*
  *May 2007 (*shortcut via multichannelmetrics.com/Brandweek*)*

This makes sense. The decision about *what* we want to buy in most cases is a separate query from *where* we want to get it. Think about what this means though. It means that a marketing campaign or search keyword that is very good at bringing shoppers to your website cannot automatically be assumed to result in offline buyers for you.

Note: Unfortunately, you can't extrapolate online metrics, such as campaign click-throughs and site engagement, into offline purchases that should be credited to the campaign.

Marketers would have it so much easier if this kind of extrapolation were a valid approach. Yet, a more accurate method for measuring cross-channel campaign results is required.

Are Multichannel Customers Automatically More Valuable?

It is often cited that multichannel customers tend to be bigger spenders than single-channel customers. For example, Shop.org released a study by J.C. Williams Group and BizRate.com that confirmed this finding after 48,000 interviews with shoppers in all channels.

> *Cross-Channel shoppers spend 50% more—and visit stores 70% more frequently—than the average shopper.*
> —Multichannel Retail Report 2001, Shop.org,
> *October 2001*

The important question for marketers to ask themselves is whether there is only a correlation here or actually a causal relationship. Do multichannel consumers spend more because they are somehow more engaged through multiple channels? Or are these consumers engaged in multiple channels because they are looking to buy so much that a single channel would not provide them enough convenience and availability for doing so? In other words, if the marketer could expand the number of channels used by a group of customers, can he expect that this group of customers will automatically start spending more?

This is a difficult question to answer. The result may likely differ from company to company. Studies have shown that multichannel shoppers are more valuable because they are more likely to respond to cross-selling and up-selling. Multichannel customers simply have more frequent interactions with the vendor making them more likely to be exposed to such offers. There is also a psychological effect of reinforcement when a brand, message, or offer that is seen on one channel is repeated on other channels. Given this relative uncertainty, the best point of view for marketers to adopt is that of a call to action.

Note: Multichannel customers are probably not automatically more valuable customers, but they can be turned into more valuable customers. However, this depends on the vendor's ability to leverage the multichannel experience not just for delivering consistent service and more convenience, but also for intelligent cross- and up-sell offers that reinforce each other.

Moreover, multichannel customers also have less-favorable characteristics. As Hung LeHong, research vice president for retail at Gartner Inc., cautioned in *Internet Retailer* in January 2007: "Retailers need to be aware of these characteristics in multichannel shoppers because they open the door to decreased loyalty." Namely, Gartner found multichannel customers to defect more easily when they can get a better price for the same product elsewhere. This makes intuitive sense because price sensitivity is among the biggest reasons why customers research their buying decision on multiple channels in the first place. Additionally, multichannel customers have been found to require better customer service probably because they want to make more informed buying decisions. According to Gartner's findings, any perceived shortcoming in the shopping experience is apt to send a multichannel shopper elsewhere. The best way for marketers to look at this is again in the form of a call to action:

> **Note:** Multichannel customers may defect more easily when price competition arises; yet vendors have the opportunity to build on the multichannel relationship in such intelligent ways that the customer perceives better service as an advantage for staying loyal.

Chicken Soup for the Troubled Marketer

Who would not be stressed out as a marketer today when buyers increasingly ignore their old-style interruption marketing, instead take control of the interaction themselves, and do so across the increasingly fragmented landscape of channels? To help marketers over their slump, a number of new approaches to marketing have been recommended over the past decades. These timely new approaches to marketing promise a solution to the marketer's plight. The marketer with the know-how and capabilities for implementing these novel approaches could establish a competitive advantage over others.

You will be very familiar with all of the following recommendations because they are repeated frequently and are commonly accepted as sound advice today. Interestingly, however, they have only been put into action by companies to varying degrees so far. The recommendations range from making marketing more accountable and integrated across media to making it more customer-centric. Given the advent of user-generated content in Web 2.0, another piece of advice is to take into account that consumers are no longer passive recipients of marketing messages, but they are active interpreters. Therefore, the marketer is also advised to find ways of amplifying the voices of customers who are raving fans.

What is meant by Web 2.0?

Wikipedia describes Web 2.0 as a "phrase which refers to a perceived second generation of Internet based services such as social networking sites, wikis, communication tools and folksonomies that let people collaborate and share information online in ways previously unavailable." The term was coined in 2004 with the first Web 2.0 conference by O'Reilly Media (for more info., see multichannelmetrics.com/Web20).

Make Marketing More Accountable

What conclusion would you draw from the fact that there are more and more choices for spending the marketing budget, yet there is a sense that not everything is equally effective at producing results? Doh! We need to measure what works and quit wasting our money on the other items. Even for our best initiatives, we ought to experiment with variations and measure their outcomes to see if we can't improve results even further.

Traditional marketers have been running analytics of various types for decades now. This is still quite a tricky job for mass marketers—for example, in broadcast media—who typically rely on various audience measurement techniques based on panels. Direct marketers have been measuring response rates to their offers across countless offer variations in order to continuously tune their outcomes. Offline marketers have also embraced modeling techniques where they study the outcomes of past marketing initiatives in order to isolate key factors that help predict the success of future marketing opportunities. Measurement, targeting, and especially modeling have reached great sophistication and are typically done by trained specialists.

With online marketers, I cannot recall a time when the desire to measure marketing results became more prominent than in the year 2000 following the bust of the dotcom bubble. Rightfully, marketing budgets were cut unless marketers could prove ROI. Once that mindset was adopted, web analytics were elevated from something that the Information Technology (IT) department looked at, past something that just counted eye balls, and on to a strategic control center for marketers. Getting web analytics reports was quite easy. However, getting web analytics right turned out to require a lot more skills than originally anticipated.

The web analytics solutions available at the time typically stopped short at reporting; therefore, they left all analysis—i.e., interpretation—for the human to do. The latter will always remain indispensable, but web analytics offerings have meanwhile evolved to provide much more direct guidance for decision support. Namely, investigative reporting now provides answers to ad hoc questions. A/B comparisons can quickly highlight differences between ad variations, visitor groups, and time frames. Automated optimization solutions adjust web pages or search ad prices to their most advantageous configurations. In that sense, web analytics has become more feasible and easier than ever. The human's responsibility has shifted slightly from manual analysis to making sure that today's analytics capabilities are generously applied to the site. There is no excuse left for ignoring the inherent measurability of the online medium and claiming to be drowning in reports without any guidance.

So, if online and offline marketers have all these sophisticated solutions for measuring results available to them today, marketing accountability should be in pretty good shape. Right? Wrong! Where is the catch?

Note: Buyers are multichannel beings. Buying cycles are cross-channel. Yet, online and offline marketers still perform their measurements of success in isolation.

Few web analysts capture offline conversions that are attributable to online activity—i.e., sales in stores or call centers that would not have come in if customers had not been researching on the website beforehand. Few offline marketers on the other hand include online browsing activity in their analysis of prospects, customers, and campaign results. Why is there this gap between online and offline when business intelligence and marketing automation technologies have been available for years? Why this gap, when online and offline marketers each within their own confines are already conducting analytics across multiple channels?

Maybe it is that collecting cross-channel data is more difficult. Maybe it is because practitioners perceive the issues to be complex and they require substantial investment that would be hard to sell to senior management. Maybe there are not yet enough examples of marketers who have tried the theoretical ideas in practice, proven their value, and are raving about them at industry events. Certainly, if it is difficult to find web analysts and other database marketing specialists for hiring, it is even more difficult to find multichannel marketing analysts. So there is lingering confusion, resistance to change, and a real lack of know how. A recent study analyzing data from 759 survey responses by marketing practitioners worldwide confirmed this.

A mere 9% of marketers say they believe their ability to measure the financial returns across all forms of marketing is "a real source of leadership" or "as good as it needs to be."
—*Lenskold Group & MarketingProfs 2007 Marketing ROI Process & Measurements Trend Study. (shortcut via* multichannelmetrics.com/LM2007*)*

Taken together with the wake-up call to marketers around multichannel behavior this suggests that multichannel metrics are a critical gap for turning marketing accountability into reality. That in turn is indispensable for maximizing marketing success.

Integrate Marketing Communications!

When all your friends voice the same opinion on a subject, it becomes very easy to agree. That is essentially the idea behind Integrated Marketing Communications (IMC), a vast body of work that was developed starting already in the late 1980s. Only, instead of "friends" just substitute "marketing channels." Namely, IMC encourages marketers to increase the effects of their marketing messages by broadcasting them consistently across multiple channels. Consistency of the message for a particular target segment is the key idea here: "If for Volvo you are communicating safety & reliability on TV, then you shouldn't communicate performance values in magazines to the same target audience. Though, additional benefits can be positioned to other relevant audiences in media that are specific to them. However, those messages should not confuse the messages to the broader audience." This example left by business consultant Zahid Adil on the MarketingProfs discussion boards sums up the idea.

Philip Kitchen and Patrick De Pelsmacker, in their book *Integrated Marketing Communication: A Primer* (Routledge, 2004), trace the birth of IMC first to practitioners in the late 1980s and then to academic interest spearheaded by Professor Don Schultz at Northwestern University. There are various definitions of IMC. I find the definition left by Laura Brooke-Smith of D.Y.B Strategies on the MarketingProfs discussion boards to be particularly informative:

> IMC is *"The co-ordination of a business's promotional efforts by determining [e.g., through measurement] the most effective way of meeting the objectives of informing, persuading and reminding customers and potential customers of the business as well as reinforcing attitudes and perceptions. The tools available to the integration process would be advertising, sales promotion, public relations, direct and online marketing and personal selling. The business will determine how much to spend on each tool not on whether they will market or not, that decision is already made."*

Implied in the definition is the fact that these communications would be coordinated in a consistent fashion across all media with which a customer segment comes in touch. Also implied is that communications, in order to be more persuasive, will start with the customer or prospect in mind and then work backward instead of starting with the products. In order for an organization to achieve this consistency in its communications, the IMC literature also invests great focus into the organizational requirements, from management buy-in down to channel expertise.

The goal of IMC is to be more persuasive with getting customers to take action. How is IMC more persuasive?

Synergies are compounded. The crux of the matter is the empirical observation that when companies communicate in such consistent and customer-oriented fashion across multiple media, the effects of repeated communications compound each other. Synergies increase marketing pressure. Customers become more likely to take notice and act. Psychologically, a marketing message may appear more believable when it is consistently heard from multiple channels even though it is really coming from the same source.

Reach is increased. The multichannel approach also ensures that the communications are delivered to all prospects in the target market by selecting the media with which the targeted individuals tend to spend their time.

Frequency is increased. On a single channel, there are practical limits to the frequency with which an ad message can be delivered before fatigue sets in. Spreading the same message to different channels can allow increasing frequency while the effects of fatigue may be somewhat lesser.

The best medium is used for each stage in the marketing cycle. Broadcast media, for example, can be leveraged for what they are best at, namely increasing awareness of a brand or product and acceptance of its value proposition. Then the Internet and direct mail can be leveraged for what they are good at, say capturing sales or leads.

Success is measured and evaluated. IMC emphasizes marketing accountability and continuous optimization for arriving at more and more effective communications

Today, we take it for granted that brands are presented to us in a consistent-enough fashion and more or less on any medium. This is probably why we rarely hear a name attached to this approach to marketing anymore, i.e., IMC. We just seem to lump it in under the multichannel marketing umbrella today. The discussion has moved on.

But wait! IMC started before the dawn of the World Wide Web and long before the era of Web 2.0. How many companies have extended IMC to include both online and offline media? Of course, most companies have a website and do a certain amount of online advertising. But on average, the level of marketing spending online is only a fraction of that offline. What would be the optimal mix between online and offline channels? In addition to website, e-mail, search, etc. how about some of the more novel online opportunities for marketing such as viral marketing, RSS, podcasts, video inserts, etc.?

Well, how could we answer that question without first measuring our return on investment from each channel? Measurement and evaluation is a key strategy recommended by IMC. Yet, we already know the poor state of adoption of multichannel metrics today. So, we can derive that very few companies must have made an informed decision for allocating their marketing spending between online and offline. What companies need so that they can make an informed decision would be a marketing dashboard with cross-channel metrics that reveals where marketing spending generates the highest returns. Because few companies have put such a dashboard in place, it would not be surprising if there is misallocation. Various studies conducted over the past years hinted that such misallocation may indeed be rampant. Namely, there is a startling discrepancy between the amount of time that consumers are spending on the Internet vs. the percent of advertising budget that marketers are allocating to the online medium.

Already in 2002, the Online Publishers Association announced the results of a study by Millward Brown Intelliquest showing that consumers with workplace Internet access spent more time in a 24-hour day online than watching TV.

Thirty-four percent of total media minutes are spent on the Internet, while 30% are spent watching television and 26% are spent listening to the radio.
— OPA Media Consumption Study,
February 2002

Yet, total U.S. ad spend online was estimated at $19.5 Billion for 2007 by eMarketer, whereas TV ad spend was estimated at roughly $75 Billion and total media spend across all channels at $285 Billion. In other words, while consumers spend more than 30% of their media time online, less than 7% of ad spend has been allocated to the Internet.

Mind you that the disparity does not automatically prove that there is misallocation. More information on the returns from each channel is required.

For some companies, it could very well be that offline advertising leads to significantly better returns so that the disparity would be justified. The best way for marketers to act on this obvious disparity is once again to take it as a call to action.

 Note: Marketers should not neglect measuring and comparing marketing returns from online and offline channels so that they can ensure that they really are allocating their advertising investments such that they produce optimal returns.

What does the IMC literature contribute to multichannel marketing measurement? It makes great recommendations on success metrics. However, the literature has not gone too deep into the practical aspects of *how* to collect such measurements across online and offline. Truth be told, survey results published by Professor Manfred Bruhn cite measurability as a key barrier to adopting IMC still today. That is the gap that this book is aiming to help close.

"Companies cite lack or defects with measuring success as the biggest barrier for the actual work of integrating marketing communications. Difficulties arise especially for measuring the interdependence of the coordinated use of marketing instruments."
—*Professor Manfred Bruhn,* Guide to Integrated Communication (Leitfaden Integrierte Kommunikation), *published in 2006 by Marketing Börse (*www.marketing-boerse.de*). Translated from the German original.*

Be Customer Centric!

You have not lived under a stone for the last fifteen years, so you already know that the rise of customer-centric marketing constitutes the primary recommendation for overcoming today's marketing challenges. In brief, a customer-centric business delivers products, services, and marketing communications in such a manner that they are more relevant and more valuable to the recipient. As a result it is assumed that they will also be more welcome. What is the distinction from IMC? If for example IMC ensured that you purchased a Volvo because the brand messages around safety repeated consistently across multiple media were relevant to your priorities, then customer centricity is concerned with your personal experience in every interaction through every channel during and after the buying process.

Yet, when it comes to details, customer-centric business strategy means different things to different people. Many flavors have been formulated and given names such as CRM (Customer Relationship Management), database marketing, direct marketing, relationship marketing, event-based marketing, right-time marketing, One-to-One marketing, permission marketing, behavioral targeting, personalization, and most recently, customer experience management. If you read up on CustomerThink (www.customerthink.com), Bob Thompson's forum for customer-centric business strategy, you will be amazed to see that even the gurus don't quite agree on a formal definition. For the purposes of this book, it shall suffice to stress some of the common denominators that are key requirements for all or most of the flavors.

Two-Way Value On CustomerThink, Paul Greenberg, who is the author of *CRM at the Speed of Light,* sums up brilliantly that "what remains unchanging is the commitment to two-way customer value." Namely, on the one hand the business is organizing itself to make every interaction with the customer as valuable an experience for the customer as possible. However, the business is not doing this for altruistic reasons but to increase the customer lifetime value—i.e., the incremental returns that it can hope to harvest from the customer over time.

Good, Relevant, and Consistent Experience In order for the experience to be valuable, it needs to be a good one. Among the many requirements for a good customer experience is that the customer perceives the interaction as relevant to his or her goals. In other words, interruption marketing is definitely out of the picture unless the interruption hits the spot. Additionally, the experience is much more likely to be a relevant one if it is consistent with past interactions regardless which other channel they occurred on.

Dialog Rather Than Monolog In order for the experience to be consistent and relevant, it needs to be born from a dialog with the customer rather than a monolog. In other words, the business needs to listen to customers and study their behavior. Otherwise, how could the business come up with relevant responses or treatments and remain consistent with past interactions?

Multichannel Mind-Set Because customers are multichannel beings and demand relevant, consistent experiences across all channels, businesses need to adopt a multichannel mind-set when listening to their customers. Otherwise, businesses may miss two-thirds of the conversation! For example, when designing a website in a customer-centric fashion, the marketer with a multichannel mind-set anticipates someone who arrives on the website to get accessories for an item he has purchased in a store.

Multichannel Metrics and Measurement at the Group Level A multichannel mind-set implies the need to measure the behavior of groups of customers across channels in order to better understand how the group wishes to interact across channels. In his inspiring article "How to Embrace Multichannel Behavior," published on ClickZ in May 2007, Jack Aaronson likened this to the folklore tale of an architect who built a college campus but did not build any sidewalks. Instead the architect said, "The students will create the sidewalks." A year later the architect revisited the school to build sidewalks where the students had created well-worn paths. As Avinash Kaushik, the author of *Web Analytics, An Hour A Day,* always emphasizes: "Don't assume that you know what your customers want! Instead measure, study, and ask them." Once you find out in which ways your company's customers want to use the channels that you have available, you can focus on making those paths as easy for them as possible.

Multichannel Measurements at the One-to-One Level Finally, here is a requirement that is common to most flavors of customer-centric marketing, but not to all. The requirement is emphasized heavily with flavors referred to as CRM, database marketing, direct marketing, relationship marketing, event-based marketing, right-time marketing, One-to-One marketing, permission marketing, behavioral targeting, and personalization. These flavors share the common goal of building a database of insights into customer history and preferences learned from interactions with each prospect and customer. This level of measurement and mass personalization was named the One-to-One level by Martha Rogers and Don Peppers in 1993. The more complete the insights available on each prospect or customer, the more relevant and valuable the company can render their next communication, offer, or service.

However, recent critiques of approaches to customer centricity have noted a possible overemphasis of this kind of data-driven automation. Bob Thompson writes in *Customer Experience Management: A Winning Business Strategy for a Flat World,* published by CustomerThink Corp. in 2006, "Customer Experience Management (CEM), on the other hand, concentrates on the customer's value proposition and includes all interactions, not just those that can be automated," (see multichannelmetrics.com/CEM).

Similarly, Bryan and Jeffrey Eisenberg warn in their book *Waiting for Your Cat to Bark?* that a strategy based on One-to-One level measurement and personalization is not suited for every business model and "Eventually the marketing costs for such a massive undertaking would outweigh its ability to contribute to revenues." Instead the Eisenberg brothers recommend *persona-lization*—i.e., the design of websites and other customer interaction channels based on *personas*. Personas represent groups of customers with shared goals in common situations. As a consequence, persona-lization does not rely on multichannel measurements down at the individual customer level. Aggregate measurements or studies suffice instead.

Regardless of which flavor of customer centricity you believe will work best for your company, a multichannel approach is a requirement that is common to all of them. Yet, knowing the poor state of adoption of multichannel metrics today, one has to assume that the implementation of customer-centric business strategies must have suffered or slowed as a consequence.

Note: If enterprises have any hope of achieving customer centricity, key requirements are a multichannel mind-set and the measurement of customer behavior across channels (whether at the group or One-to-One level).

Leverage the Voice of the Customer

Web 2.0 has opened up new opportunities for marketers to be heard by over-messaged, out-of-time buyers. The opportunity is not to spam buyers with marketing messages now delivered through RSS in addition to e-mail. Rather, the opportunity is to amplify the voice of customers who are raving fans and are happy to be vocal about it on their social networks. This may include customers' blogs, podcasts, and other consumer-generated content. The company that best knows how to amplify their fans' voices will build the best brand. The company that best knows how to listen to customers as they talk with each other and share experiences has the opportunity to build the best products.

The marketer's role is to create raving fans the old-fashioned way but then provide them with avenues and reason for sharing their excitement—e.g., viral marketing campaigns. Think for example of contests for consumer-generated commercials. Doritos & Yahoo! Video teamed up for a consumer-generated Super Bowl commercial contest in 2006 that generated significant buzz. More than 125,000 people were reported to have visited the dedicated Doritos micro site showcasing the contenders during the first two weeks of January 2007. That was ten times as many people than visited Doritos official site.

What is a Viral Marketing Campaign?

In contrast to advertising, viral marketing refers to campaigns encouraging "people to pass along a marketing message voluntarily", according to Wikipedia. To achieve that goal, the campaign may often include entertaining elements, such as a funny video or website.

"So, did we sell more Doritos?" would be an appropriate question to ask marketers. More specifically, the question should be how much customers who participated in the campaign or who were engaged through the campaign in some ways are spending versus a control group that did not participate. In most cases, this is a call for multichannel metrics because the viral campaign will likely span multiple media such as websites, e-mail, SMS, TV, etc. In the case of Doritos, purchases ultimately come in through retail stores. In later chapters, we will discuss how to assess the sales outcomes of such a campaign nonetheless.

Note: More likely than not, viral marketing or other social networking campaigns require multichannel measurements for evaluating their outcomes.

Web 2.0 also brought back attention to another opportunity for marketers. It used to be called *collaborative filtering* before the dotcom bubble burst, but it is known now as *social intelligence*. Social intelligence was made famous at Amazon through the "People who bought this book also bought …" feature. Nowadays, the concept has widened. Think, for example, of consumers' product ratings and reviews available at retailers such as Circuit City. Think of Netflix, where customers can rate the videos that they have viewed and share their recommendations with others in their network. Think of Apple iTunes or Yahoo! Music Jukebox, where musicians' albums and songs are automatically ranked by popularity. Additionally, there are cross references to other musicians that fit a similar taste. As a consequence, even if you are brand new to a musician, you can immediately know which songs you may want to sample. The social intelligence features increase loyalty to the service instead of competitors who may not offer the same.

Note: Repackaging social intelligence into an offering valued by customers can help companies counteract multichannel customers' tendency to defect to cheaper competitors.

The marketer's role is to foster the measurement of social intelligence in such a fashion that customers find it convenient to participate. For example, in the case of ranking music it suffices to collect data on how often each album and song has been clicked. There is no need to interrupt users to ask them to rate songs and albums. Once the social intelligence has been gathered, it is up to the marketer's imagination to repackage the intelligence in ways that customers appreciate. Typical goals may include increased cross-sales or loyalty. Multichannel metrics are often required to confirm whether the goals have been achieved. Put yourself in the shoes of a marketer at Circuit

City for example. Ask yourself to what extent the customer reviews of products on the website lead to more store sales versus just visits by shoppers who read the review but then purchase the product elsewhere. Later chapters recommend ways in which marketers can measure this to answer the question.

The Missing Puzzle Piece, Multichannel Metrics

As should be clear by now, multichannel metrics are indispensable for unlocking the most-anticipated solutions to today's marketing challenges. Without multichannel metrics:

- Marketing accountability remains an empty wish because marketing results that play out across a fragmented landscape of channels cannot be consolidated.
- Integrated Marketing Communications cannot be allocated to channels optimally because the effectiveness of each channel is not understood.
- Customer-centric marketing strategies remain off target because the picture of the customer is torn into multiple pieces where interactions cross channels.
- The value of viral and Web 2.0 marketing strategies cannot be evaluated because they are multichannel campaigns by nature.

Yet, as observed by the industry analysts who were quoted earlier, multichannel metrics across online and offline are missing at most companies today. In the next chapters, we will see that multiple islands of multichannel metrics are already in place within online, direct, and brand marketing, but just not across all three.

When asked why marketers have not closed this gap, some of the reasons that marketers have cited were confusion around measurement. This is true especially for measuring the interdependency of multiple touch points. Other reasons are lack of resources, buy-in, and standards for measurement. Organizational politics between different teams that are responsible for different channels with differing goals, such as prospecting versus customer marketing, should not be neglected.

Yet one has to wonder how real these cited obstacles can be given that they would also be true for each of the multichannel islands—i.e., online, direct, and brand marketing. Yet they have not held up marketers to adopt multichannel metrics for the channels within those islands. Could it be that integrated multichannel metrics across all three islands are simply the next frontier that is waiting to be tackled? Maybe we are waiting to reach a tipping point for broader adoption.

Questions Answered

The top promises that multichannel metrics make is to help marketers:

- Better understand which marketing initiatives work and which don't, by calculating the ROI realized from marketing spending across channels more accurately

- Better understand customers' preferences and experiences
  - At the overall, customer segment, or persona level, by studying the behavior of customer groups across channels
  - At the One-to-One level by reuniting each prospect and customer's interactions with the company across all channels into a more complete customer profile
- Better understand how customers like to combine multiple channels to accomplish their goals and conversely how marketers can combine multiple marketing instruments for theirs
- Better understand how products and services are combined by customers who may acquire them from multiple channels

See Table 1.3 for the kinds of questions that marketers can answer with the help of the appropriate multichannel metrics.

▶ **Table 1.3** Kind of Questions Multichannel Metrics Can Answer

Level of Measurement	Learn about Marketing Initiatives	Learn about Customers and Prospects	Learn about Channels	Learn about Products and Services
Measurements at the aggregate (or summary) level—i.e., across all customers, or for selected customer segments, or for selected personas	What works? What does not work? What's worked in the past?	What is in demand? What are current trends?	How do customers wish to combine channels and how should we do the same? How can we reduce leaks from the cross-channel funnel?	How do customers wish to combine products and how should we do the same? What social intelligence can we capture?
Measurements at the One-to-One (i.e., detail) level	Where are we in the dialog? Is there fatigue due to too many offers?	How can we be of service? How can we be relevant? What lifetime value do we predict?	Did the customer leave to a competitor or just shift to a different channel?	What is the next-best cross-sell, or up-sell offer? When is the right time to next contact the customer about a product?

The chapters in Part III of the book will outline multichannel marketing methods that employ these questions in order to turn the answers into action for better two-way value between customers and company.

Measuring Absolute Results versus Trends

The skeptical reader will have lingering doubts that multichannel metrics can be measured with absolute accuracy. The skeptic is absolutely right to be doubtful. Web analysts know that online metrics are not 100 percent accurate either despite the digital nature of the medium. Measuring the results of a TV or billboard advertisement is far more imprecise. If nothing else, it already follows from these facts that multichannel metrics can be no more precise than online and offline metrics are.

However, as Jim Sterne, chairman of the Web Analytics Association and producer of the eMetrics Marketing Optimization Summit conference series, put it during an interview with Stone Temple's Eric Enge in January 2007, "Web analytic data is not precise, but as long as the inaccuracies are consistent, then the delta is true." In other words, if you make a change to your registration form on the website and as a result completed registrations go up by 10 percent, that result is true. Similarly, if you make a change to your offer to print an online wish list for customers to take to the store and sales go up by 10 percent, then your change was a very good idea.

This suggests that multichannel metrics may be most reliable when measured over time and used for assessing the impact of changes that you make to your marketing programs. Yet, absolute numbers are too valuable to give up completely. Especially, when it comes to ROI calculations to help us choose between alternative advertising investments we do need to rely on absolute results as a guide. Take an example. You compare the ROI of a paid search keyword versus running an advertisement in the local newspaper. When you measure the resulting store sales attributable to the keyword compared to a newspaper ad, you may find that the paid keyword appears to have an ROI of 20 percent, whereas the newspaper ad only comes to an ROI of 8 percent. However, both measurements may have missed an unknown number of customers who bought from you without being identified as having used either the keyword or seen the newspaper ad.

From a practical point of view, what should you do? At what point after eliminating sources of error that you can identify, should you stop doubting, take faith in your findings, and as a result prioritize the keyword over the newspaper ad? The mathematical answer to that question would require doing the statistical analysis to determine the required sample size for acceptable margins of error. Such analysis is justified when you are making relatively large budget decisions. But for relatively small marketing investments, the overhead would be too costly. Therefore, many marketers don't invest the time and instead make a leap of faith when the sample size feels reasonable to them. Regardless of whether you take the shortcut or do the statistical analysis, once you adjust your marketing mix, I recommend that you go back to measuring the trend of sales attributable to marketing efforts. That way you can reassure yourself that the reallocation of your marketing spend has succeeded in increasing business volume.

Challenges to Overcome

It is easy to win friends for multichannel metrics. What's not to like about them when they are so incredibly useful? Well, to paraphrase Spiderman, with great opportunities come great challenges.

Data Collection and Integration Challenges

Foremost, there is the challenge of collecting customer behavior data from all channels and fusing the data to form a complete picture. Partially, the challenge is just in terms of know how. There are very few sources to turn to for advice on methods that should be used. There are analytics experts within each of the islands of online, direct, and brand marketing; however, they haven't shared much with each other in the past.

In fact, the deeper you are in any of these three disciplines, the more confusing the data can sometimes get. For example, even within just web analytics, there are multiple data collection methods that each will yield different numbers for the same website. But that kind of ambiguity has not stopped web marketers from turning web analytics into a gold mine by improving website results. Likewise, it should not stop multichannel marketers from doing the same across online and offline.

Even with the best know how, though, the actual data collection and integration still requires effort and typically a custom implementation. Every company has a different mix of systems and data items that are vital to it. Therefore, the implementation is less like traditional web analytics where the data sources are somewhat standardized. Web analytics applications come with prebuilt algorithms that can assemble raw data into a coherent picture. Instead, a multichannel metrics implementation is more like database marketing where off-the-shelf applications provide flexible capabilities for reaching and joining data sources as needed. This too, however, should not stop multichannel marketers because it is something that has already been done millions of times in direct marketing.

That same thought continues into the warehousing of multichannel data. Web analytics data has the nice advantage that most of it can be housed in generic data models that come prepackaged with off-the-shelf software. Multichannel data is less generic, especially when it comes to customer characteristics that each company stores. Hence the resulting multichannel data warehouses differ more from company to company. Yet, is that a reason to stop marketers? If it were, then no catalogs would come in the mail because the same issue is true for direct marketing.

The bottom line is, the investment needs to be committed and justified just like any other marketing effort by proving the ROI that results from employing the multichannel metrics.

The effort that is required can be reduced by using technology that was designed with multichannel integration in mind. Often, legacy technology may not have been designed for the purposes of multichannel integration. For example, data may be held captive in proprietary data silos. With the popularity of hosted, web analytics solutions, online behavior data often resides outside the company's systems at a third-party provider. Data feeds are then required in order to integrate multichannel data back into a central location. For some companies, that data transfer across the Internet may raise security concerns. If the data is to be used to drive right-time, let alone real-time, customer communication applications, then this data transfer may pose an additional risk to factor.

Yet, data is not the only challenge. In fact, the following challenges need to be overcome before we even get to the data collection phase.

Fusing the Online and Offline Marketer into a Whole Marketer

Maybe the most enjoyable aspect of working at Unica is that there are many colleagues from both the online and the offline marketing worlds. We get to compare the view points of both sides first hand. As it turns out, multichannel marketing requires more than just integrating marketing methods and metrics. It requires integrating the mind-sets of the marketers.

Kevin Cavanaugh, a colleague at Unica, pointed out the following brilliant analogy. Kevin is a veteran in the marketing industry with one foot deep in the offline direct-marketing world and the other deep in the online-marketing world.

Online marketers tend to live in a mind-set that is somewhat akin to *The Matrix*, (from the movie under the same title). There is an unbelievable detail of data streaming in about every prospect's and customer's every click, every day, every time. Having so much data at hand, online marketers use web analytics to turn the otherwise useless data into insights with which to improve the success of website design and online advertisements. What do you *not* see in *The Matrix* as easily, however? A picture of the customer as a person! Online marketers have traditionally been more focused on prospecting and aggregate-level analytics rather than paying much attention to the individual customer relationship.

What about the offline marketer's world? The offline marketer's world is more akin to the TV show *CSI: Crime Scene Investigation*. Offline marketers are not blessed with the detailed data available to the online colleague. They have to leverage every bit of information that they can extract and derive about their prospects' and customers' wishes, needs, desires, and dreams. Over time, they have become very clever at using every bit of data that they can get their hands on. Additionally, the offline marketer has typically been at this job much longer than the colleagues on the website. As such, the better offline marketers have already taken to a relationship marketing approach rather than "one size fits all" or spamming. Yet, according to research, despite the availability of technologies that enable merging the web data warehouse with the customer data warehouse, most offline marketers cite that they still lack clickstream data in their databases.

In combination, it appears that the online marketers have all the data, but the offline marketers have figured out the better questions to ask. They should talk, yes? But read on.

Organizational Challenges

The literature on Integrated Marketing Communications is highly recommended for a deep exploration of the organizational challenges that can block multichannel integration. If your company is like most others today, marketing is still divided into advertising, customer marketing, and interactive marketing departments. Employees across departments probably don't cooperate nor even communicate with each other very frequently. In my own work with customers, I have seen lead employees who frankly do not care about the other departments' goals. It can seem almost as if they were not the same company.

Remedies to this management problem are beyond the scope of this book. However, it is worth pointing out briefly that the online and offline channel experts in each department need to cooperate through overarching generalists that ensure integration. As Bruhn points out in the *Guide to Integrated Communication* cited earlier, this cooperation cannot happen in a top-down manner because the generalists are not expert in the special opportunities or limitations within each of the channels. Yet, this cooperation can also not happen in a bottom-up manner because the channel specialists may not be looking beyond their plates. As a consequence, an iterative approach of down-up management is required. In other words, multiple rounds of refining top-down plans with bottom-up feedback.

However, marketing cannot even go it alone. IT is a strategic enabler for collecting, storing, and orchestrating all the multichannel data between the company's systems. The cooperation between IT and Marketing has received a bad reputation, and maybe most noticeably so for the web channel. As a result, many online marketers have bypassed IT wherever possible by outsourcing web analytics. Yet the offline piece is so inextricably dependent on the company's information systems that outsourcing has been less of an option. As a result, online marketers who want to become multichannel marketers need to make friends with their IT colleagues again.

Hire People Who Care About Performance

Embracing multichannel metrics requires that companies first embrace web analytics and offline analytics. As Rebecca Lieb, editor in chief of ClickZ, put it: "Analytics are like exercise equipment. You don't get a great shape just from putting the equipment in your basement." If you don't make exercising one of your top three priorities in the day, it is not going to happen either!

Yet, if you are a web analyst for example, you know that the state of affairs with adopting best practices for web analytics still leaves much to wish for at most companies.

Namely, while a web analytics solution is in place almost everywhere today, it has rarely also been staffed with at least one dedicated web analyst who can give metrics the necessary attention. As a result, most companies tend to run generic reports and stop at mundane statistics such as traffic counts. Few of the solutions' capabilities for providing guidance are employed. Few metrics are shared on a regular basis. When this is the case, not surprisingly, the web business is not getting into any better shape just from having a web analytics solution around. It is worth asking why this has been happening to companies because the same obstacles, at a minimum, will also transfer to the adoption of multichannel metrics.

What is the difference between those who get a web analytics solution and those who really *get web analytics*? The following advice by Tom Harrison of DigitalAdvisor may sum it up: "Hire people who care about performance." DigitalAdvisor is an online company that uses web analytics to help them understand how visitors looking for plasma TV and LCD TV reviews and ratings are using the site in order to improve their TV buying experience.

In 2005 the discussion in the web analytics user community first turned to the phenomenon that almost all website marketers have a web analytics solution in place; yet the vast majority is leaving all the money on the table by using it solely for low-value trend reporting. Even fewer leverage the high-value analytics at their fingertips for optimizing ad spending and site conversions. Countless best practices for approaching web analytics successfully have been published since then. For example, you need to start with your site goals, translate those into key performance indicators (KPIs), make sure that you don't have too many KPIs, assign each KPI to an owner, and work an incremental cycle of testing and improvements.

While many more marketers have adopted these best practices today, to be honest, the majority of companies are still not following them. Why not? Not enough people, other priorities, too busy? DigitalAdvisor has been able to increase business results five fold. These other companies are too busy for that? Obviously, most web marketing managers must not have their priorities straight—or they don't believe in the opportunity that waits for them in the analytics because they befriend too many bad users of web analytics and not enough superstars like Tom Harrison.

Why were DigitalAdvisor and Tom Harrison so successful? Tom says, "We believe that the only way to run our business is to run it by the numbers." So the foundation is that management cares about performance. On top of this foundation Tom recommends hiring people who care about performance, as he and his colleagues do. I think that is what it boils down to. If you care about performance, you are going to find ways to get the numbers and optimize. If performance is not among your top three priorities, then you will always be too busy—too busy for web analytics and way too busy for multichannel metrics.

Hire People Who Care About People

The leading businesses do hire people who care about performance. Yet, Bob Thompson rightfully pointed out, during a conversation on CustomerThink, that the leading businesses seem even more frequently to hire people who care about people. After all, metrics are only a means to the end goal, which is to provide a better customer experience and increase two-way value. That requires people who are excited about employing the metrics and methods toward this goal.

Is it a Chicken or Egg Problem?

Finding people of this nature is easier said than done. They need to be as good at understanding business issues as they need to be at understanding data issues. They need to be savvy in marketing and in IT. They need to be strategic thinkers, care about customer service, and still need to be analytic enough to dig deep into the numbers. They need sound judgment for distinguishing fad from opportunity. They need to be neutral enough not to favor the marketing channels in which they have personal experience, but seek out the ones that promise the best returns. On top of all that, they need to be good communicators to get the couch potatoes in their organizations to come on board with the program.

They need to be true multidisciplinary superstars, in other words. Needless to say, this breed of employee does not come readymade out of the typical school program. They are more likely to be molded on the job at companies where there is already a mindset in existence of multichannel integration, performance optimization, and customer service orientation.

As a result, there may be a chicken or egg problem for creating multichannel marketers: Many companies may not get started with multichannel metrics because of lack of staff with prior experience. Yet, many business analysts may not gain know how of multichannel metrics because their companies are not prioritizing them yet.

It is time to cut through the Gordian knot now to unleash the benefits of multichannel metrics for business optimization. It is time for some marketers to be the chicken *and* the egg. Let's cross the street between online and offline to shake hands with the marketers on the other side. Somebody has to take the lead; why not you? May the rest of this book be helpful as you create your own path across the camps.

The Web Analyst Tackles Multichannel Metrics Online

Forget about the offline world for the moment; online marketing by itself is a multichannel environment. It splits across websites, e-mail, paid and organic search, comparison-shopping engines, ad networks, affiliate networks, social networks, blogs, and word-of-mouth marketing. Phew! The marketer employing these avenues has their work cut out for them. Let's see how web analysts manage to connect the dots from online marketing channels of all kinds to the website and over multiple site sessions all the way to the sales events that ultimately ensue.

Chapter Contents

A Day Without a Web Analyst?

The expertise of web analysts is indispensable for measuring ROI from the online marketing channels highlighted in Table 2.1—that is, the channels through which campaigns are executed and those through which prospects and customers respond.

▶ **Table 2.1** Marketing Execution Compared to Response Channels

Campaign Channel \ Response Channel	ONLINE					OFFLINE				
	Website	E-mail	Mobile	Blog	Viral	Viral	Mail / Fax	Phone	Direct Sales	Store
Advertising (nonaddressable) — TV/Radio/Print, Out-of-home, Events, Product Placement, In Store						Traditional Brand Marketers				
Direct Response (addressable) — Call Center, Direct Mail, Service Team, Mobile, Email, Web Ads, Search, Website	Traditional Online Marketers					Traditional Direct Marketers				

All the same, web analysts still go surprisingly underappreciated at most companies. Have you ever presented web analytics reports to your colleagues? Then you will know how hard you have to work just to keep them awake, let alone to listen or take action. Yet, at DigitalAdvisor, Tom Harrison and team draw on web analytics daily. DigitalAdvisor now operates four websites: Digital Camera HQ, Camcorder HQ, LaptopAdvisor.com, and DigitalAdvisor. Each site's reviews, real-world user commentary, and practical guidance are designed to help consumers choose the right products, and then quickly purchase them from top-rated online retailers or service providers. Since the early days of their business, Tom's team has applied intelligence from web analytics and other sources toward creating a superb experience for their website visitors—and they have the results to show for it. Online success rates have increased five-fold over the years, and visitors are almost twice as likely to come back to the site for more shopping.

Imagine yourself in the shoes of Tom and team back when DigitalAdvisor was a young startup. One day, maybe on a sleepless summer night, you come up with a great business idea. Yet, there will be so much to do in order to get the business started. In the midst of all that, can you keep your cool to set aside an hour a day for web analytics?

Steep Hills to Climb for Online Marketing

For the business to succeed, you must first attract the right visitors to the site. How can you do that? Oh well, you will just submit your site to all the search engines. You will also pay for keyword advertising. You will utilize e-mail too. Confident that you have a plan, you register your new website domain and start building your web pages. Not even a week goes by before you realize that you have not answered any of the real questions:

- Anybody can submit their website to search engines for indexing. Yet, there are so many competing websites that it does little good to be listed on page 3 of the search results. You cannot, however, be ranked highly for all search keywords at the same time. Which ones should you choose and write for your site?

- A paid keyword ad takes 5 minutes to buy. But what if you have thousands of potential search terms from which to choose? Which can you afford to pay for because you will be profitable?

- Display ads can be designed to seek a direct response or can focus on making a good impression for your brand. Which will work better?

- Anybody could e-mail spam. But which of your ideas for e-mail content are valued enough by customers for them to open, read, and take action? Additionally, how can you know which prospects clicked through from these e-mails most recently so that you might cater further offers to them?

- Even kids can create websites. Just pick from available templates! Still, most visitors never make it past the first page that they view on your site. After every click, more visitors lose interest and drop off prematurely. Having worked so hard to attract these visitors, how can you make your site as user-friendly as possible? Which site features make it easier for shoppers to discover and take advantage of merchants' product offers?

So many questions! If, like the team at DigitalAdvisor, you care deeply about customers and business performance, you will make the time for web analytics so that it can contribute answers.

Web Analytics Contributes Three Levels of Insights

What if one day you woke up and there were no more web analysts? Would only campaign and website optimization suffer? That would be bad enough, but web analysts also provide two higher levels of information and they would be lost too. Figure 2.1 outlines all three levels of insights.

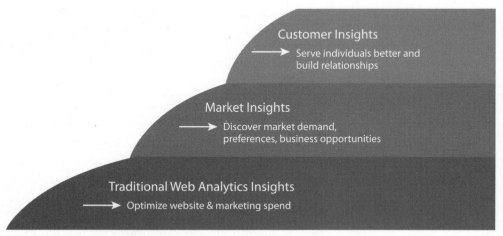

Figure 2.1 How do I love web analytics? Let me count the ways ...

Insights for making the site easier to use would remain hidden. When customers come into your brick-and-mortar stores, you can watch and help. With your website, you can only watch the lights flicker on your web servers.

- You would still do usability studies though. For example you may study lab users who arrive on the website searching for "Digital snap shooter X2000." What you might not know however is that more of your real life visitors may actually arrive searching for "easy to use snap shooters." Close, but different enough so that your website may or may not answer the question well.

- You would also still get feedback from visitors with the help of services such as ForeSee Results or OpinionLab. These will reveal extremely useful advice, e.g., that visitors were "looking for light weight snap shooters but could not find their way to the information." Without the combination with web analytics though, you may not know how to address the problem because you would not know where those survey respondents actually browsed on the site.

- You would also make use of multivariable testing solutions such as Optimost (recently acquired by Interwoven) or Offermatica (recently acquired by Omniture) who are extremely good at optimizing web pages for usability and results by automatically testing variations of page content, layout, and messaging. Without the combination with web analytics however, you might never know which pages within your site are the bottlenecks that you should focus your tests on.

Marketing efforts would be wasted. Your e-mail, ad serving, and paid search providers can all provide statistics on conversions. Do you still need purebred web analytics? Yes, because without it you would fail to learn why more of the visitors are not converting. Take search as an example:

- Visitors arriving on your site after clicking on an organic search listing may be delighted when they discover your promotional offer "20% off." However, visitors who arrive from paid search may find the same offer fishy and drop off. Why? Probably because these visitors know that they responded to an advertisement so that their level of trust is lower.

- Some of your visitors clicking on your ads for "Digital snap shooter X3000" may not convert because—unknown to you without web analytics—the full search phrase that they entered into the search engine actually was "Download manual for digital snap shooter X3000." If you knew, you would configure "Download manual" as a negative keyword to tell the search engines to suppress your ads.

- Unknown to you, visitors may still arrive on your site searching for "Digital snap shooter X2000" because of the model's high ratings by *Consumer Reports*. Yet, you may only carry the more recent "X3000."

  As a consequence, you stop advertising and optimizing your site for the "X3000" only to be surprised that business is going down. You did not realize that the visitors who did not convert during their initial visits were coming back a week later once they found out that the X2000 was the old model. Only this time, they entered the URL of your website directly so that you never gave credit to the initial ad click-through.

New business opportunities would remain undiscovered. As an entrepreneur, you constantly try to read the market to learn about customers' needs that can be turned into business. Yet, it doesn't help to have an ear on the ground if your customers are not on the ground but online:

- Lacking web analytics, you may never find out that on your site visitors enter the search phrase "Accessories for X3000" into the site search box. If you knew that there was demand, you would open a whole new department for accessories.

- You may never learn that visitors who buy a snap shooter also browsed camcorders with the capability to take pictures. If you knew, you might use the opportunity for up-selling.

Opportunities for helping individual customers would be missed. As a shopkeeper, you would know to rush to help customers at the right moment. But how can you do so online without web analytics?

- Without web analytics, you may never find out that a customer came twice to your site shopping for cameras, even started completing the online forms for the checkout process but then dropped out after all. If you knew, you might create an automated remarketing program for everyone who abandoned their shopping carts.

- You may also never detect when some of your most loyal customers start coming to the site less frequently. If you did, you might contact them to win them back.

Turn this list of examples on its head. You can then look at it as a list of recommendations for turning web analytics into action for better results. "Web analytics really is the proverbial gold mine that it's often thought to be," says Tom Harrison. "But you have to be willing to dig into the mine to reap the results."

Web Analytics Primer for Multichannel Marketers

If you are an offline marketer, this quick bottom-up introduction to web analytics can help get you on the right path.

Choosing a Web Analytics Solution

Although it may not be the best starting point, most marketers begin their endeavor into web analytics with the selection of a web analytics solution. You have the choice between software you install at your premises and on-demand solutions that are hosted for you. Some of the most-frequently mentioned vendors in alphabetical order are ClickTracks, Coremetrics, Google Analytics, IndexTools, Omniture, Unica, and Webtrends. Expected soon to arrive is also a solution from Microsoft codenamed *Gatineau*.

Aside from these purebred web analytics solutions, specialized web metrics are brought to you by providers of e-mail services, ad servers, search bid management, multivariable optimization solutions, surveys, and RSS management. Typically, their reports focus on result metrics for returns from the provider's efforts. There are three reasons for wanting to duplicate the same metrics within the web analytics solution as well. First, marketers may want to gather all their metrics into a single location for simplicity and for rank ordering. Second, some marketers may want to audit their providers' numbers by independently collecting data. Third, and most importantly, only the web analytics solution provides the complete picture of visitor behavior across all pages of the site. That in turn is required for calculating metrics such as engagement and of course for identifying bottlenecks in the step-by-step conversion process.

There are a number of great sources to turn to for advice on selecting the right solution that fits your requirements. Some of the most-frequently consulted sources are the industry analysts at Forrester Research, Gartner, and JupiterResearch. There are also buyers' guides and reports from CMS Watch, e-consultancy, Ideal Observer, MarketingSherpa, and Stone Temple Consulting. What you will learn is that all solutions have their strengths and weaknesses. That is why the best starting point into web analytics would be to figure out what your business requirements for measurement will be—i.e., your site's key performance indicators and key customer segments.

Data Is Collected via Logs or Page Tags

Before your web analytics solution can report anything, it needs to collect data. There are a number of different methods to choose from for data collection. The historical approach has been to use web server log files that automatically make an entry for every page or file that visitors access on the website. The favored approach today, however, is to instrument pages with JavaScript tags or invisible pixel-based beacons. As websites become increasingly dynamic (for example, through the use of Flash and AJAX technologies), log files lack information on behavior within pages. Still, logs retain some critical advantages over page tags, such as the ability to monitor search engine robots and spiders that index your site. Hence, a third option is to combine logs and page tags into a hybrid mode of data collection to reap some of the advantages of both.

> **Note:** Refer to Wikipedia for more info on using logs versus tags (shortcut via multichannelmetrics .com/Web_analytics).

Clicks Are Sessionized into Visits

Data on site visitors' behavior is collected click by click as visitors view pages, interact with forms, or drag the mouse to pan a map view. The set of pages and events that a visitor experienced on the site needs to be tied together by the analytics solution into what is called a *visit* or *session*. The process of doing so is called *sessionization*.

Marketers depend deeply on accurate sessionization. Without it the analytics solutions could not report on visitors' paths. More importantly, it follows that they could not report which portion of visitors, who eventually reached a "Thank you for buying from us" page, initially entered the site on a particular landing page—for example, after finding the site on Google.

Cookies Turn Visits into Visitors

In order for sessionization of clicks into visits to be accurate, web analytics solutions require a common criterion that they can find in each of the page requests. Moreover, to recognize a subsequent return visitor as an already-known unique visitor, a common criterion is needed between all that visitors' visits. These two problems are exactly what cookies help with in web analytics. Cookies can be set by the website or by the web analytics solution. For web analytics purposes, a unique ID is generated for each new visitor who does not have a cookie yet. If the cookie is configured to be of the persistent type, this ID is automatically stored on the browser's computer as a cookie. Every time the visitor returns for a new visit and clicks to a new page, the cookie is retrieved and read.

Without cookies, web analytics could not report on so-called *delayed conversions*. These are situations where a visitor may click-through from an ad while researching a buying decision; however, she may come back to the site a week later to complete the conversion. It is the cookie that enables web analytics to link the anonymous first visit with the conversion visit in order to credit the ad with the delayed conversion.

Note: Cookies are a marketer's best friends. Without them, delayed conversions could not be attributed to ad click-throughs during previous visits.

Registered Usernames Turn Visitors into People

Yet, cookies have various limits that cause the accuracy of reports to decrease. For example, those who use a computer at home, a different one at work, and also a pocket PC while on the road, have a different cookie ID stored in each. This is where registered usernames can help solve the problem. If the site is a registration site that requires visitors to authenticate via login and password, this login ID can be made available to the web analytics solution. Each of the clicks can then be associated with the registered user regardless what computer she uses. However, this strategy only augments the use of cookies rather than replacing it because it would not be wise to force visitors to register their first visit.

Jargon Alert: Cookies

Whereas logins can be compared to account or customer numbers in the offline world, cookies don't quite have an equivalent. That is, unless you could get your customers to carry a loyalty card with an RFID (Radio-frequency identification) tag that beamed their identity to detectors in your stores. Say, if the spaghetti sauce on a shelf detects your presence when you walk by, it might start speaking to you about special discounts it has to offer. Back to reality, the closest equivalent is maybe a CRM (Customer Relationship Management) or SFA (Sales Force Automation) system that keeps track of interactions with each prospective buyer.

The Big Three Metrics Form Your Baseline

You may have wondered how the terms *unique visitors*, *visits/sessions*, and *page views* are defined. So have many others before you. This was one of the contributing factors that inspired a few thought leaders to found the Web Analytics Association. The association includes a Standards Committee made up of volunteers who have worked for years to find agreeable standard definitions. The first major document that the committee signed off on was titled "Big 3 definitions," and it addressed precisely these terms. Namely, to quote from the document:

Unique Visitors   The number of inferred individual people (filtered for spiders and robots), within a designated reporting timeframe, with activity consisting of one or more visits to a site. Each individual is counted only once in the unique visitor measure for the reporting period.

Visits/Sessions   A visit is an interaction, by an individual, with a website consisting of one or more requests for an analyst-definable unit of content (i.e., "page view"). If an individual has not taken another action (typically additional page views) on the site within a specified time period, the visit session will terminate.

Page Views   The number of times a page (an analyst-definable unit of content) was viewed.

These three form the base metrics on which most other metrics in web analytics are built. In August 2007, the Standards Committee added to this set with the publication of definitions for 26 foundational web analytic metrics covering the areas of visits, content, and conversion.

Note: Go ahead and downloaded the standards from the association's website: http://www.webanalyticsassociation.org.

Key Performance Indicators (KPI) Are the Guiding Light

A sign in Albert Einstein's office read: "Not everything that can be counted counts, and not everything that counts can be counted." Most web analytics solutions can produce so many reports and metrics that web analysts often run into analysis paralysis. By the year 2005, all the pent-up frustration exploded into a crusade for highlighting the importance of KPIs for overcoming the problem. Namely, the best practice is to do the following:

1. Write down the business goals of the website—for example, providing customer service.

2. Translate these goals into five to maximum twenty metrics and targets (i.e., the KPIs)—for example, "Increase web self-service registrations and lower calls to customer service hotline by 10 percent."

3. For each goal, assign an owner who is responsible for it.

The example also demonstrates how your site's KPIs determine requirements for the web analytics solution—i.e., here the ability to combine metrics from call center and website channels into an integrated dashboard. If you know your top KPIs before you select a web analytics solution, you will make a better choice.

How does a web analytics solution measure a metric such as "Number of self-service registrations?" It is done by counting the number of instances where a visitor reached a thank-you page, also called a *goal page,* on the site. These are pages reached only by visitors who completed the registration process.

 Note: Conversions are measured by flagging visitors who reach thank-you pages. Revenue is typically measured by instrumenting thank-you pages with JavaScript tags that submit the purchased products and amounts to the web analytics solution.

Reports and Dashboards Answer General Questions

Base and KPI metrics are placed on reports and dashboards. Most web analytics tools also have a special user interface, called Overlay, that can visualize metrics by directly overlaying them over web pages so that analysts can see results in context with the site itself. See Figure 2.2 for an example.

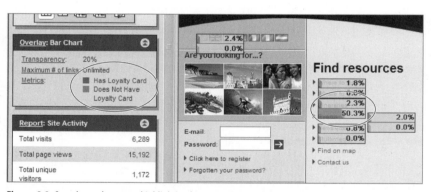

Figure 2.2 Sample overlay report highlighting how two visitor segments navigate a web page by overlaying metrics in context with the web page itself

Jargon Alert: Overlay

The online marketing term *overlay user interface* may confuse offline direct marketers because they use something called a *data overlay,* which is completely unrelated. A data overlay refers to the practice of *appending* additional data to a customer database (for example, for demographic or life style attributes).

Here are some of the most common reporting areas available in any web analytics solutions:

Marketing Analysis How are visitors finding the site and how are campaigns performing?

Content Analysis What pages or groups thereof contribute to success?

Event Analysis How are visitors behaving within pages (for example, within Flash movies)?

Visitor Analysis Who is visiting the site and what are common patterns?

eCommerce Analysis How is business? What is in customers' shopping carts?

Geo Analysis In what geographic locations are the visitors located who browse the site?

Technical Analysis Are there errors? Are there slowly loading pages?

Scenario/Funnel Analysis This is the queen of all web reports. It visualizes the drop-off from step to step in a process such as a retail website's checkout pages. However, a process does not need to be just a set of pages. For example, a scenario can also represent your sales funnel for tracking the process of turning first time visitors into engaged prospects and eventually customers.

Path Analysis Also referred to as *clickstream analysis,* this is the archetypical web analytics report that visualizes, for example, the most common next pages viewed after a selected starting point.

Segmentation Leads to Actionable Insights

The crusade for KPIs in 2005 overshot its goals a bit. Audiences sometimes left presentations on best practices with the wrong impression that KPIs were not just necessary but sufficient for achieving web analytics results. In reality, however, KPIs are only the starting point for analysis not the ending point. Analysis is performed by means of segmentation. Only segmentation produces actionable results. For example, if conversion rate is your KPI and it is 2 percent, is that good or bad? Neither. But if you segment the conversion rate by prospects' gender and find out that the conversion rate for men is 4.5 percent while for women it is only 0.3 percent, you immediately have an action item to ponder why this may be and what you can do to convert more women.

Once KPIs are defined, segmentation is at the heart of what a web analyst does to be worth her corn. Take another example. What action item can you derive from the answer to the question "What are the most popular pages on my site?" None whatsoever! Instead, ask for example: "What are the most popular pages on my site for those visitors who arrive on the site searching for easy to use snap shooters?" If too many of these visitors are not finding the pages that you know would help them reach their goal, then you have an action item to highlight those pages better.

Note: Web analytics with KPIs but without segmentation would be like a burglar alarm that doesn't tell you whose house is being robbed.

Begin web analytics by specifying the KPIs for your site. Then determine the key segments of prospects and customers that are relevant. For example, DigitalAdvisor may distinguish between consumers and professionals who are looking for advanced features. Only after you have defined your segments will you find out where the data resides that allows you to create the segments in the reporting solution. Only now are you able to evaluate web analytics solutions properly to determine whether they will support your requirements. Segmentation can be performed in many ways, for example:

Filtering A report or metric is restricted to selected visitor segments

A/B analysis A report type that compares results for two different segments of visitors

Date comparison analysis A report type that compares results for two different time frames

Drilling An investigative style of analysis where you select a subsegment in one report and retrieve further reports with more information about this group of visitors

Trending Not the activity of trending base metrics such as page views over time, but the activity of trending specific segments (for example, those who arrive on the site searching for easy to use snap shooters)

Correlation A report type that shows the interdependence of two reporting dimensions. For example, for each of the most common organic keywords that bring visitors to the site, what were the most common entry pages?

Analyze This!

This step is the key for taking action. *Analysis* is what happens inside the head of the web analyst after reporting and segmentation. Though, it alternatively refers to the use of data-mining software for discovering patterns in the data. Either way, the web analyst separates noise from meaningful insight. The analyst then derives further questions to ask or formulates theories. For example, the analyst may theorize that he could help visitors who are searching for easy to use snap shooters by improving the most common entry pages for these visitors in a certain way.

Take Action! Otherwise, Why Do Web Analytics?

The only way to test your theories is to try them out with a sample of visitors so you can verify whether they lead to an improvement for your key metrics. The team at DigitalAdvisor always has a number of such tests lined up in order to measure which option best improves usability. Gut feeling and executive decrees have proven wrong in many cases. A proposed solution that may seem so promising can turn out to be the opposite and vice versa. There is no other way to know how customers will react other than to run tests.

> ### Treasure Troves of Web Analytics Tips and Tricks
>
> Some of the best minds in the web analytics industry have shared their experience in book form. Jim Sterne's *Web Metrics* and Hurol Inan's *Measuring the Success of Your Website* published in 2002 were the original books on the subject. These were followed by Eric Peterson's *Web Analytics Demystified* in 2004 and his *Web Site Measurement Hacks* that followed a year later. The Hacks book is an invaluable reference with deep dives into 100 key questions that are not answered elsewhere in that level of detail. In 2007 multiple new books followed. One of these, *Web Analytics: An Hour A Day* by Avinash Kaushik is to be revered because the author really brought his perspective as a practitioner to shine. Another one, *Actionable Web Analytics* by Jason Burby and Shane Atchison, adds unique perspectives for the management of a web analytics program. It must not be missing in a web analyst's library either.

Attribute Responses to the Right Online Marketing Efforts

Are you burning to measure your marketing campaigns now? There is more to do before you can give credit to the campaigns that deserve credit for the business that results. You know how to track conversion events. Tracing backward from the conversion event, you know how your web analytics solution sessionizes visitors' clickstreams that lead up to the conversion event, even across multiple preceding visits. However, your web analytics solution also needs a way of knowing which visitors to the site are attributable to which marketing effort. If visitors arriving from one ad seem to be indistinguishable from those that viewed another ad, it will be very difficult or impossible to tell them apart. Luckily, there are at least five methods through which your marketing initiatives become measurable:

- Visitors arriving on your site from a referring website can be ascribed to that site with the help of referring URLs.

- Visitors arriving on your site via click-through from an ad or e-mail can be attributed with the help of tracking codes.

- Visitors coming to your site directly because they remembered an online advertisement that they viewed at an earlier point in time are said to be view-through visitors. The relation to the ad impression can be inferred with the help of cookies.

- Visitors who receive an e-mail and then visit the site without clicking through from a hyperlink within the e-mail can be inferred with the help of a direct marketing method called *matchback*.

- Visitors coming to your site because they learn of it through word-of-mouth marketing can be measured through inferred attribution. This requires however that the viral marketing campaign gets them to exhibit some kind of unique behavior that helps pick them out of the crowd.

The following sections discuss each of these five methods.

Credit Referrers by Help of Referring URLs

The two favored questions that people like to ask to web analysts are "Where did my visitors come from?" and "Where did they go after they left my site?" Unfortunately, the latter cannot be answered with web analytics, although competitive analysis solutions such as comScore, Hitwise, and Compete can provide hints based on their sample of visitors to your site. The first question on the other hand could have also been impossible to answer, but luckily for marketers, it is actually an easy one.

Whenever a visitor clicks a hyperlink, the web browser asks the web server specified in the hyperlink's destination URL for the page. When it does, the web browser typically also sends along with this request the URL of the page on which the hyperlink was clicked (i.e., the referring URL). Who do marketers have to thank for this? It is the HTTP protocol, the norm that governs how web browsers and servers *should* communicate with each other.

Say you go to the Ask search engine and enter a query for **Web Analytics Solutions**. The URL of the search results pages will look similar to the following.

```
http://www.ask.com/web?q=web+analytics+solutions&o=0&l=dir&qsrc=0&qid=D1F31B
5AFD6C91E472F1C99488B4E7EF&page=2&jss=
```

When you then click any of the search results on that page, this URL is sent along with the request for the target page as the referring URL. The web analytics solution will record the referring URL and can automatically extract a number of very useful facts:

- Based on the domain information within the URL http://www.ask.com/, this visit was referred by Ask.

- Based on the key-value pair q=web+analytics+solutions within the query string portion of the URL (i.e., the portion following the question mark), the visitor typed the keywords "web analytics solutions" into the Ask search box. (Note that the plus signs in the URL replace the blanks that would otherwise break the URL.)

- Based on the key-value pair page=2 within the query string of the URL, the visitor browsed to page 2 of the search results on Ask, which is where she found the listing and clicked.

What is described here for Ask applies to all search engines even though the URLs and key-value pairs are different from engine to engine. You don't need to worry about those differences though. You can just sit back because web analytics solutions are preprogrammed to deal with almost all major search engines automatically. The only exception is the third point, which typically does require manual configuration. See Figure 2.3 for a typical report on referrers and search keywords.

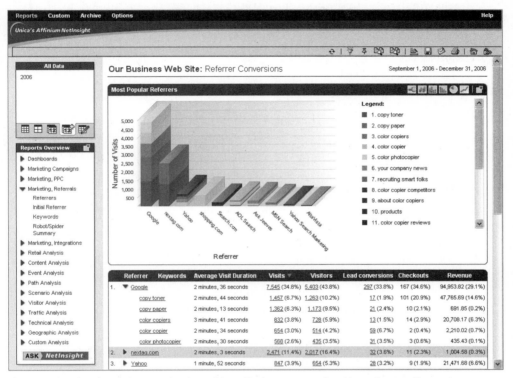

Figure 2.3 Sample web analytics report that shows visits and business events attributable to referrers and keywords

When to Rely on Referring URLs?

Referring URLs are brilliant for measuring certain marketing channels and useless for others. They are best suited for measuring the following initiatives. Common to all of them is that the user has to be clicking on a hyperlink within another web page to initiate the referral event—i.e., a click-through.

Organic Search You have referring URLs to thank for the fact that you can easily measure organic search—i.e., click-throughs from unpaid listings on search engines. Search engines can be ranked by their historical value to the business, and so can the search keywords that visitors enter.

Search Engine Optimization (SEO) Although rough, the information on the page number from which the search listing was clicked can help you assess what the relative value would be of having a search listing appear on page 1 as apposed to page 2 of search results, for example. This in turn helps justify and direct efforts for search engine optimization toward better rankings.

Referrals from news articles, partners, blogs, and other sites If it were not for referring URLs, you would never know how much traffic is referred to you through hyperlinks on news sites, partners' sites, directories, or blog posts that link to you. Because the content on those sites is outside of your control, referring URLs are the only approach for measuring them.

When Are Referring URLs Not Enough?

There is one big bummer though. Say, you read the name of a cool new product in a news article and then you search to find the website and click on the search listing. Should the credit for your business be assigned to the search engine or to the news article? The answer is complex. It is discussed in Chapter 8. For now, suffice it to say that everyone searching for keywords that include your brand names, rather than product category keywords, must have already come into touch with you elsewhere.

 Note: Just because a customer was referred to you via a particular hyperlink it does not mean that he would not have visited or purchased anyway. More often than not in web analytics, only the most recent click-through has been credited with the resulting business. Depending on your marketing programs, that may or may not be the right thing to do. Ask your web analytics vendor for advice on alternative approaches.

Yet, there are much simpler scenarios in which referring URLs are not enough. For example, what if you are running multiple variations of a display ad on the same website? You could not tell from the referring URL which creative was clicked. What if your website comes up both within organic search results and paid search ads for a particular keyword on a search engine? Referring URLs could not tell which listing was clicked. Referring URLs also don't work when a hyperlink within an e-mail is clicked. If all that were not enough, refer to the deep dive in *Website Measurement Hacks,* by Eric Peterson, for a listing of cases in which referring URLs come up empty due to technical issues. So, what to do?

Credit Ads with Click-Throughs by Way of Tracking Codes

Clever marketers have found a solution for overcoming many scenarios in which referring URLs fail. Take an analogy. When your home is for sale, and a realtor brings a potential buyer to take a look, what does the broker do so that you will remember her afterward? She leaves her business card. Marketers have thought of a way in which each ad, sort of, presents its business card whenever it sends a visitor to your website. Namely, this is achieved by configuring each ad with a unique destination URL.

Types of Destination URLS with Tracking Codes

The destination URL is the entry page on your website to which an ad's hyperlink takes visitors upon clicking. Because you control your advertisements and e-mail campaigns, you can design the hyperlinks to direct visitors to any unique destination page of your choosing on your site (for example, http://www.mySite.com/halfprice). Other than simple destination URLs, such as the previous example, there are several variations that are commonly used:

TRACKING CODES

With the enormous number of ads that you run in parallel, especially with keyword advertising, you could not afford to create a unique physical entry page for each. That is where *tracking codes* come into play. Tracking codes are destination URLs in which you append a query string of parameter key-value pairs encoding the source that should get the credit for the click-through. *Query strings* are the portion of a URL after the question mark in the URL. Query strings normally are employed with dynamically generated web pages. Query strings consist of one or multiple key-value pairs separated by ampersands. A simple example might be

`http://www.mySite.com/ads.html`**`?source`**`=e-mail123`**`&creative`**`=ABC`

For the purposes of marketing measurement, your entry page ads.html does not need to read nor recognize the query string. Your campaigns will be more successful, however, if the entry page does leverage this extra input to serve up dynamic content relevant to the advertisement. Regardless, the entire URL, including the query string, will be noted within the web analytics solution as the entry page. So, you can have multiple advertisements pointing to the same /ads.html entry page and identify the individual ads through the tracking code.

Jargon Alert: Codes

What the online marketer calls *tracking codes*, offline marketers may call *source codes* and *offer codes*. A source code refers to a unique ID assigned to a catalog or other piece of marketing collateral. An offer code is a key assigned to a particular promotional offer. Their purposes are exactly the same as tracking codes. The codes are collected when prospects and customers interact with the company. The resulting business can then be attributed back to the marketing initiative.

PERSONAL IDENTIFIABLE TRACKING CODE

Typical for e-mail campaigns, tracking codes can be extended with an additional parameter key value pair that identifies the individual e-mail recipient, for example

source=e-mail123**&creative**=ABC**&customerID**=123456

Once again, the entry page does not have to read this extra input. However the entry page could leverage it to present dynamic content relevant to the individual. Regardless, the web analytics or e-mail campaign management solution can extract the customer identifier to flag an individual customer to have not only received and opened a particular e-mail communication but also clicked through to the site. This is especially helpful if the recipients of the e-mail have not before visited the site. Until they register on the site down the road, the personal identifiable tracking code is the only information that suggests their identity.

Jargon Alert: Personal codes

What the online marketer calls *personal identifiable tracking codes*, the offline direct marketer may call *personal offer codes*. They are typical, for example, in pre-approved credit card offers.

ENCRYPTED TRACKING CODES

As a shopper, don't you love to get attention from sales people as soon as you have a question? But you don't like to feel as if you are being watched while you are just browsing. The same is true for everybody else. For this reason, tracking codes are often encrypted so that they appear as bland long strings, for example:

src=12482WAShjahs267

Some web analytics solutions generate codes of this nature that the marketer can then plug into their destination URLs when they configure their advertisements. Conversely, the encoding can also be generated within the campaign management solution. In that case, the web analytics solution is given access to a translation table for decomposing the code back into the individual pieces of information that can be derived from the tracking code. The latter approach makes more sense in e-mail marketing when you use personal identifiable tracking codes in the hyperlinks in which case only the campaign management solution could do the encryption.

When to Rely on Tracking Codes?

You need to be able to control the destination URLs so that you can set unique tracking codes. There also has to be a click-through event since nobody would bother to type in the tracking codes. Some of the most common areas of use are outlined here:

PAID SEARCH ADVERTISING

Tracking codes are especially useful for measuring results from paid search advertising with web analytics. They are stuffed with key information, such as:

The Paid Keyword This is what you pay money for when you buy ads from Google, Yahoo!, etc. Wouldn't you want to know which paid keyword was responsible for the visit? Yet, the paid keyword for which you advertise may differ from the search phrases entered into the search engine. For example, if you advertise on keyword "digital camera reviews," your ad can still be shown when visitors type in a variation such as "best digital camera reviews." A tracking code such as paidkeywords=digital+camera+reviews will reveal which paid keyword was responsible for the click-through.

Easy Ways to Set Paid Keyword Tracking Codes

It would be very tiresome if you had to manually configure tracking codes for all the keywords for which you advertise. Instead, you have multiple options. You can use bid management solutions such as Atlas Search, DART Search, Didit, Efficient Frontier, SearchForce, and others. Alternatively, the search engines offer APIs that you can program if you want to roll your own bid management solution. You can also generate your ads in a spreadsheet and simply upload it to the search engines.

Even for those who are configuring their ads manually through the search engines' web user interfaces, there are easy ways to set tracking codes. For example, Yahoo! Search Marketing offers a Tracking URLs feature that marketers can enable for all their keywords with the flip of a single switch. Conversely, Google AdWords offers macros that the marketer can employ in the destination URLs of her ads. For example, a tracking code specified as paidkeywords={Keyword} will be automatically expanded into paidkeywords=digital+camera+reviews. Check with your pay-per-click vendors to leverage these features.

Search versus Content Network Search engines can serve your keyword ads within search results or within their content networks such as Google AdSense and Yahoo! Content Match. Conversion rates vary vastly because visitors coming through search are much more targeted. Therefore, you want to distinguish them in your measurements. The search engines make this easy with macros or automated tracking codes. Check with each vendor.

Paid Keyword Vendors versus Their Affiliated Sites The major search engines are affiliated with partner sites. For example, Google paid search ads may appear within search results on AOL or Ask. In order to attribute the click to the paid search vendor and not just to the referring search engine, a tracking code of the nature "source=Google" does the trick.

Ad Type The ever-evolving search engines also offer image and video ads beyond textual ads. Stuff your tracking codes to indicate what type of ad should be credited with the click-through and resulting business.

Further key-value pairs could be added to track, for example, ad creative, ad groups, and campaigns. A resulting tracking code may look as follows:

source=Google**&keywords**=digital+camera+reviews**&adgroup**=review+keywords**&**
campaign=spring+promotion**&network**=search**&adtype**=textual**&adcreative**=123

DISPLAY AND RICH MEDIA ADVERTISING

Just as with paid keyword advertising, display and rich media ads also have a number of characteristics that marketers want to distinguish in order to devise which options work best. These characteristics include publisher media, creative, placements, ad types, and many more. Ad-serving companies such as Atlas and DoubleClick will provide advertisers reports across myriads of such attributes. In order to include some of these details in web analytics reports, tracking codes can be stuffed for display ads with the desired codes. For example:

source=Atlas**&creative**=summer+cameras**&campaign**=spring+promotion**&adtype**
=flash

However, ad-serving companies already equip their destination URLs with encrypted tracking codes so that they can collect data for the reports that they provide. You will notice, for example, how ads delivered by DoubleClick first take you to DoubleClick's domain when you click and afterward you are redirected to the final destination on the advertiser's site with a new set of tracking codes.

As a consequence, web marketers can take a different route in order to import the information into web analytics. Namely, some web analytics solutions can be integrated with ad-serving solutions. With this approach, the ad-serving company will essentially supply the web analytics solution with a translation table for their encrypted tracking codes. Web analytics reports can then break out site visit behavior by ad characteristics. Ask your web analytics and ad-serving vendors for the options they provide in this regard.

E-MAIL MARKETING

Newsletters and marketing e-mail have many components that a marketer can vary to test and optimize results. These include, for example, subject lines, sender names, creative, and content. In order to see which options work best, hyperlinks from the e-mail to the website can be stuffed with tracking codes. For example:

source=email123**&campaign**=spring+promotion**&creative**=summer+cameras
&subjectline=2**&sender**=3**&recipient**=123456

However, e-mail campaign management solutions already provide the ability to encode hyperlinks in the e-mails with a unique identifier for the message and another for the recipient. Therefore, here too marketers can choose the route of importing the detailed makeup of each message from the campaign management system. Of course, this requires that the web analytics and e-mail campaign management solution are able to integrate.

Note: Whenever applicable, tracking codes are the main mechanism used for attributing online business results to online advertising and e-mail marketing click-throughs.

When Are Tracking Codes No Help?

The concerns of cause versus correlation voiced for referring URLs in multi-touch situations apply to tracking codes just the same. Furthermore, tracking codes only help when there is a click-through. Yet, when you go to a news site, you see many ads but click only a few or maybe none of them. Just as with advertising on TV, however, you may remember the ad impression and pay a visit to the advertiser's website down the road. In fact, you may then appear as a visitor who typed in the domain name of the site directly. The marketer would like a way of measuring the impact that the ad impression had in this regard. But how would that be possible?

Infer Ad View-Throughs with Cookies

Is the primary purpose of display advertising to drive direct response or build brand equity? For a long time, online marketers focused entirely on driving direct response toward lead generation and sales. However, in parallel to the advent of rich media ads, brand advertising has arrived as well. Other than display ads it may also come in the form of video inserts, for example.

As a consequence, it has become imperative to assess the return on ad investments even when there is no click-through to the site. Unfortunately, nobody ever said that measuring brand advertising was an easy task. Offline marketers have developed a number of complex approaches; some of which are summarized in Chapter 5, "The Brand Marketer's Take On Multichannel Analytics." Internet marketers, however, rightfully wish to improve on those methods by drawing on the much better measurability of their medium. That is what view-throughs promise.

View-through measurement works by setting a cookie along with the ad impression and matching it against visitors' cookies when they visit the advertiser's website down the road. If there is a matching cookie during a visit no later than, say, 30 days after the ad impression, then the ad impression can be credited with the resulting business to a certain degree. What degree? That is subject to hot debate and will be discussed later in this section.

Jargon Alert: View-Throughs and Events

What the online marketer calls *view-throughs,* offline direct marketers may call *inferred response attribution.* With inferred response attribution, the marketer knows that a particular prospect has been targeted with a marketing communication. Yet, when the prospect responds they do so without referring to any source or offer code. The offline marketer will infer that the communication played some role in the response.

How to Measure Ad View-Throughs?

Getting view-through metrics is actually easy. Probably all ad-serving companies supply metrics not only for click-throughs but also view-throughs. However, certain limitations apply, and web analytics solutions promise to overcome those. Yet, before web analytics can capture data on view-throughs, a number of not-so-simple conditions need to be met. More on both alternatives follows:

VIEW-THROUGHS MEASURED BY AD-SERVING COMPANIES

The typical mechanism is illustrated in Figure 2.4. With most ad-serving companies, ads displayed on publishers' sites are served from the ad server's domain. In other words, if you go to the *New York Times* website and check the source of a banner ad image served through DoubleClick, you will see that the ad creative (i.e., image file) typically resides on DoubleClick's servers. While serving the ad creative, DoubleClick also sets a cookie with a unique identifier for the visitor. For example, if you delete your browser's cookies and then go to the *New York Times* site, you will see after just a few page views that you have new cookies from various ad-serving companies. The ad-serving company also makes a note on their end as to which ads have been exposed to the visitor based on their cookie.

But the story continues. In addition to all this, the advertiser places page tags supplied by the ad-serving company on key pages within their website, most notably the thank-you pages. When a site visitor reaches one of these pages, the page tag is triggered submitting the event to the ad-serving company. If the visitor has a cookie by the ad server, it is also submitted with this page tag. Connecting the dots, the ad-serving company's analytics system is then able to see how many of the visitors who converted had previously been exposed to an ad.

MEASURING VIEW-THROUGHS WITH WEB ANALYTICS

View-through measurement by ad servers is somewhat limited because the ad-serving company's page tag is typically not placed on all pages of an advertiser's website but only on a few key pages. What if the advertiser wanted to measure visitor engagement,

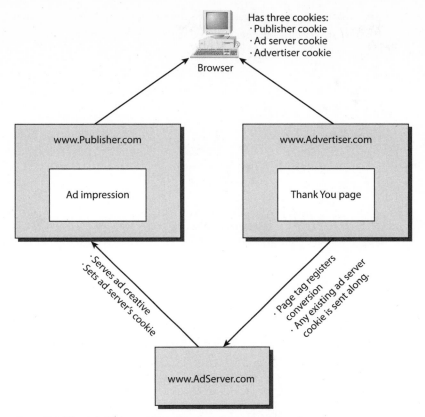

Figure 2.4 Schematic of ads served from the ad-serving company's domain

not conversions, following a view-through? That would require measuring interaction with all pages of the site, which in turn requires web analytics.

Yet, how would a web analytics system be able to get data on ad impressions? These are viewed by visitors on publisher's websites after all. Yes, the web analytics and ad-serving companies could exchange data. However, the ad-serving company uses one cookie, and the advertiser uses a different one on their site. It would be impossible to synchronize those cookies in order to match up ad views and website visits. There are two options to address this problem and enable web analytics:

Advertiser Tags the Ads Ads can be tagged such that they make one additional call back to the advertiser's website or analytics system. With that, every ad impression is recorded and a cookie can be set by the advertiser's web analytics system. While this is technically possible, it appears to be done in relatively fewer cases today. You can see this firsthand by clearing your cookies and browsing publishers' websites. While you will notice many ad server cookies appearing on your computer, you will rarely see an advertiser's cookie until you visit their site.

Advertiser Serves the Ads A new generation of ad-serving companies, such as Colorado-based TruEffect, is providing an alternative mechanism for ad serving through their DirectServe technology. Instead of serving ads from the ad-serving company's domain, DirectServe serves ads directly from the advertiser's domain. See Figure 2.5 for a schematic. In other words, if you went to a publisher's site and checked the source of a banner served with DirectServe, you would find that it resides on the advertiser's domain. Along with the image, the advertiser can set their cookie that is also used for the rest of their web analytics throughout their site. Beyond enabling better view-through measurement, this idea is very promising in that it can solve the hurdle to advertisers for integrating interactive marketing across channels.

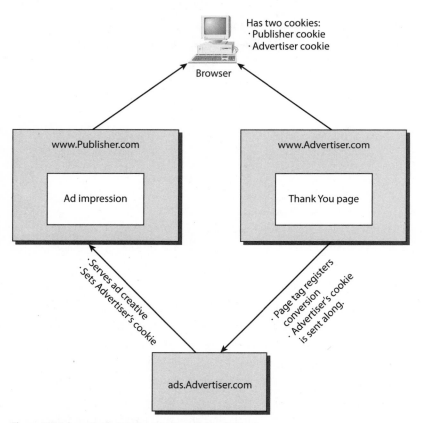

Figure 2.5 Schematic of ad serving from the advertiser's domain

Correlation versus Causal Relationship

Did you have any doubts about trusting view-throughs when you read the previous paragraphs? Well, doubts in the reliability of the metric have in fact been the greatest obstacle preventing its widespread adoption. There are good reasons for this lack of trust. People are quick to remark that there are so many ads on most publisher web pages that visitors may ignore them in many cases. Ads may even be under the fold of the scroll line and the visitor may never scroll down.

The bottom line is that what is being measured is a correlation not a causal relationship. For example, take a well-known brand such as Continental Airlines. Given how well-known the airline is and also given the common use of travel search engines, the fact that a view-through visitor bought a ticket may have nothing to do with ads to which they were exposed.

First-Party Cookies versus Third-Party Cookies

There are multiple kinds of cookies. Two that are especially important to distinguish for measuring online marketing are first-party and third-party cookies:

First-Party Cookies If a visitor visits www.mySite.com and this website sets a cookie, this cookie is called a first-party cookie. This is because the cookie is set by the site that the visitor is currently visiting.

Third-Party Cookies If a visitor visits www.mySite.com and that website contains an ad coming from another domain such as www.AdClicks.com, and that domain sets a cookie, this cookie is called a third-party cookie. This is because the cookie is set from a different domain than the site that the visitor is currently visiting.

Why should the marketer care? Because third-party cookies have both unique advantages and disadvantages:

Advantages of Third-Party Cookies Third-party cookies are generally the only way to measure a visitor's behavior across multiple websites. For example, view-through measurement requires tying behavior on the publisher's website to behavior on the advertiser's website. For that purpose, the visitor needs to be identified by the same unique cookie on both sites. That is only possible with third-party cookies. The advertiser can't read the publisher's cookie because, as a privacy and security mechanism, web browsers do not permit any one site to read cookies set by another.

Disadvantages of Third-Party Cookies As studies by JupiterResearch revealed in 2005, third-party cookies are much more frequently blocked and deleted. For example, anti-spyware software is far more likely to label third-party cookies as spyware cookies recommending their deletion. Such software can even block third-party cookies from known analytics solutions altogether. As a consequence, measurements based on these cookies suffer in accuracy. Third-party cookies used to be the norm for all on-demand web analytics solutions.

The move against third-party cookies probably began with the release of Internet Explorer's version 6 late in 2001. Focused on privacy and security features, the release by default blocked third-party cookies unless they had a satisfactory privacy policy associated with them. Especially, personally identifiable information was deemed unsatisfactory. Nowadays, third-party cookies are generally considered obsolete. The only application where they survive—due to lack of alternatives—is the measurement of behavior across sites.

The only way to distinguish correlation from causal relationship is to conduct a study with a control group. That is exactly what DoubleClick did in 2004, specifically with their customer Continental Airlines. The study is available from DoubleClick's website under the name "In-Direct Response to Digital Advertising." (shortcut via multichannelmetrics.com/IndirectResponse) The study used control groups where visitors, instead of seeing Continental Airlines' ads, were exposed to control ads by charitable organizations. The study concluded that "even with a well-established brand such as Continental Airlines, online creative has a significant role in in-direct response activity attributed to view-through." For the test campaign, 67.5 percent of the test group's view-through registrations and sales were attributable to online creative. In other words, only 32.5 percent of registrations and sales where visitors were previously exposed to a Continental Airlines ad would have occurred naturally without the online ad. That is a big thumbs-up for measuring view-throughs. Yet, the study rightfully cautioned advertisers to do their own testing as their results will likely differ.

 Note: With view-throughs (even more than click-throughs), you need to go beyond measurement and conduct tests against a control group so that you can distinguish correlation from causal relationship.

When Aren't View-Throughs Helpful?

View-through tracking relies on a common cookie or similar mechanism between ad impression and site visit. That is not always given.

- In textual paid search ads, it is not possible for advertisers to set a cookie.
- How about view-throughs from marketing e-mails? Most e-mail clients do not accept cookies.
- In most cases, in-game advertising and product placements within videos are not at the moment flagged with a cookie.
- A customer may be exposed to an ad on their laptop, but later use their smart phone to go to the website and make a purchase.
- One person may view an engaging commercial and then tell a friend about it who then visits the advertiser's site.

In these situations, what can a marketer do to still assign credit for business results to the right campaigns that deserve it? See the next two sections for answers.

Infer E-mail View-Throughs Through Matchback

The mere fact of seeing a trusted sender's e-mail arrive in your inbox may keep the sender's brand present on your mind. You may not even necessarily open the e-mail and still be more likely to visit the vendor's website when a need for their products arises. This could be called an e-mail view-through.

For example, DigitalAdvisor runs e-mail alerts to let subscribers know when desired new products become available. You would think that those e-mail programs would work primarily by getting customers to click-through to the site in order to view the new products. Yet, Tom Harrison's team found that while the customers participating in these programs did indeed become far more likely to return to the site for repeat visits, very often those repeat visits were not initiated via click-through from the e-mails. Instead, the visitors either typed in the name of the website directly or found the website again via a search using its brand name.

Measuring these e-mail view-throughs requires a different approach than measuring ad view-throughs. This is because e-mail client software such as Microsoft Outlook and Mozilla Thunderbird, even though they render HTML content, do not accept cookies. For security purposes, they don't like to execute JavaScript marking most e-mails that contain scripts as potential security threats. Finally, by default they do not render images anymore until the user prompts the e-mail client to do so. Therefore, the technique that is used for tracking e-mail opens, namely embedding a beacon image, is not as reliable as it used to be. How then can view-throughs be measured given this void of available data?

Marketers can borrow a technique from direct marketing referred to as *matchback response attribution*. Because matchback is a technique that originated in the offline world, it is explained in greater detail in the next chapters. Suffice it to summarize here that the idea is simple. Because the e-mail marketer has a list of all e-mail addresses that have recently been sent a particular message, the list can be matched against customers who visit the website and are identified either through an existing registration cookie, a login, or a new registration that includes their e-mail address on record. For the matched prospects and customers, it can be inferred that their visit should be credited to the e-mail campaign to a certain degree. Higher-end campaign management solutions have built-in capabilities for automating matchback in this fashion.

Correlation versus Causal Relationship

Just as with ad view-throughs, there will be a lot of false positives. After all, if you buy a ticket from Continental Airlines, it may have nothing to do with the fact that you are also subscribed to their e-mail program. In order to correct for the false positives, the marketer can use a control group of prospects and customers for whom the marketing communication is suppressed. If all else is the same between the e-mail recipients and the control group, and the control group is of significant size, then the lift in online visits by the e-mail recipients can be safely attributed to the e-mail campaign. Campaign management solutions are equipped to incorporate control groups into response attribution reporting. You just have to make sure you do not neglect putting the capabilities to use. Otherwise, don't blame matchback for leading you to wrong decisions!

Credit Word-of-Mouth Marketing by Inferring Viral Infection

Remember the Crash the Super Bowl campaign launched by Doritos and Yahoo!? For this campaign, Yahoo! Video along with Doritos created a micro website where consumers were encouraged to send in homemade Super Bowl commercials, with a chance for the winner to be aired during prime time. The winner was elected by votes that the public cast directly on the website. Compete, who provides free traffic estimates for websites, reported that 10 times as many people visited the microsite as visited Doritos.com during the first two weeks of January 2007.

In parallel to Doritos' campaign, Chevrolet also ran a contest for consumer-generated Super Bowl commercials, yet it generated much lower amounts of buzz if website traffic is an indicator. See Figure 2.6 for an estimate by Compete on the traffic flow to two of the microsites associated with these campaigns. (These microsite domains were not the only URLs associated with the campaigns.) Mind you, lower traffic volumes cannot be automatically assumed to mean less success. In order to assess success (i.e., ROI), you need much more information, including costs for each campaign and business results beyond just buzz and awareness.

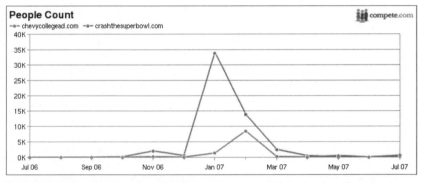

Figure 2.6 Compete estimate on web traffic to microsites crashthesuperbowl.com and chevycollegead.com

Jargon Alert: Word-of-Mouth Marketing

Measuring Word-of-Mouth marketing has many parallels to measuring lift in online activity triggered by offline mass advertising (for example, via TV or billboards). In both cases, there are neither click-throughs nor offer codes to rely on so that measurement requires other means. To compare, see Chapter 6, "Measure Lift Between Online and Offline."

Measurement is the key that enables marketers to adjust their campaign strategy based on early results. Yet, how can marketers measure viral campaigns given that they are reliant on the word-of-mouth passing from one guy to the next during late night parties, cell phone chats, IM, and e-mail? There still are a few techniques that marketers can bank on.

Correlate Trends

So you launched your word-of-mouth marketing campaign but forgot to think about measurement ahead of time? Now the boss is asking for results and you are waving your arms? Well, the least you could try is to overlay the trend of website visitation and sales with the point in time when you launched the campaign. You can see if there was a spike indicating that a lift had been achieved during that time frame and hopefully beyond. Besides relying on your own site's web analytics, you can also check competitive intelligence from comScore, Hitwise, Compete, and the like to estimate whether the campaign has helped you capture visitors who used to frequent competitors.

Of course, enterprises conduct so many marketing efforts in parallel that it would not be possible to know which one to credit with the lift. Before you go back to hiding in the restrooms, try segmenting your web traffic to isolate the group of site visitors that most closely matches the target audience of your campaign. You can filter the trend by criteria such as new versus repeat visitors, demonstrated product interest, and geographic location to see whether the correlation with the launch of the word-of-mouth campaign is more pronounced.

Use a Microsite

Just as Doritos and Chevrolet did, use a microsite for the campaign rather than your main website. First of all, you will have nicely isolated web traffic for measurement. Compare, for example, the striking up and down trends in Figure 2.6 before and after the Super Bowl.

Beyond just facilitating measurement, microsites will also raise your audience's curiosity and their expectation to encounter rewarding content rather than company messaging. If your brand is not well known, microsites can help you pick a domain name that audiences will remember more easily when they go look it up. If your brand name is well known, however, you may encounter push back for using a microsite.

The upside comes with tradeoffs too. See how traffic to the Doritos microsite is estimated to have ebbed off now that the Super Bowl has past? Well, as with all microsites that have a temporary nature, such as the one under discussion here, the question is whether Doritos succeeded in crossing these visitors over to their main site, doritos.com, or whether the opportunity was lost? A quick trend comparison of the two sites on Compete suggests that estimated traffic to doritos.com has in fact been trending upward ever since the word-of-mouth campaign. Are these the same visitors who visited the microsite? This is a question that you already know how to answer. Namely, it is a matter of measuring click-throughs and view-throughs from the microsite to the main website.

Invoke Unique Behavior That Can Be Isolated

Using microsites is only one example of enticing visitors to exhibit unique behavior that helps marketers identify them as participants engulfed in the halo of a viral campaign. Other ideas are, for example, using unique terms or code names for promotions or products that you are launching. Take the case of Microsoft Project Origami, the original code name for Microsoft's Ultra-Mobile PC device standard. Origami was pre-announced with a mysterious, viral campaign in February 2006. (See http://www .origamiproject.com) During the announcement, Microsoft deliberately withheld information on what exactly Origami would turn out to be. In synch with the announcement, Internet searches for Microsoft Origami shot up as indicated in Figure 2.7 from Google Trends. Search activity can serve as an indicator for the trend of contagion that a viral campaign achieved.

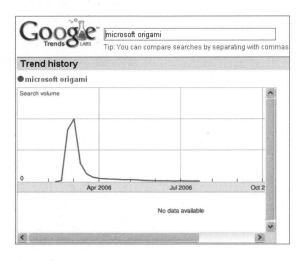

Figure 2.7

Google Trends chart for the trend of searches for keyword "Microsoft Origami" in Google's search engine

Spread the Word

Do what you can to help spread the virus, for example, by equipping the campaign's microsite with features for "e-mailing a friend." Look at the Whiteboard campaign by UPS as a brilliant example from the B2B world. You may be familiar with the campaign through its commercials available on TV and online. The microsite that accompanies the campaign (whiteboard.ups.com) includes a feature for visitors to have their own whiteboard message drawn up and e-mailed. By August 2007, more than 75,000 whiteboards had been created as UPS's Betsy Wilson reported during a presentation at the ANA B-to-B Conference.

The primary role of the feature is to increase the viral contagiousness of the campaign, of course. There is also an opportunity, if done well, to start a dialog with the individuals who are using the feature. Yet, a great side effect is the ability to measure participation.

The real measure of success on the other hand is not participation, of course, but an assessment as to whether e-mailing a whiteboard correlates with increased online purchases over time. You already know how to answer that question. It is a matter of measuring delayed conversions with the help of cookies and registered usernames.

Measure Buzz

Social networking and collective intelligence provide further opportunities for measuring buzz. For example, if your campaign contains a blog, Technorati can calculate an authority metric defined as the number of other blogs with links to yours within the last six months. Google Search in its advanced features also permits users to search for all sites that have hyperlinks to a specified URL. You get a count of how many of those sites there are.

You can also take buzz measurement to the professional level with blog and brand monitoring solutions such as clarabridge, Cymfony, Umbria, Biz360, and others. Beyond measuring quantity of mentions these solutions parse the consumer-generated content to assess tone or sentiments as much as an automated solution can derive.

All that buzz is fun to measure, but it means nothing if it does not boil down to better commercial results over the long term. You already know how to assess that though. Namely, you use referring URLs to monitor the flow of traffic and commerce to your website coming from social networking sites and blogs.

Cause versus Correlation

Did participants in the innovative UPS campaign become more likely to ship with UPS than other services? The concern voiced around cause versus correlation with all previous marketing measurements also applies to the measurement of viral campaigns. However, with word-of-mouth marketing, you can't pick the control group yourself because you don't have the virus under control. You cannot switch your campaign on and off either once the virus has been released into the world.

However, what you can do is to measure the before and after behavior of customers that participated in the campaign. You essentially ask by how much the projected lifetime value of participating customers increased compared to nonparticipants. By multiplying that difference by the number of participants, you can estimate the revenue that can be attributed to the campaign.

Online marketers are not the first to come up with this idea. For example, Jim Novo, author of *Drilling Down*, reports that during his time at the Home Shopping Network, marketing measurement faced a similar challenge. Because television is everywhere, it seemed impossible to isolate a control group. As a solution, they came up with a method of measuring increases in customer value. Refer to Jim Novo's book and website for more information (http://www.jimnovo.com).

Note: Among the many things that require careful planning with word-of-mouth marketing campaigns, a strategy for measurement is among the key requisites. Otherwise, you miss out on critical feedback from analytics and lose the ability to manage adjustments towards greater success.

Success Metrics for Online Marketing

Now that you have attributed responses to the campaigns that deserve the credit, you are ready to ask the big questions:

How successful are my online campaigns?

What can I do to make them more successful?

Almost every web metric and report ever defined plays some role in answering these two questions. This is because online marketing optimization is very different from optimizing a stock portfolio, for example. That is to say it is not just about picking the campaigns that promise the greatest gain. Rather, it is also about tuning every single step along the conversion process starting from the ad impression over the click-through, to the landing page, into the interior of the site, across multiple subsequent visits, and finally through the conversion pages until the visitor reaches the thank-you page. Even there, the marketer's work is still not done. Namely, maximizing the returns on a campaign also implies working to maximize the lifetime value of the customers acquired through the campaign. That in turn calls for delivering a combination of excellent customer service with skillful customer marketing.

For the purposes of this book, we will limit the online success metrics that we review to the ones that are most narrowly related to the campaign itself and the customers who are acquired. The books on web analytics that were recommended earlier are terrific references for metrics and methods around website conversion optimization and customer service.

Campaign-Centric Success Metrics

We are finally getting down to the metrics! Campaign metrics fall into three categories. Quantitative and qualitative performance metrics are the most frequently used. However, they are only intermediary indicators of success. Only ROI metrics are truly reliable success metrics for decision making. Most of the metrics listed here are commonplace in web analytics solutions today. However, some of them—such as reach, cost, and consequently ROI metrics—require integrating web analytics data with data from other marketing systems.

The definitions proposed here lean on those put forward by the Web Analytics Association (WAA) whenever available. At the time of writing, the WAA's standardization process is still in progress, however, so that many of the metrics listed here have not yet been standardized.

Quantitative Performance Metrics

Probably everybody began their dealings in web analytics with some of these metrics. In this day and age, however, do not be caught relying solely on these!

Campaign Impressions or Reach The number of times that an advertisement or e-mail has been viewed. Unless you are serving your ads directly, this metric is available only from the ad network, paid keyword vendor, or e-mail campaign management system.

Note: in this and all the following metrics you can substitute *campaign* with the specific level at which you wish to measure a marketing investment. For example: *paid keyword ad* impressions.

Campaign Click-Throughs and Click-Through Rate The number of times links to the website from ads, e-mails, or other referrers were clicked by a visitor. The rate metric is defined as the number of click-throughs for a specific link divided by the number of Campaign Impressions.

Campaign View-Throughs and View-Through Rate The number of visits to the website following an exposure to an ad or e-mail. The rate metric is defined as view-throughs divided by Campaign Impressions.

Unique Campaign Respondents (Visitors) The number of unique visitors who visited the site in response to a campaign no matter whether as a result of a referral, click-through, view-through, or word-of-mouth.

Qualitative Performance Metrics

Should you prioritize the campaign that brings the most visitors to your site? Not necessarily. What if those visitors are not converting to customers? You could joke that the only business model where counting click-throughs would be sufficient is the model of those who specialize in committing click fraud on pay-per-click advertisements. Everybody else requires qualitative performance metrics. They are not perfect for decision making either but are used as shortcuts when ROI metrics are not within reach. The specific definition of *quality* depends on each site's business goals.

Engagement Metrics Engagement metrics aim to measure in how far visitors take an interest into the content offered on the website.

> **Campaign Bounce Rate** This metric expresses the portion of click-throughs where visitors viewed only the entry page and then left. It is defined as single page view visits divided by all Campaign Click-Throughs. The higher the rate, the lower is the quality of the traffic.

> **Percent of Engaged Campaign Visits or Visitors** The definition of engagement will differ from site to site. No standards exist. You could, for example, flag every visitor who viewed at least 10 key pages or stayed at least for 5 minutes as an engaged visitor. The higher the percentage, the better is the quality of the traffic.

Page Views per Visit for Campaign Respondents The number of page views by Campaign Respondents in a reporting period divided by number of visits (i.e., Campaign Click-Throughs).

This metric is of special interest for ad-supported publishing websites because their primary business model is to engage visitors across as many page views and, therefore, ad impressions, as possible.

Conversion Metrics Engagement is nice. But most websites are designed with the goal of enticing visitors to complete calls-to-action such as an online registration form or a purchase. For these sites, conversion metrics are the minimally required indicator of campaign performance.

Campaign Conversions (Same Visit or Delayed) The number of times that a respondent to a campaign completes a target action, such as submitting an online form for lead registration or completing an order. If the conversion occurs in a subsequent visit (for example, within 14 days of the original ad click-through), the event is called a delayed conversion. If credit for a conversion is divided among multiple campaigns that were involved in the run up, then the metric may be assigned a fractional value. See more about this in Chapter 8.

Campaign Conversion Rate (Same Visit or Delayed) The ratio of Campaign Conversions to Unique Campaign Respondents. Some web analysts prefer to define this metric as the ratio to campaign response (i.e., visits) rather than unique respondents as the denominator. Refer to *Web Analytics: An Hour A Day* by Avinash Kaushik for a detailed treatment of the tradeoffs. An advantage of using unique respondents as the denominator is that the conversion rate will not be penalized for visitors who visit multiple times before they convert. Conversely, a higher conversion rate will result when a visitor visits multiple times and completes a conversion each time. This seems to be in line with marketer's expectations as to how the metric should behave.

Conversion rates remain tricky to interpret. For example, you may make a very successful advertising investment that leads to such high volumes of respondents that conversion rates take a dive. Yet campaign conversions may spike. This is why you cannot rely solely on conversion rates for assessing campaign success.

Online Revenue Metrics Should a retailer prioritize the campaign with the most conversions? No. The order values need to be taken into account, of course.

Campaign Revenue (Same Visit or Delayed) The revenue from campaign respondents collected directly or shortly after their exposure to the campaign. The purchase may occur during the first visit in response to the campaign or during a subsequent visit (for example, within 14 days). If credit for a purchase is divided among multiple campaigns that were involved recently, then each campaign may only be credited with a fraction of the revenue. See more about this in Chapter 8.

Campaign Average Order Value (Same Visit or Delayed) Campaign Revenue divided by Campaign Conversions (i.e., number of orders). The higher the value, the more attractive is the campaign.

Campaign Lifetime Revenue (Historical and Forecasted) The total sum of revenue realized and/or forecasted from campaign respondents across all their subsequent purchases that would not have occurred if it were not for the campaign.

If a company ran only a single campaign, this would simply be the sum of all subsequent revenues from Campaign Respondents. When companies run ongoing customer campaigns, however, each new campaign's lifetime revenue becomes impossible to calculate with standard web analytics. This is because existing customers who responded to the new campaigns already had a lifetime value before they were targeted with the new campaign. So the lifetime value that is credited to the new campaign should only be the amount of increase in lifetime value. Otherwise, we would be double-counting the value that is generated by our marketing investments.

Obviously, this metric is as complex as it is powerful. Yet, a number of methods exist for estimating it, such as using control groups and customer valuation models. These methods have been honed among direct marketers for many years. Chapter 4, "The Direct Marketer Digs into Multichannel Analytics," will discuss how they go about it.

Campaign Cost Metrics The campaign that brings the most revenue or largest average order values must surely be the one that marketers should prioritize? But what if that campaign costs proportionally much more than other campaigns do? Before she considers costs, how can the marketer honestly say whether a campaign has been a success or a failure?

Campaign Costs The total costs of a marketing investment into a campaign whether based on a pay-per-click model, cost-per-thousand impressions model (CPM), or a fixed-price model (such as for the purchase of a target e-mail list). Neither the cost of goods and services delivered nor overhead costs are part of the equation, however.

Campaign Cost per Click-Through or Visitor Campaign Costs divided by Campaign Click-Throughs or Unique Respondents respectively.

Campaign Cost per Acquisition (i.e., per Conversion) Campaign Costs divided by Campaign Conversions. If you compare two campaigns and find that one leads to a lower cost per acquisition, you would prioritize that campaign if and only if all other factors can be assumed to be the same (i.e., same amount of campaign conversions, lifetime revenues, mix of products purchased, etc.). If those factors are not the same between the two campaigns, however, using the cost-per-acquisition metric can lead to bad marketing decisions.

ROI Metrics

Should the marketer favor the campaign with the lowest cost of acquisition? But what if that campaign also brings proportional lower revenues? ROI metrics are the only true measure of financial success for a campaign. But look out! There are multiple kinds that are crucial to distinguish:

ROAS (RETURN ON AD SPEND)

Campaign Revenue divided by Campaign Costs. As powerful as this metric can be, it is dangerous unless you understand its definition correctly.

It is startling that ROAS is often mistakenly assumed to be interchangeable with ROI. A definition is frequently not even provided. What is the metric good for? It is a performance indicator for campaigns. As such, it is a much better indicator than relying solely on revenues or costs. ROAS relates campaign costs to revenues within a single indicator.

Note: ROAS is actually not a true ROI metric! I recommend that you call this metric by a more correct name than the one that has established itself unfortunately. Call it "Revenue over ad spend." An ROAS of 100 percent means that you unfortunately just wasted your time by spending exactly as much on your ad costs as you brought in as revenue during the sale. Worse than that, however, the ROAS of 100 percent means that you just lost money. Why? Because you have costs for fulfilling the sale, such as the costs of goods and overhead costs. Say you bought an ad for one dollar that enabled you to sell a product for one dollar. Yet, that product costs you 50 cents to build or buy. Your ROAS is 100 percent, but you just lost 50 cents.

If you compare two campaigns and find that one has a higher ROAS, you would prioritize that campaign if and only if the products sold in both campaigns lead to the same gross margin. That is unlikely, however, if the company sells more than a single product. Gross margin between products typically differs. Using the ROAS metric can then lead to incorrect prioritization.

ROI (RETURN ON INVESTMENT)

In his eye opening book, *Marketing ROI,* James Lenskold defines the ROI metric as

$$ROI = \frac{Return}{Investment} = \frac{Gross\ Margin - Marketing\ Investment}{Marketing\ Investment}$$

Gross margin is defined as the forecasted Campaign Lifetime Revenues minus Cost of Goods Sold minus Incremental Expenses. Additionally, Gross Margin is adjusted to its present value by discounting revenues that occur later in time.

These definitions are only the starting point for Lenskold's investigation into the practical use of the ROI metric for prioritizing the most promising marketing efforts. The book is especially enlightening for online marketers who are frequently exposed to faulty definitions of ROI metrics that may put them at risk for taking bad business decisions.

By combining complete costs and revenues, the ROI metric is the definitive financial indicator of a campaign's historical pay off. Say you bought an ad for one dollar that enabled you to sell a product for two dollars and 50 cents. That product cost you 50 cents including overhead costs. Your ROI is 100 percent:

$$(($2.50 - 50c) - $1) / $1$$

At the end of the day you had total costs of $1.50 but generated $2.50. You did not just get the one dollar back that you invested into this marketing campaign, but you made an extra dollar on top. How different compared to an ROAS of 100 percent.

During a series of postings on the subject, Craig Danuloff, president of search-marketing company Commerce360, published a translation table for ROI to ROAS in his blog. Given the definitions of ROAS and ROI previously stated, ROAS can be expressed as a function of ROI and percent gross margin as follows:

$$ROAS = \frac{Revenue}{Marketing\ Investment} = \frac{1 + ROI}{Percent\ Gross\ Margin}$$

Filling in values for ROI and Percent Gross Margin Craig Danuloff arrived at the table in Figure 2.8. For example, even an ROAS of 1000 percent leads to 0 percent ROI if Percent Gross Margin is 10 percent. To confirm, take an example: You buy an ad for $1 and gain revenues of $10 (i.e., 1000 percent ROAS). Since your Percent Gross Margin is 10 percent that means that $9 go to costs of goods sold and overhead expenses. That leaves $1 with which you can pay for the advertising but will have nothing left to show for from the activity.

ROAS to ROI Lookup			
With This Margin	You Need This ROAS		
90.00%	111.11%	166.67%	222.22%
80.00%	125.00%	187.50%	250.00%
70.00%	142.86%	214.29%	285.71%
60.00%	166.67%	250.00%	333.33%
50.00%	200.00%	300.00%	400.00%
40.00%	250.00%	375.00%	500.00%
30.00%	333.33%	500.00%	666.67%
20.00%	500.00%	750.00%	1000.00%
10.00%	1000.00%	1500.00%	2000.00%
	To Earn 0% ROI	To Earn 50% ROI	To Earn 100% ROI

Figure 2.8
ROAS to ROI Lookup, by Craig Danuloff of Commerce360

However, most web analytics implementations today are not configured to include the costs of goods in reports, let alone forecasted lifetime revenues. As a consequence, most online marketers fall back to performance metrics as shortcuts for decision making. That can be fine if the marketer is aware of the associated risks. Going to the other extreme, many businesses have built homegrown systems for pay-per-click bid management that control bids based on ROI instead of ROAS. Most frequently this is the case in the retail and travel industries where margins are slim and differ from product to product. It also applies to the publishing industries where margins vary from day to day based on ad inventory.

BALANCED SCORECARD METRICS

Is success only about financial gain? Balanced scorecards weigh financial metrics against other kinds of metrics such as customer satisfaction. For example, an e-mail spam campaign may result in excellent short-term financial ROI since its costs are negligible. Yet, it will probably damage a company's reputation, which should be weighed in decision making.

Customer-Centric Success Metrics

Imagine you walked into a store and instead of listening to you, the sales rep just rattled down the list of products he wished to sell you. Ah, that would never happen, you say. But one of the jewels in the Eisenbergs' book *Waiting for Your Cat to Bark?* is the observation that good sales people really listen to their customers in order to respond in a meaningful way and marketers do so much more rarely. When the Eisenbergs say so, they actually mean to really listen and talk with customers to understand them. From a one-to-one marketer's perspective though, the minimum technology requirement is to at least keep a record of what has been communicated to the prospect or customer so far and what her reaction was. In other words, keep the promotion and response history. These make up the first two components of a more complete customer profile that will be discussed in Chapter 7, "Measure 1:1 Interactions Between Online & Offline."

Online Promotion History

The *promotion history* is the record of communications, offers, or advertisements to which the individual has been exposed:

Original Online Promotions These may list the promotions that are credited with originally acquiring the customer. For example, the original display ads that she has been exposed to and the search keywords through which she found the website. For actionability, it will help to keep track of the date, campaign, channel, offer type, and product orientation for each of the promotions

Most Recent Online Promotions In the same manner, the most recent promotions that the individual has been exposed to should also be noted. The marketer can take this information into account while devising the next communication that makes sense to send to the individual. However, this information will also help avoid contact fatigue, where an individual would be overloaded with too many promotions at the same time.

Online Response History

For each of the promotions in the history, note the response by the individual. The response can be of multiple types (for example, a visit to the website, a registration, subscription, purchase, or an opt-out). A response may also be scored with a qualitative measure. For example, the visit to the website could be scored depending on the degree of engagement that the visitor demonstrated. Taken together with the promotion history, a picture of RFM, i.e., recency, frequency, and monetary online response per prospect or customer, will emerge. Online marketers can extend the age old RFM idea by adding engagement as a new metric to the mix. Instead of *RFM*, this could be abbreviated as *RFEM*.

> **Note:** So what? That is exactly the right question for marketers to ask, as Avinash Kaushik points out with his "triple so-what test." All these flags and metrics are valuable only in so far as they enable the marketer to provide customers with a better experience and the business with better results. Refer to Part III, "Multichannel Marketing Methods," for ideas on working with the metrics in that regard. Because there is also a cost associated with building the customer records, marketers should evaluate the projected ROI first, just as they would with any other marketing investment to prioritize correctly.

The Offline Marketer's Bag of Tricks

3

The seasoned offline marketer has built a deep bag of tricks. It contains a wealth of methods from which multichannel marketers can draw. Yet, few colleagues from the online side of marketing have risked looking inside the bag. Years after the dotcom bubble burst, online and offline marketers still don't talk to each other very much. If their jargon were not so different from each other's, they would realize that they already share many methods between them. More gems are still waiting to be discovered by marketers on the other side of the fence. Let's explore how the viewpoints differ and why.

Chapter Contents

Blame Evolution, Not Ignorance!

Remember how the "eChannel" got started way back? It began as a separate entity staffed by a new generation of marketers. The old marketers were still skeptical about whether "this Internet thing" was going to last very long. All the while the younger team had no time to delve into offline marketing traditions. Online, everything seemed different anyway, and there was no time to lose in the race to get eyeballs to the website.

Meanwhile, as eCommerce took off for real, traditional marketers' skepticism turned into the fear of being cannibalized by their online colleagues. The fear was very real because P&L (Profit & Loss) and employee compensation plans were in conflict between online and offline. So, of course the marketers had few words for each other and differing languages developed even for similar ideas. Examples of the latter are found in the Jargon Alert boxes throughout the book.

However, beyond this unfortunate historical development, the conditions for marketing online have also been ever so slightly different from those offline, as we will explore next. Those differences have also predisposed marketers in each camp to evolve in different directions.

Different Starting Points Rocketed Marketers to Separate Orbits

When it comes to business, there is no such thing as eBusiness versus offline business. There is just business. We learned that lesson during the dotcom bust. When it comes to marketing, however, online marketing traditionally has had slightly different conditions to work with than offline marketing. See Table 3.1 for some notable differences.

▶ **Table 3.1** Slightly Different Starting Points for Traditional Online and Offline Marketers

	Conditions Online	Conditions Offline
Life cycle phase in which channel has come to play	Typically, only starts in the Consideration phase *	Typically starts with the Awareness phase
Direction of inquiry between vendor and marketer	Inbound first—i.e., prospect inquires with marketer *	Outbound first—i.e., marketer invites prospect to inquire
Costs of ad production and delivery	Relatively lower	Relatively higher

* Except with display ads

The biggest discrepancy between online and offline marketing comes from the observation that buyers have typically interacted through online and offline channels during different stages of their customer life cycle. Namely, as we saw in Table 1.2, the website traditionally came into play only after the customer was already aware of a particular product category or maybe even the brand. Before the advent of broadband

Internet access, rich media ads, and video inserts, common thinking was that the Internet simply was not well suited for brand advertising.

Not surprisingly, most (though not all) of the channels online seem to be of an inbound nature. When prospects do a search, click a hyperlink, or come to a website directly, they typically have a goal in mind, such as to answer a specific question or inquire about a particular product. For this reason, the online marketer's primary focus over the past ten years has evolved to center on two things:

- To be easy to find when prospects formulate a goal
- To bend over backward to close the sale while the prospect is on the website, knowing that competitors are just a click away

The result ended up being a mindset focused on short-term acquisition and conversion of visitors into leads or customers. Offline, it is not that marketers don't care about those same aspects. They do. But before they can worry about them, they first have to flip their oblivious prospects into aware and curious ones. For that purpose, marketers are trying to reach their potential prospects wherever they happen to be, on the couch, in the car, or out and about. Most marketing dollars offline are spent for an outreach with the goal of growing some legs on those couch potatoes—i.e., creating or revitalizing demand.

Note: Offline marketers work with more potential prospects or potential repeat customers than active prospects. Through advertising, offline marketers aim to create active consideration for buying. With the exception of display advertising, online marketing on the other hand has focused more on those who already are active prospects.

Add to that the fact that most advertising programs offline are a lot more expensive to produce, test, change, and deliver than the traditional online ad has been. The sum of all these differences is to blame for driving online and offline marketers to fairly different perspectives. See Table 3.2 for the five most notable differences in perspective that arose as symptoms.

▶ **Table 3.2** Different Analytics Focus for Online and Offline Marketers

	Online Marketer's Traditional Tendency	Offline Marketer's Traditional Tendency
Type of Analytics	Mostly descriptive	First predictive, then later descriptive
Perception of Customer Life Cycle	Acquire, Convert, Retain	Raise awareness, improve brand perception, facilitate research, offer trial, convert, service, up-sell & cross-sell, gain loyalty, prevent attrition, and win-back should that fail

Continues

	Online Marketer's Traditional Tendency	Offline Marketer's Traditional Tendency
Perception of Marketing Cycle	Produce, test, improve	Predict value of alternative ideas, test on sample, produce, improve
Perception of ROI Metric	A rearview mirror metric that results from marketing initiatives	First, a predictive metric whose outcome is selected based on choices, only later also a rearview mirror metric
Perception of Lifetime Value Metric	A rearview mirror metric that results from marketing initiatives	The predicted value of existing customers that the marketer is toiling to grow

Let's study these viewpoints more closely so that we can appreciate why the seasoned offline marketers have developed the extreme diligence in their methods that they have.

More Comprehensive Perspective on the Customer Life Cycle

When online marketers divide the customer life cycle into stages, they typically distinguish three different ones: namely acquisition, conversion, and retention.

Acquisition The task of attracting visitors to the website, typically through means of advertising or other types of marketing campaigns.

Conversion The task of persuading a visitor to complete a targeted action, such as submitting a registration form or making a purchase. Depending on the nature of the website, there can also be other types of targeted actions. For example, a publisher's website that is supported by advertisement may target that visitors will view many pages so that many ad impressions can be delivered. A customer service website, on the other hand, may consider a successful self-help resolution to represent a conversion.

Retention The goal of enticing repeat visits and especially repeat business from existing customers.

This three-stage cycle turns out to be a somewhat limited perspective, however, as can be seen by comparing it to the viewpoint of traditional marketers who may distinguish all the life cycle stages seen in Figure 3.1. The narrower focus of online marketers mirrors their inbound and acquisition-marketing-centric attitude to which we pointed in the previous section.

Granted, this is not true for everyone in online marketing. Back in 2000, Jim Sterne and Matt Cutler described the life cycle much more comprehensively within their trend-setting paper, *E-Metrics*. Their perspective was similar to the one that offline marketers would also take. Yet, only the Acquire, Convert, and Retain stages struck a chord with most online marketers. This was probably because they correspond to the tasks with which these marketers have been most concerned—namely, the tasks of advertising the site, making it easy to find in search engines, increasing site conversions, and bringing customers back for more business.

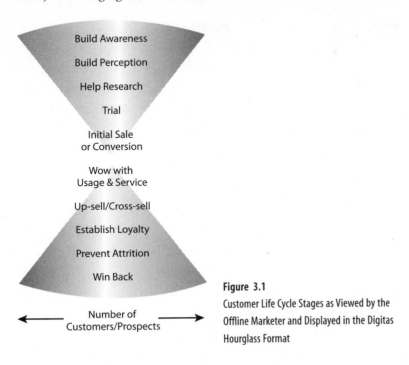

Build Awareness

Build Perception

Help Research

Trial

Initial Sale
or Conversion

Wow with
Usage & Service

Up-sell/Cross-sell

Establish Loyalty

Prevent Attrition

Win Back

Number of
Customers/Prospects

Figure 3.1

Customer Life Cycle Stages as Viewed by the
Offline Marketer and Displayed in the Digitas
Hourglass Format

Offline marketers on the other hand, at their best, would take into account not just the funnel stages leading up to the initial sale (i.e., awareness, perception, research, and trial), they would also take into account stages post initial sale (namely usage, service, cross- and up-sales, loyalty, attrition prevention, and win back). The digital and direct marketing agency Digitas displays the pre- and post sale parts of the life cycle in the form of an hourglass instead of the traditional sales funnel form. Putting all these ideas together, Figure 3.1 indicates the offline marketer's perspective onto the customer life cycle.

Example: Local Retail Bank Say you just took the helm of the marketing function at a local retail bank. You want to show that you are worth the big bucks by growing your bank's business. The life cycle model helps you identify where the bottlenecks are for success. For example, the shape of the top half of the hourglass may indicate that many prospects inquire about the services in the bank but much fewer actually convert. Then you may conclude that the offer terms are not persuasive enough. If, on the other hand, customers sign up for a checking account but frequently leave within the first year it would suggest that there may be dissatisfaction with your bank's service. Granted, the bottom half of the hour glass does not really need to be shaped like a funnel. Hopefully, you will have more loyal customers than customers with high risk of attrition.

Other than process optimization, the life cycle model has another purpose that is equally helpful. It guides you to think about *what kinds of offers or services will make sense* to extend to your bank's prospects and customer at each stage of the cycle. Surely, newly acquired customers require different treatment from high-value customers with multiple accounts and others who are at risk of attrition? These segments and others can form the stratified segments for which you will design differing marketing offers and communications.

Then, when it comes to *whether*, *when*, and *where*, *which* of these offers should actually be extended to each customer within the segments, this is something that the offline marketer determines during the course of the marketing cycle. The marketing cycle is described next.

More Comprehensive Perspective on the Marketing Cycle

Once it has been determined *what* initiatives you will extend to prospects and customers in each of the segments within the customer life cycle, Figure 3.2 indicates the circular process that the offline marketer follows. There are stages in this process that most online marketers have not prioritized to the same degree as their offline colleagues.

Planning The planning stage may start the marketing cycle. For example, in your plan for the local bank, you would split budget, revenue goals, and team responsibilities across all the initiatives that you will conduct in order to grow your business.

Analysis Meanwhile, in the predictive analysis phase, statisticians determine which subset of the segments will be targeted with which of the offers over which channel and at what point in time in order to maximize the forecasted returns.

Design & Production In the design and production phase, your team will collaborate to create and approve the related advertisements, commercials or direct response offers.

Execution The projects then move into the execution phase which involves more than just the delivery of the offers though. For instance, in direct marketing, customer segments will be randomly subdivided into offer cells, some of which will serve as control groups and others as test groups for offer variations.

Measurement In the measurement phase, response data from each offer cell is gathered in order to produce descriptive analytics on the outcomes. Based on these results, the original plan and predictive analytics will be enhanced. The cycle begins anew.

As the cycle spins, the marketing team produces a growing body of plans, workflows, digital assets, customer models, scores, business rules, and measurements. Collectively, these assets are referred to as the *marketing meta data* or the *marketing system of record*. Its purpose is to prevent marketers from reinventing the wheel every time the cycle spins instead of reusing what has already been produced.

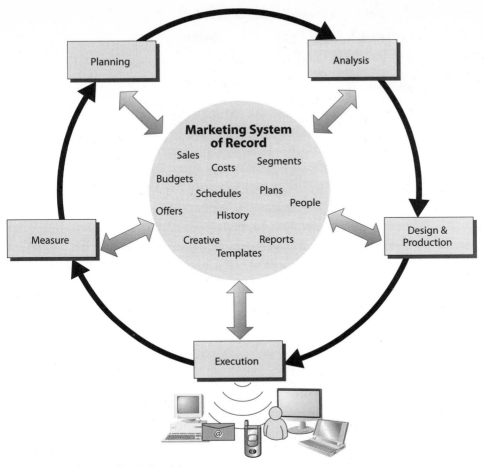

Figure 3.2 Stages of the Offline Marketer's Process

Enterprise Marketing Management

Software suites that are designed to support the marketing team through all stages of the marketing cycle and across marketing channels are referred to as Enterprise Marketing Management (EMM) platforms. They also help with managing the marketing system of record by replacing the typical chaos of spreadsheets, documents, and notes taken on napkins that marketing teams have relied on traditionally. The goal with using EMM software is to increase both the effectiveness and the efficiency of the marketing cycle. The top rated platforms in the space come from Aprimo, Oracle-Siebel, and Unica.

Not Just Descriptive Analytics, But Also Predictive

Offline, targeting is not optional. Offline marketers seem much more aware that their efforts have no chance of breaking even unless they are targeted toward the most suitable subsets among their prospects and customers. Take an example from direct marketing. Say that you want to cross-sell brokerage accounts to customers who have nothing but a checking account at your bank. This will grow the wallet share that you have with customers and make them less likely to leave to competitors. You design an attractive offer that will be sent by direct mail.

But to whom should you mail the offer? You want to play big, but should you really blow your entire budget by sending the brochure to everyone in your customer list with a single checking account? Well, does each of the households have the same likelihood of opening a second account? Certainly not! If you can focus on those who are more likely to respond, you will achieve a better conversion rate. Say the conversion rate would be 1 percent across the entire applicable customer list of 100,000 households but 3 percent for the most promising group of 10,000 households. Table 3.3 shows different sizes of mailings and their effect on your profits:

▶ **Table 3.3** In Offline Marketing, Targeting Is Not Optional.

	Mailing to Entire List	Mailing to Top 20%	Mailing to Top 10%
Number of contacts mailed	100,000	20,000	10,000
Costs of campaign (at $3.50 per contact)	350,000	70,000	35,000
Conversion rate	1%	2%	3%
Conversions	1,000	400	300
First year margin (at $250 per conversion per year)	250,000	100,000	75,000
First year, contribution	−$100,000 loss	$30,000 gain	$40,000 gain
First year ROI of campaign (= margin minus costs divided by costs)	−100%	43%	114%

If you select the target group too broadly, you will have no chance to break even. This is why the offline marketer has been obsessed with improving conversion rates by targeting the most promising segments. By predicting the most promising subset of contacts, the direct marketer can reduce the size of mailings to the most fertile target audience and consequently *select a forecasted ROI* at a desired configuration.

If you were sick for a month and your colleague from online marketing had to take your job at the local bank, she might approach the problem very differently. Online marketers have been absorbed with *experimenting* with different channels, keywords, creative, and landing pages. Then ROI is *measured* to *select the winners*. This tends to manifest itself in ad or page-level optimizations instead of offer-centric optimizations. Applying this traditional online marketing mindset, your colleague would probably design multiple envelopes, messages, etc. and send each variation to a sample of households to test which works best. She would then take the winner and see if she should send it to the entire customer list. She would likely conclude however, that not even the winning design would enable you to break even since the costs are simply too high. Upon your return, you might therefore find a yellow sticky note saying that there is no money to be made this way and that you should consider an e-mail campaign instead.

Offline marketers agree with their online colleagues about the value of such test-and-learn strategies. However, offline direct marketers use the results for building a predictive model. In our example, the model could take as input available responder (and nonresponder) attributes such as

- gender
- age
- occupation
- distance to nearest branch office
- type of customer segment
- typical tenure at the bank
- average number of product holdings
- and revenues associated with these holdings.

The purpose of the model is to identify the characteristics of the target audience that will allow the offer to achieve the desired ROI.

Targeting Online

It is not as if targeting doesn't exist online though. On the contrary, the selection of the right search engine keywords for which to run paid advertising implicitly corresponds to the offline marketer's activity of selecting the right target group. Our local bank could select between broad pay-per-click keywords such as "checking account" and specific ones such as "Manhattan Upper West Side no-fee checking accounts." The conversion rates for these keywords will differ because the visitors typing in the more specific search phrase are a much more preselected group of prospects. Assuming that our local bank is located in the Upper West Side and offers low-cost checking accounts, the online marketer is much more likely to find takers among them. Instead of trying to predict the outcomes, however, it seems so much quicker to just run a test online, so that is what most online marketers have been doing.

Predictive Analysis Online

Does that mean that predictive analysis is unnecessary online? Not at all. For example, how could our local bank test the revenue streams that will come in during second and later years of the relationship with the customers? It would be impractical to run tests for such long periods of time. Too many external factors would change during this time. This is what predictive analysis has to offer online marketers. Yet, sometimes online marketers mistake predictive analysis to mean that every click of every website session should be mined to make sense of it. Plus, online marketers are still too busy optimizing short-term results because the testability and measurability of their medium gives them so many levers with which to work.

 Note: Quite the reverse from offline marketers, online marketers have typically left predictive analysis for the genuine optimization of results including the long-term perspective to be tackled later.

Differences Between Online and Offline Marketing Are Shrinking

As the online and offline worlds are converging, sales cycles are spanning across both. If nothing else, it is for this reason that offline and online marketing are crossing paths and can benefit from each other. Yet, there are also other reasons why online marketers are increasingly now facing the same challenges that their offline colleagues have had to find sophisticated solutions for:

Outbound advertising is on the rise. While the inbound nature of search marketing and website optimization still dominates the agenda, the outreach for finding unsuspecting audiences wherever they happen to be browsing on the Internet is on the rise. Clever rich media ads are no longer as quick and cheap to create as previous generations of banners have been. Video inserts can be full-blown commercials and as expensive to develop as their offline counterparts. Viral marketing aims to create a buzz where there was none by using ideas such as fake personal pages on MySpace and entire virtual presences on Second Life.

Moreover, display advertising can be behaviorally targeted to individuals based on their past behavior. Advertisers can assign frequency caps to avoid contact fatigue. These trends do not just put more control in the hands of the advertiser. They also put the responsibility in their laps to segment who they will prioritize for targeting. Thus, online brand advertising is faced with a confluence of traditional direct marketing and brand marketing concerns.

Search bid costs are rising. The cost per click of bidding on search keywords has been on the rise for a while. For instance, the cost per click on some keywords around mortgages can even be well above 10 dollars. At those rates, advertisers are looking to retreat to more targeted keywords to be able to break even.

Search advertising has new targeting capabilities. Introduced by MSN Ad Center, new capabilities for targeting are coming to search advertising. Marketers can direct their ad purchases not just by geographic regions, but also by demographic profiles. That prompts the marketer to predict the expected value of a prospect based on their profile in addition to keyword selection.

Initial acquisition may be unprofitable. An effect of rising advertising costs and murderous price competition in comparison-shopping engines is that the initial acquisition of a customer may be unprofitable. Predicting the future customer value becomes necessary in order to calculate the marketing allowable correctly.

Loss leader offers may be adopted. A well-established method in offline retail and other transactional business models is to have a loss leader promotion to get customers into your store. Online marketers can adopt this method. The profit of the offer needs to be predicated on getting shoppers to buy additional higher margin items during their visit.

Focus on customer retention and customer experience will increase. In any early market, most businesses first focus on acquisition to gain market share. Then, as markets mature companies recognize that retaining loyal customers is less expensive than acquiring new ones—and loyal customers tend to be less price-sensitive if you are delivering a better customer experience (see Reichheld's Loyalty Effect). Growing the value of already acquired customers is necessary in order to afford the acquisition costs. Therefore, just as with offline marketers, lifetime value is bound to become more of a goal-oriented metric than the rearview mirror metric that it has been in web analytics.

Online business models have grown beyond e-commerce. Retailers, B2B (Business to Business), and ad-financed businesses have been at the forefront of the Internet boom and have shaped the way web metrics have traditionally been done. However, there are many other businesses whose income models require predictive analysis for success measurement. Think of insurance companies, such as GEICO or Progressive, where customers can buy policies online. The amount of the initial transaction is very clear. However, the length of time the customer will stay with the insurer needs to be predicted in order to truly understand the value.

The same is true elsewhere. Consider subscription services, such as Yahoo! Music or Netflix, or consider pure online banks, such as ING Direct and eTrade.

The web analyst may be quick to offer a shortcut to this problem, namely to use the *average* historical customer value as a placeholder for predicting individual customer value. Technically, that can be done very quickly and easily. Yet, success in the face of competition depends on getting the answer more correctly than the competitor. As an analogy, if an insurance business charged all drivers of red convertibles the same rate, they may do alright. But if insurance statisticians at one firm figure out that the drivers of red Thunderbirds are much less likely to be involved in accidents, they can extend a better price to this target segment and, therefore, generate a higher ROI.

Target web visitors based on behavior. Having come pretty far with ad and page optimization, online marketers are now starting to look into automated behavioral targeting to increase site conversion rates further. Yet, targeting offers to a visitor online without knowing their offline behavior history has great limitations. For example, a travel operator may target ads for vacation resorts in the Greek islands to a return visitor to the site because that is the travel destination that the visitor may have browsed a week ago during her last visit. Yet, meanwhile the customer may have purchased a trip to Sicily over the phone already so that the ads go fail.

Offline and online marketers have many reasons to work together. By combining their insights from interactions with customers, they could refine their targeting to show more relevant offers. For example, if the visitor in the example is registered on the travel operator's site, she could retrieve her itinerary that was booked over the phone and be targeted ads relevant to Sicily.

Spam carries high opportunity costs. The cost of a marketing e-mail is negligible compared to the costs of mailing a high-gloss brochure. What is difficult, however, is to get the recipient to pay attention to the e-mail instead of deleting it or marking it as junk mail.

 Note: Although the cost of sending an e-mail or flashing a real-time offer on a website is negligible, there is an opportunity cost associated with presenting the wrong offer to the wrong customer at the wrong time. Namely, the loss of permission for future marketing may result. As such, online marketers and offline marketers have the same reason to embrace predictive analysis and contact optimization.

The Direct Marketer Digs into Multichannel Analytics

Direct marketers have been dealing with multiple channels since day one. Offers are delivered over certain channels, whereas responses come through others. Many direct marketers today are juggling 10 to 15 channels. These channels range from direct mail to websites, mobile devices, and plenty of others.

How are these marketers solving the multi-channel metrics challenge? We will study the direct marketer's approach that was originally developed for offline channels. However, the same ideas can also be borrowed to help us bridge the divide between offline and online channels in order to shape the customer experience for the better.

4

Chapter Contents

The Direct Marketer's Goal

The friendly shop keeper at a local corner store knows all his best customers. That makes it easier for him to predict the products that will be of interest to each: "You have to taste the new Prosciutto that just came in. It tastes just the way you like it." Thanks to his personal relationships, he has insights enabling him to make his offers relevant.

Relationship-oriented direct marketers challenge themselves to re-create as much of this personal customer experience as possible, given a mass audience. Therefore, analytics for intelligent customer decisioning are at the heart of direct marketing. Every step of the direct marketing cycle depends on learning from customers' behavior. The insight is to be used for deciding which service or communication to offer at what point in time. The traditional direct marketer has been applying this process to the offline channels outlined in Table 4.1.

▶ **Table 4.1** Marketing Execution Compared to Response Channels

Campaign Channel / Response Channel	Online					Offline				
	Website	E-mail	Mobile	Blog	Viral	Viral	Mail/fax	Phone	Direct sales	Store
Advertising (nonaddressable) — TV/radio/print, Out-of-home, Events, Product placement, In store							Traditional Brand Marketers			
Direct Response (addressable) — Call center, Direct mail, Service team, Mobile, E-mail, Web ads, Search, Website	Traditional Online Marketers						**Traditional Direct Marketers**			

Set a Strategic Communications Plan

For a top-down starting point, the direct marketer begins with the strategic communications plan. This is typically developed during an annual planning construct. Objectives are established across the top tier of strategic customer segments. Think of the example from the previous chapter — our local bank. Here, the customer life cycle model may lead direct marketers to pay special attention to segments such as new customers, high-value customers, and at-risk customers. If you were the chair of the strategic planning committee, what data would you ask your staff to bring to the meeting to support decision making? You would want to know:

- What has worked well in the past and what has not?
- Who are your customers and what opportunities do you have?
- What are the status and historical trends for each of the customer segments?
- What has been the trend of new customer acquisition?
- How many products do customers use over time?
- How many customers grew from low- to high-value status and how many became at-risk customers?
- What is the estimated amount of value compared to opportunity or risk in each of the segments?

These and many more questions are likely brought to the table. Typically, the answers are obtained from an enterprise data warehouse with the help of business intelligence solutions from vendors such as Business Objects (acquired by SAP in 2007), Cognos (acquired by IBM in 2007), and MicroStrategy.

Specific marketing goals are set for each of the customer segments. In our example of the local bank, you may aim to:

- Increase new customers by 10 percent
- Increase the number product holdings per customer
- Meanwhile reduce attrition by 4 basis points

Derive Tactical Communications

Tactical campaign communications are derived to fit the strategic goals. Offers are designed and prepared as candidates that can be extended to prospects and customers in each of the segments. When and where these offers will be extended depends on the nature of the communication:

Ad-Hoc Tests

Until 10 years ago, most marketing campaigns were run manually. Whenever the business decided on a new communication that was to be sent to customers, the database specialists would be called to prepare the list of recipients on an ad-hoc basis. Marketers would design the creative and get the campaign out as a one-off matter. This was a time-consuming process.

Today, the most important use of ad-hoc campaigns is probably for testing new campaign ideas — e.g., a new product bundle. Direct marketers always have many ideas for possible promotions. Therefore, the faster marketers can test their ideas by trying them on a sample audience, the quicker they can fail promotions that don't seem to be triggering enough interest. Marketers can then focus their attention on those ideas that survive the testing phase. These will be subjected to further scrutiny and then potentially developed into automated production campaigns.

Scheduled

Regularly scheduled campaigns are the most basic form of automating campaign execution. Our local bank may, for example, run customer acquisition campaigns on a monthly basis. The bank may also extend cross-sales offers to its existing customers by attaching them to their monthly billing statements.

Rule Based

Campaigns may also be executed based on business rules. For example, at most banks, everybody who opens a new credit card account will also be encouraged to sign up for credit loan insurance.

Event Based

Scheduled and rule-based campaigns can hardly be called customer centric. After all, they happen on the marketer's schedule. In contrast, event-based campaigns are a step toward a more meaningful dialog with customers. Simple event-based campaigns may be triggered by predictable events such as a client's birthday. However, more sophisticated event-based campaigns are triggered by the behavior of individual customers. For instance, a retention campaign may be activated for an individual checking account holder if he stops his direct deposit and also the mortgage payment. A cross-sales campaign may be set off if a client deposits a sum of money on their account that is more than a standard deviation above the regular average for this client.

Next Best Offer

Even if there is no unusual event that occurs, you will want to be ready with the most relevant offer for each client. The offer will be extended when an opportunity arises. For this purpose, next best activity campaigns precalculate a number of offers per client based on the client's history and product holdings. The offer may be delivered as part of a scheduled communication or in response to an inbound inquiry (for example, via the call center).

For instance, if a bank customer already has checking and savings accounts, and there have been significant direct deposits, the next best offer may be an IRA. If on the other hand, the account balance is always near zero or sometimes even negative, maybe the next best offer is a fixed interest rate loan.

Real Time

Next best offers may be calculated on a daily basis or at less frequent intervals. However, such pre-made plans may need to be thrown overboard based on the momentary situation. For example, a client may call into the local bank's call center with a question about ATM access during his planned vacation to Turkey. In this moment, does it make any sense to extend the IRA offer that may have been precalculated as the next best? Maybe you should be raising the client's credit limits so that he can bring home a few Oriental rugs as souvenirs.

Link Marketing to Targeting

Once the Marketers have charted the course of marketing communications to come, it is time for the *targeters* to get to work. Targeters are the specialists that refine which customers within the strategic segments should receive which offer at what time and over which channel.

Reader: Targeting? Why yet another round of refinement?

Direct Marketer: Well, should every at-risk customer receive a retention offer, for instance? What if the customer has never been profitable?

Reader: Yeah, but, they could still turn into a profitable customer by accepting the right kind of retention offer!

Direct Marketer: Very true. So a decision is required as to which at-risk customers should receive which retention offers and in what format.

Reader: Hmmm... How would you do that?

Direct Marketer: We start by predicting the future lifetime value of at-risk clients based on their past behavior and based on the behavior of similar clients. This calculation can be based on statistical models. Once we have predicted the value, we can derive how much we can afford to spend on retaining the customer. If the predicted value is really low, then we can only spend very little on discounts or on delivering the offer.

Reader: That sounds complicated. How about I skip retention campaigns and just do scheduled campaigns for acquisition and cross-sales instead?

Direct Marketer: Don't you remember the example of the local banker from the previous chapter? If you blanketed your entire customer base with cross-sales offers, you will spend a lot of budget yet probably never break even. Targeting is needed here too. You need to predict the subset of your potential audience that is most likely to appreciate your offer, so that you can save costs and make money.

This is generally the point where the predictive modeling team is brought in to advise which subset of customers within the segments should be targeted. Their job is also to predict how much value is expected when these customer are targeted with each candidate offer. In this chapter, we will pay quite a bit of attention to this predictive analysis phase because it is probably the part that is most different from online marketing practices.

Jargon Alert: Key Performance Indicators

What the direct marketer knows as the *strategic communications plan* has an analogy in online marketing in the establishment of *key performance indicators (KPIs)*. The KPI process includes not just metrics that describe a site's mission but also goals for these metrics that the business wishes to attain. Website KPIs have typically been suggested as site-level goals however. In contrast, the strategic communication plan is formulated at the level of strategic customer segments. It is used to derive communications and offers for the segment.

Segmentation is no less important for online marketers. Therefore, online marketers would be well advised to ensure that their KPIs will reference the targeted customer segments that they pertain to. In addition, Megan Burns from Forrester Research recommends that a plan of action is associated with each KPI, for situations when the metric crosses certain thresholds.

Predict Individual Response and Value

Think for a moment. How would you analyze your prospects and customers in each of the strategic segments if you want to come up with useful predictions that you can pass to your colleagues? Studying customers in order to understand their wishes is complicated and involved. Data analysis is only one aspect, and even that aspect is complex.

Within data analysis, the typical starting point is to first *discover characteristics* of people who are most likely to behave in similar fashion. The second step is to create a mental or mathematical *model* with which the marketer *scores* the likelihood that each person in the segment will respond to specific product offers. The models also estimate a *valuation* of the amount of business that is predicted with each prospect. Finally, one more step is necessary given that it would not be acceptable to bombard the resulting target audience with all product offerings at once in the hopes that some offer will stick. Namely, the marketing team has to *optimize* by deciding which customers will receive which offer.

More about the three steps follows. However, before you can begin with them, you first have to figure out what customer data you should look at during the predictive analysis phase.

Select Customer Data to Inform Predictive Analysis

What types of data about customers are best to use as input into predictive models so that you can refine who should be contacted? Marketers choose from geographic, demographic, socioeconomic, psychographic, and behavioral data bits. The exact choice will differ for each business and is part of their secret sauce that companies keep to themselves. Marketers want to exploit any data that they have available and that their privacy policies permit.

Demographic, Socioeconomic, and Geographic Data Go back to our example of the local bank from the previous chapter. Of the people that live in town, are certain *demographic* groups more likely to open a checking account with you? Yes, for example, if student loans are a major focus for the bank. If this is your target audience, then demographics will of course be helpful in narrowing down your direct mail list.

The last time you were in your bank's branch, however, did it seem that most customers were of similar demographics? Probably not. In many cases, demographics are a poor determinant of who is going to be a promising prospect.

How about *socioeconomic* data then? Surely, if your offering consists of private banking services, you want to target the *geo locations* in town where the more affluent live. Yet, a regular retail bank may in fact prefer customers from a mix of income levels. For example, our local bank may benefit more from those who are likely to keep debt balances on their credit cards. Although geographic, demographic, and socioeconomic data should be useful for many kinds of businesses, our local retail bank probably would not get enough out of them.

Psychographic Data How about *psychographic* data such as *attitudes, life styles*, etc.? Well, our local bankers could find out for themselves by surveying a sample of their most valuable customers. The marketer might learn that her most valuable customers tend to be urban DINKS (downtown dwellers with double incomes and no kids). She might also learn that they are of liberal mind-set and travel abroad frequently. With this insight, the marketer could better target messaging to this crowd. She may decide on messaging and graphics that signal how the bank is open-minded and global, just like its customers. Therein seems to lie the greatest value of psychographic data, namely to help decide how to market to a target group rather than selecting the target group.

Behavioral Data That leaves us with *behavioral* data such as customers' past product choices and their history of responding to marketing communications. Direct marketers regard past behavior as the most predictive for future behavior. However, behavioral data by itself is not perfect either. Without attitudinal data, for example, it does not reveal why people behaved in the way that they did—i.e., what goals they were pursuing.

In the offline world, behavioral data is often unavailable for prospects who are not customers yet. Hence, acquisition-oriented marketers would have to fall back to descriptive data. Yet, a popular alternative is to outsource the customer analysis process to companies such as Epsilon and Acxiom, who maintain large prospect databases including transactional data.

RFM The best known behavioral data scores used in direct marketing are recency, frequency, and monetary (RFM) scores. Did you ever make a donation to a charitable organization and found in surprise that more and more requests for donations come in the mail? Fund raisers know that the most promising prospects are those who most recently and most frequently gave the most sizable monetary contributions. Therefore, they continue contacting the same donors or they may look to obtain lists of those who have been giving to other charitable organizations.

The idea has been studied and confirmed by commercial marketers. Among the three scores, recency is typically considered to be the strongest indicator. Jim Novo, in his book *Drilling Down,* provides intuitive instructions for turning RFM scores into high-value customer segments for targeted marketing.

Latency Jim Novo also suggests latency as an indicator — i.e., the time that passes between interactions or purchases. For example, if a customer is part of a segment that typically interacts every 30 days, then a pause of 40 days may suggest that something is changing in the customer's pattern of behavior. It could be that the customer is defecting. In other cases, it could be an opportunity to offer new services to address changing needs.

Event-based marketing puts this idea on steroids. It automates the detection of changes in patterns of behavior. It does so for each individual, based on their personal past behavior patterns instead of segment average behavior.

RFM Scores, What Are Those?

Take your customer file and sort it by the date that indicates when each customer's last contact with you occurred — i.e., sort by recency. Now group the list into a number of buckets, say five. Everyone in the bucket with most recent interactions, say within the last month, receives a top score, 5 in this case. The next most recent group gets a score of 4, and so forth.

Similarly, each customer will also receive a frequency score between 1 and 5, depending on how often per month they interact with you. Finally, they will receive a monetary score between 1 and 5, depending on the size of the transactions. The scores can also be added to obtain an overall RFM score between 3 and 15. Our marketers would rank order their customer file by these scores and start calling everyone with the top scores first.

In summary, the direct marketers at our local bank may use a combination of data items to narrow their target group. Among these, behavioral data is the most promising, and psychographic data helps tune the messages that will be delivered. If nothing else, demographic, socioeconomic, and geographic data can at least help eliminate people from the target group who are the least likely to be interested.

 Note: Given that behavioral data is the direct marketer's favorite type of data, it is a shame that, according to studies, most direct marketers do not study and analyze the online behavior data.

Discover Segments with Exploration and Clustering

In everyday life, we often take shortcuts to help us cope with the complexity of our days. Relying on average numbers is one of those shortcuts without which we could not do. In marketing analysis, however, averages kill our chances of discovering pockets of opportunity hidden in the data. For example, if you were a tutor looking for students, you would probably pass on a class where the grade point average is a wonderful A–. But if you grouped the students in the class by their actual grade points, you could discover that five of the students got a C or D and would be excellent prospects.

If your data set does not contain prohibitively many characteristics about each person, discovery can be achieved by exploring the data visually. Figure 4.1 shows how a visual analysis and reporting solution such as Tableau from Tableau Software can make sense of many dimensions of data within a single, intuitive chart. The chart explores opportunities for tutoring across grade points (*X*-axis), class grade (*Y*-axis), recency of grade points (color), and frequency of grade points (circle size).

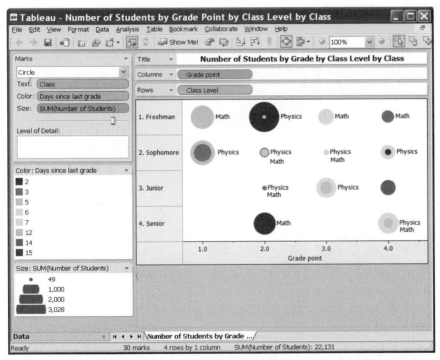

Figure 4.1 Visual exploration of data on opportunities for tutoring (based on Tableau, a visual analysis and reporting solution from Tableau Software)

Data visualization can be used and understood by many people, whether they are trained in statistics or not. Yet, when more and more dimensions are added to the analysis, it gets increasingly difficult to discover clusters through dimensional visualization. For that reason, data-mining software solutions automate the discovery process through clustering algorithms. The goal of clustering is to define segments of prospects and customers who are relatively similar to each other but relatively different from people in other segments. Algorithms such as k-nearest neighbor or k-means clustering create multidimensional cluster centers. They then calculate the n-dimensional distance between entities to determine to which cluster a customer's set of attributes is closest. Clustering is not a goal in itself, but just a step along the way to identifying the most promising segments.

Predict and Score Outcomes with Modeling

Which groups in Figure 4.1 are most likely to respond to your offer for tutoring? Do you think it would be the groups where students received the worst grades, more recently and more frequently? If so, you just built a mental model based on three input variables. Your output variable from the model was a score — i.e., a prediction for the likelihood that each segment will respond to the offer for tutoring. The output is a function of the inputs. For example, your assumption was that the worse the grade, the higher the propensity to respond to an offer for tutoring.

Jargon Alert: Clustering

Web analytics reporting often relies on average numbers to suggest typical behavior. Good web analysts go beyond averages, however, and segment results across multiple dimensions. The whole purpose of slicing and dicing web analytics reports (i.e., segmentation) is to discover pockets of behavior. In fact, web analysts know that without segmentation, it is very difficult to get any meaning out of web analytics reports.

The clustering used by direct marketers goes beyond segmenting data by individual dimensions. This becomes clearer if you consider that in each cluster there may be a different combination of dimensions that are close among entities within the cluster. For example, one cluster may be a group of students who are similar to each other mainly because they received a low grade point, recently. Another cluster in the same analysis could be other students who are similar to each other mainly because they took a math class and are seniors or juniors.

Build the Model

But do we really know that D students are more interested in tutoring than C students? It could be that D students have given up hope whereas C students see that Bs are within reach and will seize the opportunity to improve. It's a good question. This is why models are better built by using a sample of historical data instead of gut feeling. For our case, we will need historical data not just about students' past grades but also their responses when presented an offer for tutoring.

Regression Analysis and Machine Learning Models

Regression analysis expresses a model as a mathematical equation (the regression equation). The equation ties input variables together to calculate the value of the output variable (the prediction). After exploring a sample set of historical data that includes both, the input and output variables, a statistician may guesstimate the rough makeup of the regression equation. The statistician will then write out this equation by including regression parameters — i.e., a number of variables that are yet to be filled in. For example, a simple, linear regression equation for our example with a single variable, namely student's grade points, might look similar to the following:

$Y = a + b \times GradePoint$

In this case, the statistician would be postulating that the grade point multiplied with some regression parameter b and corrected by another regression parameter a would result in the output Y that is a score for the likelihood that students will respond to the offer for tutoring. The process of regression analysis is primarily about determining the makeup of the regression equation. Secondly, it is about determining the best values of the regression parameters so that the resulting equation comes as close to matching the value of the output variable in the sample data as possible.

There are many types of regression analysis, ranging from regression for single or multiple input variables to discrete choice models that involve variables that take discrete values instead of continuous ones — for example, either "Yes" or "No" to tutoring.

When it comes to machine learning models on the other hand, there are also a number of different kinds. The most famous among these are neural networks. A neural network is trained on a set of input versus output variables. It builds an internal model that is inspired by brain neurons. A large enough network of nodes simulates brain neurons in the sense that each node is connected with other nodes. They fire a response when a certain combination of their neighbors are in turn stimulated by input.

One way of training the network is by stimulating the designated input nodes with the historical input variables and stimulating the output node with the historical output variable. The internal nodes adjust their connections so that the trained model from there on will by itself produce the output signal when only the input nodes are stimulated.

The upside of a neural network is that it is not limited to predictions that can be expressed as linear equations. A neural net captures nonlinear relationships by virtue of its algorithm. The downside is that the network is a black box in the sense that it does not reveal why it predicts what it has been trained to predict.

Getting that data is hard enough. But how can it then be turned into a model? That is the work of a statistician, typically drawing on data-mining software for assistance. Together they will build one or multiple models using a choice of statistical techniques. These techniques can be grouped into regression analysis and machine learning types. One of the go-to books for a description of both types of techniques as applied to direct marketing is *The New Direct Marketing* by David Shephard Associates.

Marketing modeling software solutions and generic data-mining software can automatically generate many different models for a given set of data. They can offer the statistician results from regression analysis as well as neural networks. The statistician can then pick the type of model that they prefer and that performs best to predict results.

For instance, one model may depend on 15 input variables, some of which are difficult to collect. If there is another model that is equally descriptive yet requires fewer and easier input data, then the statistician may likely prefer it.

Verify and Calibrate the Model

Regardless which method you pursue for building the model, it needs to be verified on another sample of historical data that has not been used for building it. This is especially obvious for machine learning methods. Take a famous example of a failure. Rumor has it that somewhere, someone tried to train a neural network to distinguish between aerial photographs with military vehicles parked under trees and photographs with no military equipment under the trees. When the proud scientists validated the model on a new set of photographs, however, it failed miserably. The scientists were disappointed. After much deliberation, it dawned on them that all the training photos that included military equipment had been taken during the same time of year, namely fall. The neural network had learned how to distinguish a fall forest from a summer forest.

This is no trivial problem. It exemplifies that a model will only be as representative as the historical sample of data that was used to build it. The only way to effectively verify a model is to do non-inbred testing. Data that the model has not seen before is used to confirm whether the model generalizes properly.

In an equation-based model, it would be possible to calibrate its predictions if they are not a close fit yet. This would be done by slightly altering regression parameters until the predictions are more accurate on new samples of data. With a neural network, on the other hand, one would probably have to start from scratch.

Run the Model

Putting our model for tutoring students to work, we will feed it the entire file of prospective students. For each of the students, the model will score the likelihood that they would sign up for tutoring. We will then rank order the entire file by that probability score.

The next step is traditionally to divide the ordered list into 10 deciles (buckets) of equal size. Why 10? There's no particular reason actually. For each of the deciles, we can calculate the average forecasted conversion rate and revenue. If the costs of our campaign communication are already set in stone, we can calculate the expected ROI from each of the deciles.

Table 4.2 presents an example with 10,000 prospective students. It assumes marketing costs of $3.50 per prospect, or $3,500 per decile. In this case, we would pick deciles 1 through 4 and target them with our campaign. Decile 5 still breaks even, but our money might yield a better return if invested into a bank CD instead of this initiative. In other words, the opportunity costs are higher. So we would forego marketing to deciles 5 through 10.

▶ **Table 4.2** Expected ROI from Marketing to Each Decile of Prospective Students

Decile	Predicted Conversion Rate	Predicted Average Contribution	Predicted Total Contribution	Gross Margin	ROI
1	4.1%	$210	$8,610	$5,110	146%
2	3.7%	$190	$7,030	$3,530	101%
3	3.5%	$180	$6,300	$2,800	80%
4	3.3%	$165	$5,445	$1,945	56%
5	2.3%	$159	$3,657	$157	4%
6	1.8%	$149	$2,682	−$818	−23%
7	1.5%	$136	$2,040	−$1,460	−42%
8	1.1%	$100	$1,100	−$2,400	−69%
9	0.9%	$80	$720	−$2,780	−79%
10	0.2%	$60	$120	−$3,380	−97%
Total/Average	2.2%	$168	$37,704	$2,704	8%

Figure 4.2 shows another way of selecting a reduced target audience for our campaign. This method depends on the output from modeling software. Namely, instead of grouping by deciles, the software rank orders the entire customer file. It plots file depth compared to the predicted percent of responses that can still be achieved at each file depth. For example, reducing the size of the target file to the most promising 60 percent of potential prospects, the model predicts that the campaign would still achieve 94 percent of the responses that it would achieve if the campaign was sent to 100 percent of the customer file. This type of report is known as a *lift chart*.

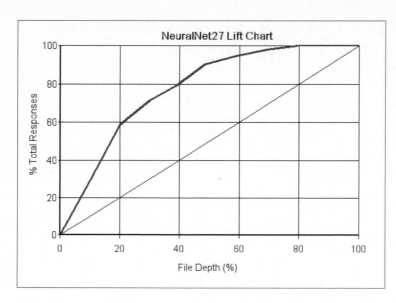

Figure 4.2

The lift chart predicts percent of responses based on reduced target audience sizes.

Modeling software can combine the lift chart with information on expected marketing costs and profits in order to calculate a rollout profit curve. Figure 4.3 shows an example of that. We see that based on a given cost per contact of $1 and an expected profit per response of $25, the rollout profit curve is maximized by marketing to the top 475,600 of 1,000,000 contacts in the database. As you can see in the table of Figure 4.3, the modeling software divided the customer list into 20 buckets in this case, instead of 10.

The Model Perishes

We have come such a long way, and we are almost ready to execute our campaign. At the most inopportune moment, our chief executive decides to lower the price of the tutoring service. She also changes our marketing message from "Want better grades?" to "Don't want your friends to think of you as a loser anymore?" Oh boy. The conditions have changed and our model has just become stale. It cannot predict what it has not been built to predict. If formerly C students had been our prime target segment, now they may decide they can very well tutor themselves. They don't think of themselves as losers after all. Yet, the D students may respond better now, get off the couch, and turn into our most promising segment. If we don't correct the model, our campaign may target the wrong group.

Direct marketing programs may stay stable for a few months or maybe even a year before they are adjusted. But marketing in general thrives by constantly developing new ideas and quickly reacting to ideas that the competition develops. Therefore, a practical requirement for the use of modeling for marketers is the ability to build models as quickly and cost efficiently as possible. This requires statistical know-how and

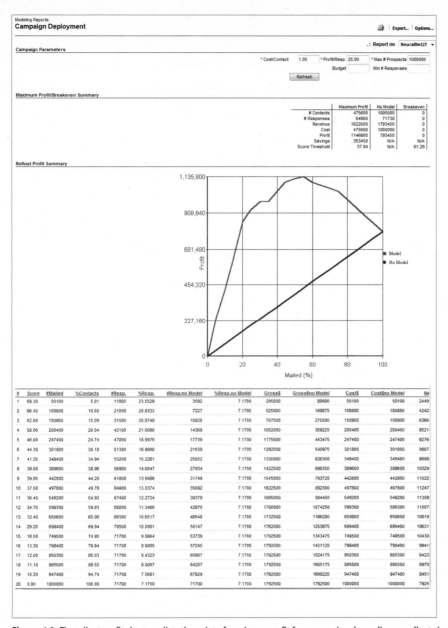

Figure 4.3 The rollout profit chart predicts the point of maximum profit for a campaign depending on rollout size.

resources. The use of modeling software solutions that are connected with the marketing system of record helps reduce the number of steps that are involved for building the models. Enterprise Marketing Management (EMM) platforms aim to provide such an environment.

Case Study of Contact Optimization at Wachovia

Providing each customer and prospect with the most suitable offer, at the most welcome moment, can be a challenge even in a small business. Let's take a closer look at a "real life" example of a diversified financial services company headquartered in Charlotte, NC. Wachovia is the fourth largest bank holding company in the United States with 13 million households and businesses as customers. Their services include not just retail banking and brokerage but also asset and wealth management as well as corporate and investment banking.

The Insight and Innovation (I&I) team at Wachovia has the unique challenge of centrally managing customer and prospect marketing contacts across the four lines of business at the bank. The consultative role of the I&I team in cross-functional projects is to:

- Provide targeting expertise gained through campaign analyses
- Create value and response modeling
- Conduct intense data mining

The I&I team's function directly impacts the company's bottom line. The goal of its modeling efforts, specifically, is to contact the optimal target group with the most valuable offer to both the recipient and the marketer. Angenique Breeland, Senior Consultant of I&I's Customer Contact Management team, described the classic optimization problem as "ensuring that we provide the right offer, to the right customer or prospect, at the right time of need. Maximizing the relevancy of each marketing communication is critical in our environment where coordinating contacts across various product and business lines is intentionally constrained on a recurring basis by contact channels." The optimization process at Wachovia integrates modeling, targeting, and channel optimization to ultimately increase value to customers and the bank — a win-win achievement!

Previously, the actual prioritization of alternative offers was coordinated manually for any given set of proposed contacts in each prescribed timeframe. This was performed by a committee of consultants specializing in targeted marketing. In their review, the consultants would net opt-outs and other campaign specific criteria. Where there was overlap between product offerings for the targeted audiences, the group would meet to determine the best target audience for each campaign. Obviously, they would have to resolve competing business goals and objectives in this process. "As you can imagine, a contact fatigue issue was perpetual with a 'first come, first serve' procedure and no over-arching value metric utilized," as Breeland recounts. This was a complex undertaking that added unnecessary delays to campaign execution.

Clearly, there had to be room for improvement. The I&I team took on the challenge of increasing the efficiency of this process by automating it through an optimization software solution. At the same time the team set the bar high by seeking to increase the resulting customer revenues by 10 percent. Optimization can be automated with the help of software solutions from vendors such as Experian, SAS, Teradata, and Unica. The software performs its algorithms to provide an optimal contact plan. One of the challenges seen at Wachovia was convincing marketers to relinquish control and trust the software's advice.

The Insight and Innovation team's initiative to switch from manual coordination to automated optimization was critical for Wachovia to shift from product-centric to customer-centric marketing. Previously, the product marketers drove the targeted campaigns. They were worried now about the seeming loss of ability to meet sales goals by controlling campaign quantity. The new optimization scheme did not always provide a fixed or desired quantity of contacts for each product. After all, the most optimized contact plan was centrally inclusive of all product groups and contact channels.

Rightfully, the product managers challenged the Insight and Innovation team to prove that the same or better returns could be achieved with lowered costs under optimization. In order to get buy-in, the team gained trust through a period of parallel testing of the old and new methods. A selection of campaigns that Wachovia was executing on a regular basis became the testing ground. Wachovia ran the new, automated optimization in parallel to continuing the manual coordination. Using the models, Wachovia scored the outcomes predicted for the manual versus the automated contact plan. Indeed, the automated optimization was able to prove an overall 60 percent improvement in expected returns measured across the test period.

Since then, the automated optimization has been placed into production. Wachovia has achieved a 34 percent increase in expected results and a 12 percent increase in five-year customer valuation from their monthly campaigns. The goal of a 10 percent increase in customer revenues was exceeded.

The Insight and Innovation team created the graphic in Figure 4.4 to summarize the benefits of optimization. The graphic indicates that when firms switch from silo'd product marketing to manual coordination, they achieve higher ROI but the effort is highly inefficient. By figuring out how to entrust the optimization to an automated process, Wachovia was not only able to maximize returns but also efficiency. Targeted marketing has to evolve to the point of increasing bottom-line value and maximizing marketing budgets in a more efficient way. Kevin Daly, Vice President of I&I's Customer Contact Management team that centrally owns the optimization process, says the next strategy is to apply value at a household level to drive optimization. "If we optimize at the household, long-term value level, we can really grow revenue," which is the overall goal of any organization engaged in targeted marketing.

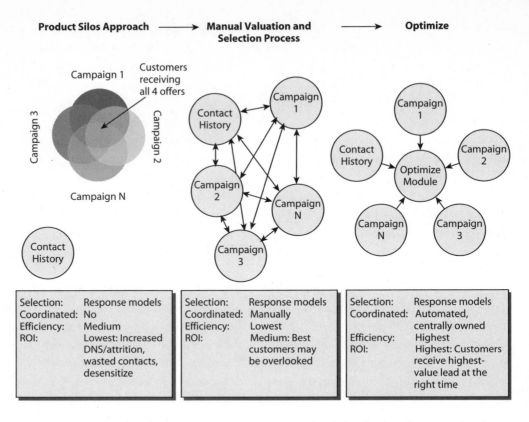

Figure 4.4 Graphic created by Wachovia's Insight and Innovation team to explain the benefits of moving from a product silo approach over manual coordination to automated, centrally owned optimization

Execute Campaigns

So, now we have optimized who should receive a marketing communication and which one at what time. We are ready to bring our campaigns to the market. Yet, the execution phase is anything but chopped liver. There are many more hurdles, especially if our campaign is not just a one-off effort but a regular occurrence such as Wachovia's monthly campaigns. In that case, the marketer wants to automate "lights out" operations by configuring the business rules once and having the campaign management system fill in the details each time a new wave is executed.

Batch-Oriented Execution The campaign management system needs to pull and merge data from the customer data warehouse and other systems. Duplicate records need to be purged and incorrect addresses cleaned out. The latest suppression rules need to be obeyed and verified. Customers with contact fatigue need to be given a break. The final recipient lists, including their offers, need to be delivered to the channel distribution applications, mail houses, or call centers that will get the offer out.

Marketers can define repeatable execution plans. These capture the business rules around each campaign into a format that both the campaign management system and the marketer can understand. Figure 4.5 illustrates an execution plan as a flow chart. Some elements in the flow chart are responsible for pulling and transforming customer information, others for customer decisioning or creating offer cells. Yet others are responsible for generating output for passing to the marketing channels.

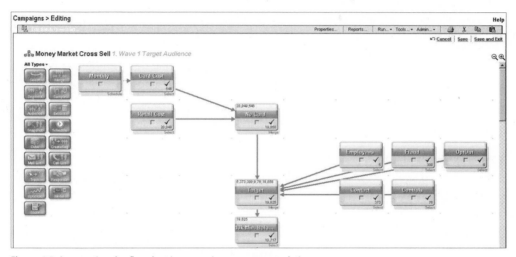

Figure 4.5 An execution plan flow chart in a campaign management solution

Event-Based Execution with Customer Decisioning For event-based execution, the campaign management system needs to be connected to all required data marts in order to listen for trigger events and then initiate campaign execution on a one by one basis. An automated customer decisioning process has to decide which offer the customer will receive. This will, however, not just be based on the trigger event (e.g., a cancelled product subscription). It also needs to take into account everything else known about the customer's status at that time (e.g.. their purchases on other channels).

Take the example of a retargeting campaign. The shop keeper at a small corner bodega in Manhattan may get worried when a loyal customer that came in for milk every day does not show up for two weeks. The shop keeper may give the customer a call to make sure everything is all right and invite him back to the store. A big box retailer for office stationary wanted to implement essentially the same idea for all their customers across all their stores. Customers who have not been shopping in the stores as frequently as their usual patterns were to receive a discount coupon to win back their business. However, if a customer's business had merely shifted to the telephone or Internet, the coupon should probably be suppressed. The value of the coupon and the channel through which it is delivered should also depend on the value of the customer. These are the kinds of choices that an event-based customer decisioning process can make during campaign execution given access to up-to-date customer data.

Inbound, Real-Time Customer Decisioning The customer decisioning process has to become even more real time if an offer is to be extended while the customer is still on the website or on the phone with the call center. (In comparison, event-based execution may occur nightly.) For this purpose, the customer decisioning process has to have available information on the live website session or the current phone conversation.

That requires systems specifically designed for this purpose. For example, a web analytics solution cannot complete sessionization because the session is still in progress. Yet, data about the recent clicks still need to be streamed into the decisioning engine. The recommendation engine needs to be scalable enough to get the output to the call center system or website in time.

Offer Cells for Test and Control

With all this going on, the direct marketer at last reaches the step that is so familiar to the online marketer. Namely, to test different versions of the same message in order to select the winners and use them in future waves of the campaign. Even before A/B testing became a mainstream term in online marketing, the offline colleagues were using a Test and Control approach for testing. For that purpose, the segments that were created during the analytical phase were randomly subdivided into smaller cells, each of which received a slight variation of the offer.

Even after a clear *champion* has established itself as the most successful offer variation, direct marketers can keep testing possible *challengers* in future waves of the campaign to see if an even greater champion will emerge.

Jargon Alert: A/B Testing

What the online marketer calls A/B testing has been known in direct marketing as a Test and Control or Champion – Challenger approach.

We also want to measure ROI of the campaign. For that purpose, one of the target cells will serve as the control group which will receive no offer at all. This is despite the fact that the group is made up of promising prospects who are just as likely to value the offer as anyone else in the target group. A trap to avoid here is being too stingy and making that cell too small to be statistically significant.

Given the complexity of the direct marketing process, it is easy to see why many companies outsource the entire management of their campaigns. Marketing service providers who expertly run campaigns and customer data marts on behalf of their clients include: Acxiom, Epsilon, Equifax, Experian, FairIssac, Harte-Hanks, Target-base, and many others.

Measure and Attribute Responses

Finally, we are back to measurement. Not the predictive analytics that the marketer performed in the beginning, but descriptive analytics that report how the campaigns performed across all the offer cells. The direct marketer's take on response attribution is of particular interest to our cause because of the inherent multichannel nature. With few exceptions, most direct marketing messages are delivered on certain channels while customers respond on others—say, catalog to phone purchases. If the offline marketer can measure that response, then surely the same technique will also help us measure catalog to online channel responses.

Interestingly, offline marketers routinely use a number of relevant terms and techniques that online marketers and web analysts hardly ever consider. In the hopes of convincing online marketers to adopt them, they are listed here:

Response Attribution

An inquiry or purchase is referred to as a *response* if it has been triggered by a direct response advertisement or campaign. The process of measurement becomes the process of collecting data from all channels with the goal of attributing each interaction or transaction back to the campaigns that deserve the credit.

For collecting this data, the campaign management system needs the ability to pull transaction-level data from the locations where it resides. This may be within a customer data warehouse or directly at point-of-sale data marts and call center records. Collecting the data is only the first step of response attribution. The secret sauce is in identifying the campaigns that deserve the credit. That can be done through a variety of matching techniques, as follows next.

Direct Attribution via Source Codes

Say Mary Meyers received a 10 percent discount offer from Best Buy and used it in a purchase. How will the marketer responsible for the program be able to take credit? At the register, the discount coupon is keyed in along with the payment information. The marketing system pulls information on all transactions and looks for available reason codes. Thus, it can sum up the transaction volume and attribute it to the related campaign.

Viral Response Attribution via Source Codes

What if Mary Meyers received a direct mail offer with a discount, but Paul Peoples buys the advertised product using the discount code? Paul is not in our list of offer recipients. Surely, somebody must have leaked him the information. This is counted as a viral response.

Inferred Attribution via Matchback

Let's face it. The vast majority of advertisements and transactions involve neither coupons nor source codes nor unique phone numbers. So how can the marketer still attribute a purchase to an earlier campaign touch point? If the response attribution technique did not have anything to offer beyond source codes and unique phone numbers it would be a quick failure. The trick that helps the direct marketer keep their pants on is matchback response attribution. We introduced this briefly in the previous chapter in regard to e-mail measurement. It has been a standard method in offline direct marketing.

The campaign management system maintains the list of customers who were targeted with offers including offer characteristics. Say Mary Meyers is one of these recipients on a Tuesday. If Mary also makes a purchase in the store the following Saturday, it can be inferred that the transaction should be attributed to the campaign.

The attribution could be further refined by requiring that the product category in which Mary made a purchase should be related to the marketing message that she received. For example, Mary's bank may mail her a balance transfer offer with a specific low-interest rate. The campaign management system may later detect in Mary's customer data that an account with exactly that low-interest rate has been opened. The system can then infer that the original offer should be credited with this response.

Campaign management systems provide functionality that automates matchback response attribution so that no custom business intelligence solution needs to be built for the purpose.

CAUSE VS. CORRELATION

However, just as with online view-through reporting, there is nothing to prove that Mary made the purchase because of the offer that she received. She may not have seen the direct mail because her husband committed it to the trash bin on the way from the mail box. Even if she saw the offer, maybe she was going to make the purchase anyway, so that the discount offer caused a loss to the company rather than a gain. What to do?

As with online view-through reporting, the recommendation is to compare offer recipient's behavior to control groups. These control groups should consist of people who are just as promising prospects as Mary but who do not receive the offer. As long as the control group is of statistically significant size, the difference in purchase behavior can be attributed to the campaign.

Campaign management solutions facilitate the use of control groups as a standard feature, but not all marketers use them. That can be a big mistake, as author and multichannel marketing veteran Kevin Hillstrom points out on his blog MineThatData.com.

Note: Online marketers should adopt the practice of using control groups from their offline colleagues. It should become a routine measure in order to separate cause from mere correlation when attributing responses to e-mail or display advertising.

Householding for Matchback What if Mary Meyers received the direct mail offer, but Mark Meyers goes to buy the product? Using publicly available data sources, individuals can be related to their households so that the matchback technique can be extended accordingly. Often times, this process is outsourced to marketing service providers who can also provide the necessary data.

Jargon Alert: Matchback

Matchback is in essence the offline equivalent of ad view-through reporting. However, instead of using cookies to perform the matchback, the connection can be made based on the customer's name, for example. Information on the customer's name would be available in the transaction record if the customer used a credit card. If the customer is using a loyalty card the matchback will of course be even more straightforward. After all, this is part of the purpose of loyalty cards.

Some stores also ask for phone numbers at the checkout. Matchback may also be achieved with 70 to 80 percent accuracy if only the name on the credit card is available and paired up with a zip code. Even with cash transactions, if the teller can obtain a zip code or telephone area code for the customer, the revenue can at least be matched back to marketing activities within the customer's geographic area.

Other industries have it much easier. For example, when you visit your mobile phone vendor's stores, the clerk will probably pull up your account by your mobile phone number. When you bring the car to the garage, your account will be accessed in the CRM system. When you visit your insurance broker or bank, they will also open your account and register any transactions right there.

Halo Response Attribution with Matchback Mary Meyers received a direct mail offer for a credit card from her local bank. She goes to the branch to open a checking account instead. Because Mary is in our list of campaign recipients, the campaign management system can match the response back and attribute it to the halo effect of the credit card campaign.

Multi-Touch Response Attribution What if Mary received multiple offers before she went to the store to purchase? Which of the offers should receive how much of the credit? You must have been waiting for this one! In real life, this situation is almost always the default. Extending the matchback mechanism, some campaign management solutions offer flexible methods for distributing credit to multiple preceding touch points. They enable marketers to assign credit to the most recent campaign or spread the credit in parts to multiple campaigns. We will leave the details around these attribution options to be discussed in Chapter 8.

Response Types So far we have measured completed responses — i.e., conversions or sales. A response may be of other types too. For instance, a response may be an inquiry about the products and may or may not turn into a conversion. A response can also be a request to opt-out from further contacts. These intermediary response types can be attributed to the marketing campaign in the same fashion as completed responses. The attribution can be automated by the campaign management solution as long as the data is made available to it.

Figure 4.6 shows an example of a campaign summary report that brings together all attributed responses per campaign and calculates a number of metrics including, for example, costs and profits.

Blind Spot of the Offline Direct Marketer

If Mary received a credit card offer by mail and decided to respond, quite likely she would do so online via a website. If Mary completed the application online, our offline direct marketers would receive the transaction record. This would enable them to perform the matchback to the direct mail just as if Mary had used the phone or local branch for her application. But what if Mary began the application online, got lost somewhere within the forms, and finally gave up?

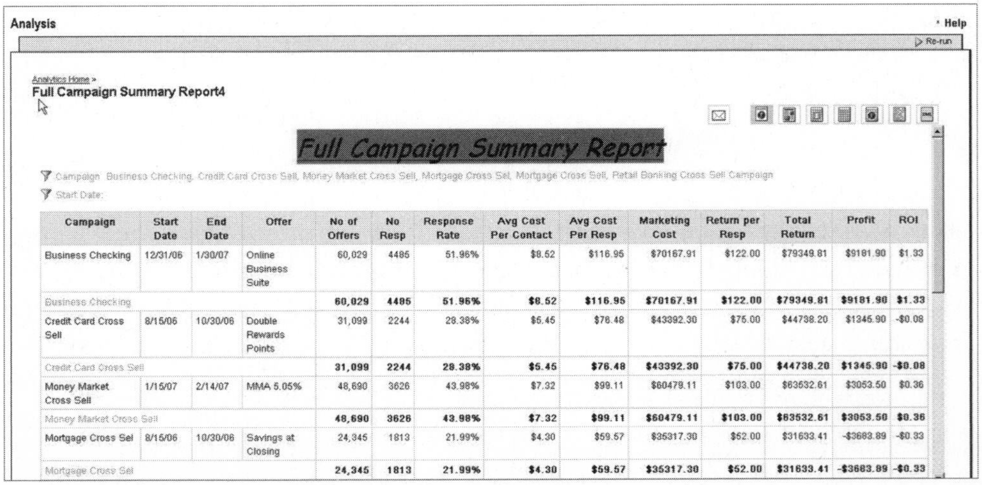

Analysis   · Help
                                                                                                                         ▷ Re-run

Analytics Home »
Full Campaign Summary Report4

Full Campaign Summary Report

▽ Campaign Business Checking, Credit Card Cross Sell, Money Market Cross Sell, Mortgage Cross Sell, Mortgage Cross Sell, Retail Banking Cross Sell Campaign
▽ Start Date:

Campaign	Start Date	End Date	Offer	No of Offers	No Resp	Response Rate	Avg Cost Per Contact	Avg Cost Per Resp	Marketing Cost	Return per Resp	Total Return	Profit	ROI
Business Checking	12/31/06	1/30/07	Online Business Suite	60,029	4485	51.96%	$8.52	$116.95	$70167.91	$122.00	$79349.81	$9181.90	$1.33
Business Checking				60,029	4485	51.96%	$8.52	$116.95	$70167.91	$122.00	$79349.81	$9181.90	$1.33
Credit Card Cross Sell	8/15/06	10/30/06	Double Rewards Points	31,099	2244	28.38%	$5.45	$76.48	$43392.30	$75.00	$44738.20	$1345.90	-$0.08
Credit Card Cross Sell				31,099	2244	28.38%	$5.45	$76.48	$43392.30	$75.00	$44738.20	$1345.90	-$0.08
Money Market Cross Sell	1/15/07	2/14/07	MMA 5.05%	48,690	3626	43.98%	$7.32	$99.11	$60479.11	$103.00	$63532.61	$3053.50	$0.36
Money Market Cross Sell				48,690	3626	43.98%	$7.32	$99.11	$60479.11	$103.00	$63532.61	$3053.50	$0.36
Mortgage Cross Sell	8/15/06	10/30/06	Savings at Closing	24,345	1813	21.99%	$4.30	$59.57	$35317.30	$52.00	$31633.41	-$3683.89	-$0.33
Mortgage Cross Sell				24,345	1813	21.99%	$4.30	$59.57	$35317.30	$52.00	$31633.41	-$3683.89	-$0.33

Figure 4.6 A response attribution report in a campaign management solution

Jargon Alert: Drop-Off Report

Measuring the drop-off from intermediary response types, such as inquiries to completed conversions, has an analogy in online marketing. Namely, the queen of all web analytics reports is the conversion funnel also called scenario, or drop-off report. It too measures drop off from step to step in the conversion process, say landing page to product catalog, to checkout, to order confirmation in the case of a retail site.

Maybe the primary use of the conversion funnel report in web analytics is to experiment with changes to the site, messaging, pricing, etc., to see whether the drop offs can be minimized. Offline marketers can follow the same experimentation process for their media.

The direct marketing concept of *intermediary response types* would apply here. However, DMNews cited research by Forrester, who surveyed 108 database marketers in 2006 and found that website behavior data was missing from an astounding 82 percent of customer databases? So, 82 percent of offline marketers would never find out about Mary's intermediary response — i.e., her abandoned attempt to open an account. They might continue mailing her or they might stop eventually, thinking that she must not be interested. Little do they know!

Figure 4.7 shows a web analytics funnel report to underline the kind of blind spot to which an offline direct marketer may be subject. If the marketer were not working with his colleagues on the online side, response attribution would show that only 139 customers completed an application online. However, as can be seen in the funnel report, the web analyst could reveal that 338 prospects entered the source code online to check their offer. A whopping 4,036 came to the website prompted by the direct marketing offer. The sample funnel report pinpoints the critical paths for optimizing this direct mail campaign. Namely, the direct marketer should really be working with his website team to experiment with variations to landing pages, offers, and forms. If a configuration can be found that increases the completion rate for the funnel process by just 1 percent, it would mean 40 additional applications. That would be a 29 percent increase over the original number of 139 completed applications.

Note: Given all the amazing sophistication, why wouldn't offline direct marketers close their obvious gap in regard to online behavior measurement? "Too busy!" is a response heard frequently. That sounds silly at first to online marketers who have been able to tune their conversion rates by many hundred, sometimes even thousands of percentage points. But after walking through everything that colleagues on the offline side have on their plates, we can sympathize easily with their feeling even if we cannot agree. To overcome the impasse, it is probably necessary to get company-wide recognition for the huge ROI opportunity that is left on the table.

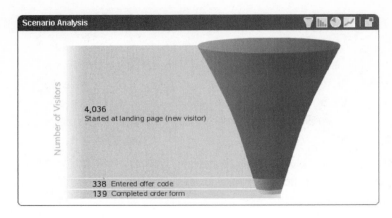

Scenario Analysis

Number of Visitors

4,036
Started at landing page (new visitor)

338 Entered offer code
139 Completed order form

Figure 4.7
A web analytics funnel report showcasing the blind spot of the offline direct marketer

Success Metrics for Direct Marketing

It is amazing how much sophistication goes into response attribution. Now that you have thought through the hard work that is required for measurement, it is time to formulate success metrics. Staying true to the direct marketer, let's look at metrics and flags at the level of the individual first.

Customer Centric Metrics and Flags

Customer-centric metrics for direct marketing can be measured at the level of the individual prospect or customer, their household, or the entire segment to which they belong. In addition to typical metrics such as the number of products per customer, there are also a variety of non-numeric flags to note — for example, the contact and response history.

Marketing History Flags

As we saw earlier, keeping track of marketing communications that have been sent to individual prospects and customers is the key requirement for enabling matchback response attribution. Other than that, it also helps with avoiding contact fatigue by making it possible to enforce rules that limit the number of contacts per period. Another benefit is that marketers can place their next communication such that it builds on previous ones. Finally, the data is also vital as a source for calculating campaign centric metrics such as response rates and conversion rates.

Contact or Promotion History The promotion history contains the initial and the most recent marketing communications to which each individual recipient or household has been exposed. This kind of history also needs to be kept for members of control groups. Thankfully, campaign management systems maintain this information automatically for direct marketing communications.

Response History For each of the promotions that an individual received, the response history lists the reactions that have been matched. Included should be qualitative measures such as:

- The response type (e.g., an inquiry, trial, purchase, or opt-out)
- Status of response (e.g., active sales opportunity)
- Monetary value, if applicable

Response data can be captured from order-processing systems, call center logs, CRM systems, etc. The campaign management system can access this data to execute response attribution rules. Results are then stored within the campaign management system.

Behavioral Flags

The shop keeper at the corner store can observe the habits and preferences of his best customers directly and remember them eventually. Asking enterprise marketers to do that would be a bit much. So, instead they maintain behavioral flags in their customer databases that institutionalize their learning.

Behavioral flags can help marketers devise the next meaningful action for each customer either based on rules or with the help of predictive analysis. Some of the most typical behavioral flags are the following:

Interaction History The history of an individual's interactions with the company is typically recorded in a CRM or SFA system. This includes not just sales interactions but also service interactions, such as help requests and complaints. However, only a subset of these interactions is relevant to marketers, namely the ones that represent events that should trigger a follow-up marketing treatment.

Transaction History Depending on the business model, the transaction history may refer to different kinds of entries. Retailers may list product purchases, whereas subscription oriented businesses may list accounts that have been opened or contracts that have been signed.

Segment Membership History Yes, the customer is king! Yet, some customers are more deserving of being treated like royalty than others. So, most marketers group their customers into different buckets; value to the business is one criterion.

For example, a bank may distinguish customers who have direct deposit and a mortgage payment set up for their account and others who don't. One group is more firmly married to their bank, whereas the others may leave more easily. It is typical for marketers to ask at the end of each period how many customers have been moved from lower value segments to higher value segments.

Life Cycle Status Remember the customer life cycle model from the previous chapter? A status flag within the customer record can indicate where within the life cycle model the prospect or customer appears to be. For instance, if the flag shows that the prospect is in the "purchase consideration" phase, the marketer can prioritize certain communications. If the flag shows "risk of attrition," this may trigger other communications.

Behavioral Scores and Metrics

Behavioral observations cannot be expressed with flags alone. Instead, they can consist of numeric scores and metrics such as the following:

RFM Scores The marketing history taken together with other behavioral history can be abstracted into recency, frequency, and monetary scores of behavior. We discussed these earlier already.

Number of Products per Customer or Household In saturated markets, such as with mobile phone services, it is really hard to acquire new customers because they need to be lured away from the competition. Therefore, growth in those markets is often achieved by growing the wallet share of existing customers. A metric that keeps track of success with this endeavor is the number of products held by each individual or household.

Loyalty Scores and Attrition Rates For the never ending battle of fixing service defects and closing leaks that lead to lost customers, it is helpful to measure attrition rates. Break the numbers down by customer segment so that you can identify where the biggest leaks are.

For similar purposes, you can calculate loyalty scores that express how hooked a customer is to the company's products or services. This can be computed, for example, as a formula combining tenure of relationship with the company, number of product holdings, and the average latency of interactions.

With further analysis, you may find that highly loyal customers do not need a lot of pampering to keep them buying. In contrast, promotional offers may be better spent with less loyal customers where the offers may make a bigger difference.

Predictive Scores

Scores that are calculated by predictive models for each customer are also part of the customer database. Among the various kinds of scores that we discussed, customer value scores come closest to being a success metric. Marketers ask how actions that they have taken impacted the customer valuations.

Predicted Customer Value The predicted customer value is the net present value of all the margins that the marketer expects to earn from the customer. If this value is calculated over the lifetime of the relationship, it is called the lifetime value. But it may also be calculated over shorter periods of time (for example, as a *five year net present* value).

Note: Online marketers agree that customer value metrics are great ideas, but most contend that they are out of reach for all practical purposes. In this case, it is the online marketers who will feel "too busy" to worry about predicting the value that a customer represents to the business over the long run. Most online marketers have enough on their plates when it comes to increasing short term conversions and sales. They don't usually have a staff of statistical modelers available to estimate future purchases by customer. While seasoned direct marketers can sympathize with that feeling, it would seem silly to them. They know that customer value scores are in fact the only way to evaluate marketing results in many industries.

Take as an example the Insight and Innovation team at Wachovia that was introduced earlier. When Wachovia's customers open additional accounts, how much value should the Insight and Innovation team assess to these new accounts? The actual value will manifest itself over time depending on how the customers fund and leverage their new accounts. Therefore, the value of the marketing effort has to be calculated as the difference between customer valuations before and after the marketing initiative.

The analytical model used for predicting the customer value before and after targeting in a campaign should be the same one. Only by using the same model can it be assured that apples and apples are compared. As Kevin Daly from Wachovia says, "For this purpose it does not even matter so much whether you compare lifetime value or five year net value as long as you select one and stick to it consistently."

Campaign-Centric Success Metrics

For all that customer love and attention, direct marketers still need to prove that their campaigns are profitable. They need to keep tuning their campaigns to improve returns as much as possible. Campaign-centric success metrics can be used to help. They can be measured at the level of the business initiative, the underlying marketing projects, the related products, or the offer cells. They help the marketer assess what works well and what does not.

Reach Metrics

Remember the question that the product marketers at Wachovia asked the Insight and Innovation team? They asked what reach they could expect for the monthly promotion related to their area of responsibility. Although reach is not a success metric, knowing it enables the product marketers to predict what their marketing funnel will likely shape up to be.

To answer the question, the campaign management system provides contact counts calculated for every level of a direct marketing campaign — i.e., at the overall initiative level, per segment, and per offer cell. The value is applicable to channels such as direct mail, call center, e-mail, SMS, MMS, and similar.

Jargon Alert: Lifetime Value

Both online and offline marketers talk about the lifetime value (LTV) metric, but they understand the metric differently.

The online marketer thinks of LTV as something that is associated with campaigns (i.e., the sum of *sales revenue* that has been realized from all customers who were initially acquired through a particular marketing initiative). LTV then becomes the total, historical revenue attributable to that marketing initiative. The campaign that brought a larger LTV amount is thought to be the more successful one. Hopefully, marketing costs and costs of goods sold will also be considered by the marketer when they make this assessment.

Offline direct marketers, on the other hand, associate LTV with customers, i.e., as the sum of historical and future margins expected from the customers. The prediction may be based on subscription contracts, historical experience, or statistical modeling.

Direct marketers use marketing initiatives to increase the LTV of their existing customers. They realize that the LTV of customers is always at risk of being diminished through accidental bad moves or external factors. For example, a customer service blunder at AOL was famously recorded and distributed on YouTube. A customer wished to cancel their account but did not seem to get his request across to a particular service representative. Yet, the customer recorded the conversation and the news spread through both Internet and TV news. As you can see, it even made it into this book in your hands even though AOL has addressed the issue.

Quantitative Performance Metrics

For the purposes of this book, *quantitative performance metrics* are those that express a volume of inquiries regardless of whether those inquiries led to purchases or not. This definition has been borrowed from online marketing where a quantitative metric expresses the volume of traffic on a website regardless of the quality of that traffic. To make it easier to compare metrics between chapters, we will use the same classification here.

Number of Responses The number of responses can be broken down by response type for further detail. A response can be a completed purchase or conversion, but it can also be an intermediary response such as an inquiry, opt-out, or other type of interaction.

Number of Unique Respondents Each person may inquire multiple times. The Unique Respondents metric counts every unique person only once. The person is typically identified by their contact, account, or payment information.

Response Rate The response rate is the number of unique respondents divided by the number of contacts. Similar to the argument around conversion rates with online marketers, this metric can alternatively be defined as the number of responses divided by the number of contacts.

Jargon Alert: Click-Through Rate

What the offline direct marketer calls *response rate,* the online marketer may think of as a *click-through rate.*

Qualitative Performance Metrics

Leaning on the online marketer's definition, qualitative performance metrics indicate the business volume generated by a campaign. When qualitative performance metrics are used, judging the success of a direct marketing initiative begins to get interesting.

Number of Conversions This is the number of responses where customers made a purchase or completed a different kind of call-to-action such as a lead registration. Depending on the way that multi-touch conversions are split between different campaigns, each may receive credit for only a fraction of a response. When that happens, the Number of Conversions metric can have a fractional value. We will discuss that in more detail in Chapter 8, "Measure Multi-Touch Conversions."

Conversion Rate The conversion rate is the number of unique respondents with purchases or conversions divided by the number of contacts. The difference to the response rate is that the latter also counts responses that are inquiries but don't represent a business value.

Lift Over Control Group As an alternative to matchback response attribution, another method for success measurement is to compare the behavior of customers in each campaign offer segment to their control group. The number of conversions by campaign recipients divided by the natural number of conversions from prospects in the control group constitutes the percentage lift attributable to the campaign.

Number of Saved Customers Not all campaigns are about sales. Just as important are campaigns aimed at changing the hearts of customers who are set to leave for a competitor. A retention campaign's performance can be judged by the number of customers who have been saved from attrition. For example, a Telco may count the number of customers who had terminated their contracts but were won back in the end to sign up for a new contract period.

Revenue Metrics Not all conversions are created equal, which is why we want to measure associated revenues too.

> **Revenue (Actual or Predicted)** For a financial institution it is obvious that monetary success coming out of a campaign needs to be measured as contractual or estimated revenues that the institute can earn over time. Retailers would also be advised to do the same given that it may take multiple purchases before a newly acquired customer becomes profitable.

In all cases, only the incremental revenue that would not have come in without the campaign should be attributed to the marketing campaign. This is obviously not easy to do. We will discuss possible methods in the chapter on multi-touch conversions. The revenue that comes in can be split over multiple preceding campaigns that deserve credit in order to avoid double counting income — even then it remains a judgment call.

For that reason, an alternative is to look at lift in revenue versus the control group. Of course, that requires having a control group who received all the other marketing campaign offers, except for the one that is being measured.

Revenue per Conversion   This metric divides the actual Revenue metric by the number of conversions to calculate the average value. For example, in retail this would be the average order value.

Cost Metrics   Even a dilettante marketer can trigger lots of responses if enough budget is blown on the project. That is not a sign of success. Instead, generating responses at an affordable cost is what makes the difference between a successful and a bad marketer. Therefore, direct marketing analysis without the cost side would be missing a key point.

Dollars Spent versus Budget   Managing the budget is an art in itself. The actual amount that has been spent to date is measured at each level of the campaign for purposes of ROI analysis. Compare the actual dollars spent versus budget allocation to make sure that the project is on course.

Costs per Response   This metrics divides the actual costs of the campaign by the number of responses. Depending on the response type, this can be a cost per lead or a cost per sale.

ROI Metrics

As with online marketing, ROI metrics are the only true indicators of a campaign's financial success, because they contrast revenues and total costs, not just marketing investments.

SALES ROI

Offline marketers can be too quick to follow their online colleagues by saying that ROI should be defined as incremental *revenues* attributable to a marketing campaign. Ideally, ROI should be defined as incremental *returns* — i.e., past and future gross margin minus marketing investments divided by marketing investments. The desire to shortcut costs of good sold is understandable, but it can lead to dangerous decisions as outlined in the previous chapter.

The word *incremental* in the definition of the ROI metric suggests that customers who responded to marketing initiatives might have purchased naturally or due to other campaigns with which they interacted.

For example, you may receive a discount card from your favorite fashion retailer and go to the store to buy a pullover and a shirt. It is tempting to credit the coupon with the entire purchase. Yet, it could very well be that you were going to buy the pullover anyway. The coupon may have led you to buy the shirt in addition though. In that case, the incremental value produced by the coupon is the purchase of the shirt minus the discount on the pullover.

Obviously, this is a challenge to measure. See Chapter 8 for some hints. Also see the Lift In Customer Valuation discussion for an alternative.

MARKETING ALLOWABLE

In *Marketing ROI*, Jim Lenskold defines the Marketing Allowable metric as the "maximum cost per targeted prospect for a specific campaign objective and market segment." If the marketer wants to hit a certain minimum sales ROI, called *sales ROI threshold*, and the marketer projects a specific conversion rate and average gross margin from each respondent, the allowable represents the maximum cost to spend on each targeted prospect. If you spend more than that, then according to your projections, you will not be able to hit the desired sales ROI threshold. For example:

- Desired sales ROI threshold: 25 percent
- Projected conversion rate: 5 percent
- Projected average gross margin per customer: $10

Together that amounts to a projected gross margin per prospect of 50 cents. Given that

$$\text{ROI} = \frac{\text{Return}}{\text{Investment}} = \frac{\text{Gross Margin} - \text{Marketing Investment}}{\text{Marketing Investment}}$$

we can solve for the Marketing Investment and obtain the following formula on a per prospect basis:

$$\text{Maximum Allowable Marketing Investment Per Prospect} = \frac{\text{Projected Gross Margin Per Prospect}}{(1 + \text{Sales ROI Threshold})}$$

In our example, that amounts to 50 cents / (1 + 0.25) = 40 cents. We can confirm that result by plugging the marketing allowable of 40 cents per prospect back into the ROI formula. We see that the projected ROI = (50 cents − 40 cents) / 40 cents = 0.25 — i.e., 25 percent as desired.

Refer to Jim Lenskold's book for many practical examples of using the marketing allowable metric in various situations.

Jargon Alert: Allowable

The marketing allowable is somewhat akin to setting a maximum bid in search keyword bid management. Both values represent the maximum marketing investment that should be spent on a prospect so that ROI goals are not jeopardized. In both cases, the marketing allowable comes from underlying assumptions as to the expected conversion rate, revenue, and gross margin. If the assumptions are incorrect, the allowable or max bid will also be incorrect.

To keep from underestimating the allowable or max bid, the expected gross margin should take into account not just the initial sale but the incremental lifetime value per customer achieved through the marketing investment.

LIFT IN CUSTOMER VALUATION

An alternative to the difficult business of isolating the incremental impact of each campaign is to use the lift in customer valuation as a success metric. Sum up the valuations predicted by the analytical models for all customers in an offer cell or segment. Compare that result before and after the direct response campaign has been run. You can also compare to control groups. The difference will suggest the value generated by the campaign.

To some, especially online marketers, it may seem unsatisfactory that this calculation is only a prediction. However, as mentioned before, in businesses such as finance, nothing else would make sense. Even in retail, the actual value may have nothing to do with the initial sale. For example, think of low-cost printers compared to expensive and proprietary ink cartridge costs.

Direct and online marketers may have gone their separate ways in past years, yet as we have seen they have more in common than they would guess in their wildest dreams. Beyond the similarities, however, the direct marketing mind-set also offers fantastic additional practices that can fill gaps in the traditional online marketer's agenda. For that reason, every direct marketer ought to find themselves an online marketer to work with. No online marketer should remain alone either. One is not complete without the other. Like the yin without the yang or the couch without the couch potato, the traditional separation between the camps is no longer sustainable. In the next chapter, let's see what brand marketers can contribute to this party.

The Brand Marketer's Take on Multichannel Analytics

Nobody knows better than the brand marketer just how difficult measurement can be. Brand marketers in traditional offline media have had no clicks to work with, no cookies, no coupons, and no names with which to match them. Impacts could manifest themselves in a week, a year, or later. Even so, the genius of these marketers has produced many sophisticated measurement techniques. Might their methods hold the keys to unlocking the multichannel puzzle? Let's review how traditional brand marketers and advertisers have gone about measurement so that we can borrow suitable methods to apply across online and offline.

5

Chapter Contents

The Brand Marketer's Goals and Challenges

Marketing often times may not feel too different from the circus art of plate spinning (see video at multichannelmetrics.com/PlateSpinning). Just as circus artists hustle to keep their plates spinning, marketers bustle to keep sales going and growing. You could picture direct marketers as spinning plates that have "customer life time value" written on them — i.e., they are looking to grow their customer relationships. In such cases, brand marketers are instead spinning plates that have "brand equity" written over them — i.e., their job is to maintain and grow *brand equity*.

What Is Brand Equity?

To provide a metaphor for brand equity, MarketingNPV, an advisory firm specializing in marketing measurement, refers to a quote from Tim Ambler of the London Business School. (See multichannelmetrics.com/MarketingNPV.) Ambler likens brand equity to a "reservoir of cash flow earned but not yet released to the financial statements." It is like potential energy that has been stored in buyers' minds and that still needs to transform itself into actual purchases and increased shareholder value.

How Do We Detect Brand Equity?

Although immediate sales results are one outcome produced by brand marketers, they do not represent the complete picture of their work. Another part of the picture is stored as invisible energy within brand equity. In fact, the short-term sales effects achieved by brand marketing may often not be sufficient to justify its costs. So it becomes extra important to assess what longer term value the campaign has added to brand equity. For that reason, brand marketers are looking for the equivalent of a battery tester to measure how strong that brand equity actually is. The difference in strength before and after a marketing campaign is thought to go to the credit of the effort.

The *voltage* of brand equity manifests itself in multiple forms for which a battery tester of sorts can probe. Namely:

Coverage in Media and Consumer-Generated Content It can be a great asset if media and target audience are frequently covering the brand, as long as they mention it in a positive context. Some of the marketer's key questions are

- What is the brand's *reputation,* when judging by news and consumer-generated articles?
- How often are media *covering* the brand, and in what context?
- How positive is the *tone* or *sentiment* in consumer-generated content?
- What is the *share of voice* in comparison to the competition — i.e., not just in respect to advertising volume, but total communications to the target audience?
- To what degree do key influencers in the market give the brand its fair share of mentions?

Brand Perception Being famous and on everybody's lips can be great. But if it does not translate into a desire to do business with the company, fame is fruitless. So the next set of questions to ask is about the perception that buyers in the target audience have about the brand. It can greatly impact their buying decision. Some of the questions that marketers are looking to assess are

- What is the *share of mind* of the brand — i.e., how often do buyers' think about the brand when they think about the related category of products?
- How likely are people in the target audience to associate attributes with the brand that represent the key value proposition or differentiators for its products?
- Do people in the target audience express *intent to purchase*?

Willingness to Put the Money Where the Mouth Is Brand equity measurement that stops short at perception has been coming under fire increasingly. After all, what good is *intent* to purchase if that purchase never happens? Therefore, brand equity researchers are pushing further to see whether the target audience's brand perception links up with financial outcomes. To phrase it more bluntly, are buyers willing to put their money where their mouth is? As Jonathan Knowles writes on the MarketingNPV website, some possible indicators are the following:

- Are buyers willing to pay a premium for the brand's products?
- Is the target audience willing to recommend the brand to a friend? Quoting from Reichheld's Loyalty Effect: What is the net promoter score? This is defined as the number of people willing to recommend the brand minus those who are not willing to do so.

Sales Ultimately, brand equity comes down to sales. However, it is very difficult to split the sales volume into the amount that was due to brand equity and to other factors such as product preferences. How could the marketer (or even the buyer) know where to draw the line? That is why the preceding questions typically serve as surrogates for assessing brand equity strength. Instead of calculating the ROI of brand equity, marketers may more often focus on ensuring that it is growing and is a positive contributor.

When it comes to brand advertising, however, marketers are frequently asked to calculate ROI. While the question remains difficult to answer there too, it is much more feasible because advertising is a more definable impulse. As we will see, analysts can work to isolate its impacts as much as possible in order to size them up.

A wide variety of marketing measurement firms are offering an equally wide variety of measurement services for brand equity and advertising. We will discuss a number of these methods in the context of brand advertising. Many of the methods are used for measuring either advertising or brand equity. That is because brand advertising is often measured by assessing the strength of the brand before and after the advertising effort.

How Do We Build Brand Equity?

While the rest of this chapter will focus mostly on brand advertising and its measurement, there are many other ways in which marketers work to build up their brand equity. Those too require measurement in order to manage the efforts. For example:

Customer Experience Management Without a good customer experience, forget about it! Product and customer service probably have relatively greater impact on the customer experience than marketing. Yet, marketers need to keep their eyes open too and contribute what they can. If nothing else, their communications are directly part of the experience. Are they going to be of service or a nuisance?

A direct way of measuring customer experience is with the help of customer satisfaction surveys. Providers of syndicated research such as J.D. Power and Associates conduct independent and unbiased surveys of customer satisfaction, product quality, and buyer behavior. What makes the surveys even more valuable is that satisfaction is compared between competitors. As a management tool, employees' salary bonus can sometimes be tied to the company's J.D. Power ratings.

Media and Key Influencer Strategies Getting the media and key influencers to pick up news on the company often requires some level of effort. One typical strategy is to look for key opinion makers in the market, whether those are particular broadcast shows, publications, journalists, gurus, or entertainers. Getting them on board with the brand may be a matter of persuasion or sponsorship. The latter case can well be treated as a form of advertising.

The amount of coverage in the media is measured by reputation management services. Firms such as Factiva and Biz360 employ software solutions for text analytics in order to automate the process. Factiva, for example, taps into the newswire to parse out how often a brand is covered, in which contexts, and by which key influencers. The solutions also aim to assess the tone of the coverage — i.e., whether the sentiment is positive or negative. A paper available from Lexalytics, a reputation management software provider, describes just how difficult that is to do automatically. Namely, the same paragraph may talk positively about one thing while being negative about another (shortcut via multichannelmetrics.com/Lexalytics). Give the downloadable demo from Lexalytics a try which is available from their website.

Consumer-Generated Content According to *Time Magazine,* who was the key influencer of 2006? Who was *Time*'s person of the year? It was you! The content *you* generate across websites such as YouTube, MySpace, and Wikipedia can rival the impact on brand equity from news and advertising.

Reputation management services also perform their text analytics on user-generated content online to offer similar insights. Two additional examples of providers are Cymfony, owned by TNS Media Intelligence, and Clarabridge.

Marketers are not passive in the light of user-generated content. Leveraging *your* voice to build brands through viral marketing campaigns is very much a skill that marketers are looking to hone. In Chapter 2, "The Web Analyst Tackles Multichannel Metrics Online," we touched on examples and possibilities for measurement.

Advertising Strategy Advertising is, of course, the most visible aspect of brand marketers' work and usually the most expensive. While brand marketers are responsible for advertising, they may draw on specialists to design, deploy, and measure advertising campaigns. Often times, these specialists reside in outside agencies, the well-known breed of advertising agencies.

Brand marketers would be forgiven for trembling with nervousness just for the sheer costs of brand advertising, especially on TV, but there is also the contest to produce ever more creative and entertaining ads in face of equally talented competition. Whose head is on the chopping block when sales of a commodity product are down? All of this would be sufficient to make anyone forget to eat their lunch. Now, add on top of all this the difficulty of measurement!

Measuring brand advertising is a great challenge but it also promises a solution to brand advertiser's woes. Namely, metrics are the key to managing investments confidently and improving outcomes over time.

Why Is Advertising So Difficult to Measure?

The fundamental problem is that all the traditional brand advertising channels in the offline world are nonaddressable, as you'll see if you look back to Table 1.1. That means that exposures of individuals to ads are not generally measurable, and hence their responses are difficult to attribute. Brand advertisers had to overcome this problem by developing clever methods to infer the outcomes of their investments.

In order to rise to the occasion, brand advertisers proceed by balancing creativity with methodic processes. Just like their colleagues on the direct marketing side, they follow a marketing life cycle process that starts with analyzing what has worked in the past to derive guidance for future advertisements. Marketing ideas are then derived and pretested on select audiences. The winning ideas are developed into production and executed. Meanwhile, measurement is applied before, during, and after the campaigns in order to gauge their success.

In this chapter, we will restrict ourselves to the traditional offline channels highlighted in Table 5.1 for brand advertising. In later chapters, we will see how the same measurement methods have been extended to online and cross-channel situations as well.

► **Table 5.1** Marketing Execution Compared to Response Channels Measured by Metrics and Methods

Campaign Channel ╲ Response Channel		Online					Offline				
		Website	E-mail	Mobile	Blog	Viral	Viral	Mail/fax	Phone	Direct sales	Store
Advertising (nonaddressable)	TV/radio/print Out-of-home Events Product placement In store							**Traditional Brand Marketers**			
Direct Response (addressable)	Call center Direct mail Service team Mobile E-mail Web ads Search Website		Traditional Online Marketers						Traditional Direct Marketers			

Analyze and Predict Advertising Opportunities

Imagine you wake up one day, and find in surprise that overnight you have become a brand marketer in charge of a breakfast cereal product. On your calendar you find a meeting scheduled to plan the coming year with your advertising agency. What should the coming year's ad strategy be? Some of the biggest questions that will require a decision from you are

- What are the messages that you would like to convey?
- How will you communicate those messages?
- In which media will you invest how much advertising budget?

A great amount of analysis goes into answering each of these. The investments at stake are huge and your competition is eager to undo your efforts. To answer the first question, the brand may invest in primary research with consumers to understand their shopping behavior from an emotive perspective. An analysis of current brand equity will come in handy now, especially in regards to the attributes that buyers associate with your brand. For example, healthiness may be a key reason why people choose your cereal over others. Then you would ask now whether your brand is top of mind when buyers think of healthy breakfast cereals. If not, it may suggest the direction that your ads should take. If instead you find that your brand is perceived as "healthy but boring," that would suggest another direction.

Once the message has been decided, the next step becomes to design the ads that will bring it across effectively. As you develop your ideas into prototype ads, together with the advertising agency, early assessments of their strength are analyzed. Pre-market tests for that purpose might include focus groups where you show basic versions of your ads and gauge reactions. You may even invest into theater testing where an audience will see a number of commercials during a seating, including yours. The audience's perception of the ad is evaluated with a survey at the end.

The third question, however, is where we will focus because it is closest to our multichannel topic. Which media should receive how much advertising budget to build enough pressure in the market so that your company can achieve your lead generation and sales goals? How much budget is enough to move short term and long term sales goals to their desired levels? If you cannot get a sufficient budget, what expectations should you set with the business? Just as public companies are responsible for giving revenue guidance to Wall Street, marketers are responsible for providing guidance regarding the amount of demand that they predict they will generate. To answer these questions, brand advertisers, especially within the Consumer Packaged Goods (CPG) industry, have developed an analytical approach named marketing mix modeling.

Marketing Mix Modeling

Essentially, marketing mix modeling correlates historical market conditions and marketing investments across channels as input variables, with sales outcomes as the output variable. The purpose is to run the model for future marketing investments to predict their effects, as in Figure 5.1.

More specifically, marketers have developed models that predict the incremental sales that can be expected from investing an extra dollar into each advertising channel, similar to Figure 5.2.

Brand marketers are highly aware that external factors also impact their brand and marketing outcomes. These market conditions also need to be taken into account in the marketing mix model. Otherwise, the historical data will be interpreted incorrectly. For example:

Seasonality More advertising will probably be needed to sell ice cream in the winter than in the summer. If the summer is hotter than usual, the sales of ice cream will go up by itself.

Jargon Alert: Modeling

Brand advertisers use marketing mix modeling to predict aggregate impact on sales. Direct marketers use modeling to predict response by individuals and their value to the business. By summing the results for all individuals, direct marketers can arrive back at a value for total sales.

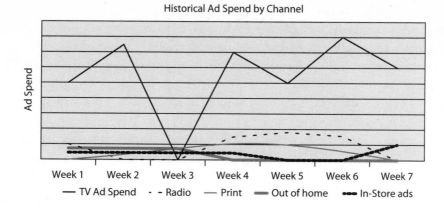

Historical Ad Spend by Channel

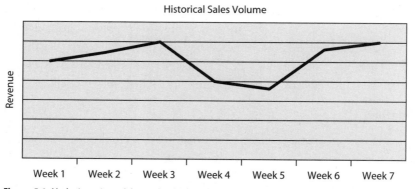

Historical Sales Volume

Figure 5.1 Marketing mix models correlate historical market conditions and campaign investments with sales.

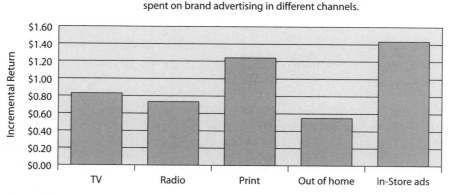

Incremental return predicted for one incremental dollar spent on brand advertising in different channels.

Figure 5.2 Incremental sales predicted by a fictitious marketing mix model for an additional dollar of investment into brand advertising on various channels.

Awareness The same amount, or frequency, of advertising will have a different impact depending on the degree that the target market was already aware of a brand or a product. A new introduction may require considerably more ad spending.

Brand Development Index (BDI) and Category Development Index (CDI) The same amount, or same frequency, of advertising will lead to a different impact depending on the percentage of the target population that is already purchasing the product (BDI). The higher that percentage in a market, the harder it will be to find additional buyers. That assessment can be refined using the CDI — i.e., the market share of the brand relative to competitors in the same category. If CDI and BDI are already high in one area, then advertising might be better spent elsewhere.

Total Price of Ownership The price of a product is not the only cost of owning it. For example, when gas prices go up, sales of gas guzzlers is expected to suffer.

Competitive Advertising Levels For example, if Kellogg spends three times as much as you do on TV advertising to tout their Froot Loops, these messages will probably drown out the advertising investment you may be making to promote your cereal. Do marketing modelers have to watch television 24/7 across hundreds of channels to collect data on how much the competition is advertising? Luckily, there is an easier way. TNS Media Intelligence provides a go-to service when it comes to obtaining competitive advertising information across channels.

Developing the Model

When it comes to developing the actual mathematical model, the process followed by statisticians has similarities to the one used in direct marketing. Namely, historical data on marketing mix, market conditions, and sales outcomes flow as input into regression analysis. The resulting mathematical model equation will be only as expressive as the historical data permits. For example, in order to predict the value of an incremental dollar spent on television compared to billboard advertising, the historical data needs to permit isolating the historical influence of each channel.

Ideally, the company will have run ads on only one of the channels during some historical period, enabling modelers to get data on the impact of each channel by itself. The company may have run ads in parallel but in different geographic regions. However, such controlled testing is not a mandatory requirement. For example, Vinit Doshi of Marketing Management Analytics (MMA), the recognized industry pioneers, points this out in his article "Marketing Mix: Truth and Fiction in the Quest for Marketing Performance Measurement." The article is available from the firm's website (shortcut via multichannelmetrics.com/MMA). Doshi states that the problem is challenging but "can be overcome through the use of granular data, analytic treatments, and proper interpretation of results." The level of investment per channel needs to, at the very least, be varied and must not be completely parallel to spending levels on other channels. Statisticians can often tease out the different impacts per channel on sales.

As you can sense, it is a serious challenge. Ordinary marketers for that reason may find it difficult to follow the reasoning used in the statistical analysis to understand how the model's predictions came about.

Just as in direct marketing, marketing mix models also need to be validated before they are used to predict the future. As with direct marketers, the marketing mix models are applied to a second historical period of data. Statisticians review whether the model closely predicts the aggregate sales volume in this new period given only the market conditions and brand advertising volumes as input. Model parameters can be calibrated to tune the model.

While the process of crafting the models is similar to the one in direct marketing, the model specifics involve many unique details. Because of that, marketing mix modeling is done by a distinct set of specialist consulting firms such as Marketing Management Analytics, Marketing Analytics, and Dratfield Analytics. Even then, consensus seems to be that the advice that is derived should not be the sole factor that leads to decision making.

At its best, however, the model can predict baseline sales compared to incremental sales derived from advertising in each channel:

Predicted Baseline Sales This represents the baseline of business that would occur naturally without any marketing efforts. That baseline is not a fixed level because it is influenced by external market factors, competitors, and seasons.

Incremental Contributions by Ad Channels Beyond the baseline, the model can show the predicted impact of brand advertising broken down by each of the channels. You can picture this similar to Figure 5.3.

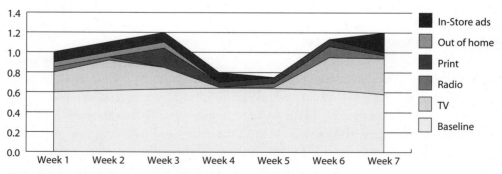

Figure 5.3 Contribution of each advertising channel to predicted or historical sales volume

Marketing mix modeling is said to be the most popular with the largest consumer marketing companies who can afford the necessary studies and help of specialists. Costs can run in the multiple hundred thousands of dollars up to millions. So, the statement is probably true when it comes to formal marketing mix modeling. However, in practice all companies perform some ad-hoc form of it. For example, marketers at a B2B (business-to-business) will measure historical lead flow from trade shows, advertisements, e-mail lists, and online advertising. Using these historical results, the B2B marketer will form an expectation as to the outcomes that can be realized from splitting the coming year's marketing budget across these channels.

> **Note:** The B2B marketer can formulate expectations on the performance of tradeshows, direct mails, e-mail lists, etc. because of the direct response (addressable) nature of these channels. That makes it relatively easy to attribute a sales lead to the source through which it was acquired. When it comes to brand advertising without direct response, however, this is no longer so straightforward. That is precisely where the value of the correlation analysis of historical data comes in.

Interaction Effects

One of the greatest feats of marketing mix modeling may well be its suitability for capturing the interdependencies between multiple marketing instruments. Many marketing mix models can help marketers quantify the additive effects of running messages across channels at the same time or in similar periods. For example, it is possible to assess the effect of broadcast TV ads and direct mail efforts running separately compared to running them simultaneously. The lift of returns from the direct mail program in the latter case is referred to as an *interaction* or synergy effect.

We are talking about the kind of situation where one plus one can yield three. That is just what was suggested by the Integrated Marketing Communications (IMC) theories we discussed in Chapter 1, "With Great Opportunity Come Great Challenges." How does the marketing mix model know when one plus one makes three? There is no magic involved. Rather, there has to be suitable historical data as input into the model. The various historical campaigns must have partially overlapped over some periods of time within the same markets. The model can then "learn" from historical sales results what the outcomes tend to be from running the campaigns independently or synergistically.

Correcting the Marketing Mix Model for Ad Quality

Once the marketing direction has been set for the year, the rest of the twelve months are spent toiling to produce the most effective ads that the team can formulate. Some ideas work out great, others not so much. Marketing mix models can gloss over that fact and just assume that future ads will meet average historical ad quality. Otherwise, accounting for ad effectiveness within the models would first require getting that kind of data for historical periods.

Now, how would you go about judging the quality of historical ads? That is the difficult part. In order for the marketing mix model to include characterizations of individual ad campaigns, it needs that much more historical data. Some ad campaigns may also have been too small in volume to impact sales enough for it to be statistically significant. Models that gloss over individual ad campaigns and just include ad spending by channel are called *media mix models*.

Correcting for Diminishing Returns and Decay via Advertising Adstock Models

A danger with interpreting Figure 5.2 is to assume proportional returns when increasing your investment into each ad channel. From your personal experience though, you know that a commercial's effect wears off the more you are exposed to it. Clearly, there are diminishing returns on increasing ad volume and frequency, as indicated in the graph of Figure 5.4. Advertising Adstock models represent this fact with mathematical equations such as the logarithmic function.

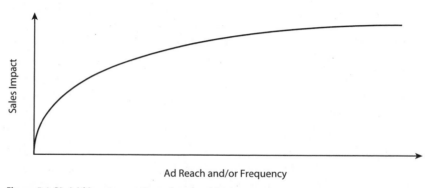

Figure 5.4 Diminishing returns on increasing advertising investments

Adstock also models the notion that the impact of an ad exposure will probably continue a little longer but in a decaying fashion. For example, have you ever placed a classifieds ad on Craigslist? If you have, you will know from personal experience that you receive a lot of inquiries on the first day, fewer on the next, and isolated inquiries even weeks later. The ad's impact fades similar to the graph in Figure 5.5. Adstock Models express this decay using mathematical equations similar to the ones used for modeling the decay of radioactive materials. Adstock modelers even speak of the half-life time when an ad's impact is only half as strong as it was immediately after the campaign.

Advertising Adstock models combine the effects, decay, and diminishing returns into a single mathematical equation. Parameters in the equation control how quickly an ad's impact is thought to decay and how quickly additional ad investments lead to saturation. How would the marketer know what the correct values are for these model parameters? As usual, statisticians need to study historical levels of investment into advertising to fit the equation to historical levels of outcome that have been measured.

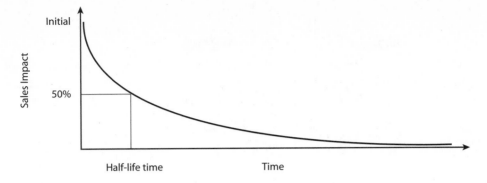

Figure 5.5 Decay over time of the impact on sales of an advertisement

Critique of Advertising Adstock Models

Brand advertisers opinions are split over whether the effect of advertisement exposures really does continue for a significant time. For example, in his article "Adstock and Media Planning," media-planning guru Erwin Ephron wrote: "Short of modeling, there is scant evidence of Adstock effects in the U.S. Most data show immediate sales response to advertising is brief." The article is available from Erwin Ephron's website (shortcut via multichannelmetrics.com/EphronOnAdstock, site requires registration).

Ephron's recommendation is to distinguish the short term sales impact of advertisements from their impact on brand equity. Although the former actually has been found to dissipate quickly with U.S. consumers, the effect of the latter does linger. With heightened levels of brand awareness, Ephron writes that any subsequent campaigns (e.g., direct mail) continue to receive a boost.

Applying the Advertising Adstock Model

So, say you developed a pretty good Adstock model equation that describes historical results. What now? You would use it to determine how continuously you schedule advertising impressions. If you think that ad pressure continues for a while following an ad impression, you will probably spread out your schedule. If you think that the effect dissipates quickly, you will schedule advertising more continuously. Therefore, it is necessary to figure out what the case is for your own campaigns.

Although it is primarily the bigger consumer marketing brands that use Adstock modeling formally, all marketers apply the idea intuitively. For example, you try not to over-advertise in one channel when you sense that returns are diminishing. A B2B business will naturally time the tradeshows that they attend over the course of the year such that their sales teams are kept busy. When leads from previous marketing activities ebb off, the marketing team aims to replenish the supply by engaging in another lead-generating event.

How can brand advertisers measure when effectiveness diminishes in their world? It is time to switch to the methods that they use for doing just that.

Jargon Alert: Diminishing Returns and Decay

Online advertisers can apply the Adstock idea not just for describing the effects that they expect from online display advertising but also in search marketing. Think of a chart that plots returns based on keyword rank. The chart will show the incremental value expected from improving the keyword *rank*. There are diminishing returns on improving ranking further. Say, a second rank may perform almost as well as a first rank.

Decay effects play a role beyond advertising too. Think for example of site visitor's loyalty in terms of return visits. The online marketer may look at the increasingly smaller portion of visitors that return to the site each week after having clicked through on an advertisement at some point. The half-life time can be said to be the point at which only half of the original visitors are still frequenting the site. The online marketer can measure whether changes to content or site usability succeed in prolonging the half-life time.

Measure

Measurements are taken at different times for different reasons:

Perform pre-market testing. As mentioned earlier, ads are pretested to help determine whether they should be aired in the first place.

Take a baseline before running the ads The status before running the ads is measured so to assess a baseline for brand equity and sales.

Conduct in-market testing during the ad campaign. After the advertisements begin to run, measurements are taken to verify that the campaign is on the right track. Another benefit is insight into the impact of repeat exposures to the ads. The marketer can tune the frequency by which the ad is exposed to the target audience, for example on TV. We will review the effects of *effective frequency* in Chapter 8, "Measure Multi-Touch Conversions."

Conduct more testing after the ad campaign. At the end of the ad campaign, another round of measurements are taken to calculate the difference to the baseline — i.e., the lift.

Let's see the most established methods for taking measurements next. The techniques span media coverage reporting, audience research, and various kinds of customer research.

Use Reputation Management Solutions for Reporting Media Coverage

Part of the results from advertising should become visible in the form of increased coverage through media. The volume of consumer-generated content should increase along with increased share of mind. The reputation management services that were mentioned earlier provide trend reports showing the levels of coverage over time. Just as the online marketer looks for spikes in traffic to the website, these media coverage reports can be reviewed to look for spikes in coverage.

Of particular interest in both cases is not just whether the tone of the coverage is positive, but whether the messaging goals of the campaign are reflected. Are the key differentiators for the brand's products being covered more often when the brand or its products are mentioned? The reputation management services look for that with the help of text analytics.

Use Audience Measurement for Reporting Media Exposure

So that your advertising campaign has a chance to build brand equity, it first needs to reach as many people in your target audience as possible. It is the job of audience measurement solutions to assess just how many have been exposed to the ads.

Audience measurement of offline media such as print, radio, and TV has been conducted since at least the 1950s with the help of panels. The panels are built by carefully signing up a number of volunteers who form a representative sample of the population. The behavior of the panel is then mathematically extrapolated across the entire target audience.

A number of different audience measurement services have established themselves for different channels. For television ratings, the best-known solution comes from Nielsen Media Research. For radio audience measurement, Arbitron's ratings are the standard. Mediamark Research (MRI) is the destination for magazine ratings.

These services are so established that they are referred to as the *currency* for buying and selling advertising slots on the media. Namely, air time for advertising is priced by the size of the audience that will be exposed to the commercials. These services are the ones that networks and advertisers rely on for assessing that exposure.

How Do Audience Measurement Solutions Measure Exposure?

Most audience measurement solutions started out by collecting media behavior data in the form of diaries that participants completed manually. Since the 1990s, however, the products have moved to electronic data collection. For example, television consumption is monitored with an electronic device that plugs into cable set-top boxes and satellite dishes to record what channel is being watched. However, as Carl Bialik wrote in the *Wall Street Journal* in February 2007, the systems often still rely on some manual input. Namely, panel audiences press a button on the monitoring device to log the fact that they are beginning or stopping to watch.

Another limitation of cable set-top box monitoring has been that only viewers who see the programs live as it airs are counted. With the proliferation of digital video recorders such as TiVo, significant audiences are watching the programs time-shifted. Even more importantly, they may skip the commercials when doing so.

To keep up with the times, audience measurement solutions have become increasingly sophisticated. For example, Nielsen started capturing data through an agreement with TiVo. In May 2007 a "live plus three commercial rating" was introduced. Not only does it report time-shifted watching behavior up to three days past the original date of each program. But most importantly, it rates the audience during the commercial break minutes and not just the programming itself, as had been the case previously. The *Wall Street Journal* reported in October 2007 that "as much as one-fifth of the audience for television's most popular shows are skipping the commercials, according to the first round of commercial data for the new fall season, released by Nielsen Media Research."

Extrapolating Media Exposure to the Target Audience

Volunteers participating in audience measurement are registered and have provided detailed data about themselves. Given that, marketers can slice the behavioral observations by criteria, such as demographics, to zoom into the behavior of the target audience that they are after.

However, there is a caveat. If a panel does not contain a representative set of members from the target audience, the extrapolation will be inaccurate. For example, if your television commercials were geared toward college students, you would seek ratings for audiences watching from dorm rooms. Yet, you were out of luck until the beginning of 2007, because no television sets in dorm rooms were part of Nielsen's panel before then. While that has changed now, the general point remains—namely, the more specific the demographic is for which a marketer is looking to understand behavior, the more difficult it may become to find an appropriate panel that allows doing so.

Use Surveys to Measure Qualitative Results

Audience measurement by itself cannot provide any insight into the impact of advertising on brand equity. For that purpose, we need a way to measure qualitative effects of the ads. That is typically done through surveys.

Surveys are generally employed to measure the strength of brand equity independent of campaigns. In order to measure the impact of ad campaigns, surveys can be compared before and after the campaign. They can also be compared between people who have been exposed to the ads and others who have not.

Surveys can take an immense variety of shapes. They can be in-person, one-on-one interviews, such as when you are stopped in the mall. They can also be taken by telephone, by mail questionnaires, or online.

Survey questions are aimed to probe for the signs of brand equity that we discussed earlier. Statisticians devise clever ways of getting answers to their questions without asking them directly. For example, it may be relatively simple to investigate share of mind by posing questions such as "Which are the top three breakfast cereal brands that you can think of?" However, it is much more difficult to survey brand equity attributes such as the willingness to pay a premium. How can you determine which attributes really prompted buyers to prefer the cereal that they ended up buying? As you will recall, the latter are much more significant measures of brand equity. So, how do you get answers?

Surveying for Willingness to Pay a Premium The Brand Price Trade-Off (BPTO) method works by asking survey participants a set of iterative questions. Namely, the participant is asked to pick one of multiple competing brands or products based on a changing set of prices that are provided for each of them in every round of the survey. The method observes which price level causes participants to change to a different product. In other words, it determines the shape of the demand curve at different price levels. Market research firm Dobney Corporation provides an interactive demonstration of BPTO on their website dobney.com (shortcut via multichannelmetrics.com/BPTO).

If the ad campaign was able to raise brand equity, we would expect to see an increased willingness to pay a premium price for the brand's products. When you compare the results from two advertising campaigns, you may find that one increased the willingness to pay more than the other. This insight can serve as a criterion for prioritizing the former campaign, assuming all else is equal.

Surveying for Appreciation of Specific Benefits Surveys can look for an increased appreciation of a brand's key attributes among survey participants. For this purpose, a variation of the BPTO method by the name of Conjoint analysis can be applied. It uses features and benefits instead of price levels. Namely, survey participants are run through a number of What-If questions that prompt them to pick between two unnamed products based on their feature sets that are specified. The set of features or benefits is varied from round to round so that the survey will eventually be able to derive the value ascribed to each individual feature. Dobney.com also provides an interactive demonstration of Conjoint analysis (shortcut via multichannelmetrics.com/Conjoint).

If the survey is repeated before and after the advertising campaign, it should show a greater number of participants who appreciate the benefits associated with the advertiser's offering. If one campaign is more successful at accomplishing that than another one, this can serve as a criterion for selecting between the campaigns, assuming that all else is equal.

Use Scanner Data to Illuminate Purchase Behavior

When push comes to shove, a brand's value lies in its ability to motivate prospects to reach in their pockets and vote for the brand with their dollars. Surveys could also ask participants whether they have been using or purchasing the brand's products recently. However, wouldn't it be better if this could be measured more directly? That is precisely what a series of solutions that share anonymous purchase data from points of sale at participating vendors do.

For instance, InfoScan from IRI taps into grocery checkout scanner data from participating retailers. According to the firm, InfoScan "processes raw data from over 34,000 stores on a weekly basis across the grocery, drug, mass merchandiser, and convenience channels." As a result, manufacturers who are IRI clients gain reports on their products' relative market share within the category in which they compete.

For illuminating the impact of advertising, marketers can observe whether their share of market improves in correlation with the campaign. In order for this to be possible, however, the ad campaign needs to be of sufficient size so that its impact becomes noticeable. It is also clear that finer nuances, such as the impact of frequency of exposure to ads, may be more difficult to tease out from the data. Additional controlled experimentation may help with that, though.

Use Single-Source Research for Tying Media Exposure to Purchase Behavior

The beauty of scanner data is the accuracy and the huge sample size that it provides. Yet, the impact of advertisements is still inferred through a correlation method. There is no way to detect at the retail checkout which customers have or have not been exposed to particular advertisements. The marketing analyst combines two separate data streams, namely media exposure data and scanner data, to correlate them mathematically.

What if you could observe the media exposure of individuals and then directly observe the same individuals' purchase behavior? That should enable a finer grain of learning as to how people behave following ad exposure. The premise of a technique called *single-source research* answers that wish. It is a panel-based method that relies on a set of volunteers who are panelists both for audience measurement and for purchase behavior measurement. For the latter, solutions such as Nielsen's HomeScan and MyScan panels enable participants to use scanning devices at home to manually record every purchase that they make.

In Chapter 8, we will see how single-source research has been used to investigate the impact of frequency of exposure to ads.

Controlled Experimentation

Brand marketers can, of course, also run test ads in certain geographic regions while suppressing them in other regions that will serve as control groups. The difference in behavior between the two regions can indicate the impact of the test ads, assuming that all else has remained equal between the regions. Similarly, tests can be run over time. In that case, it is important to correct for any market conditions that may have changed between the time frames (for example, competing ad campaigns).

> **Jargon Alert: Audience Measurement**
>
> Audience measurement is well established in the online world too. Multiple vendors offer solutions. comScore and Nielsen//NetRatings collect data on the online browsing behavior of participants in their panels. Just as with offline panels, information such as demographics is registered for panelists and permits marketers to slice and dice behavior accordingly. Hitwise, which is owned by Experian, measures a large panel of anonymous visitors by collecting data through its relationships with ISPs. Alexa measures a panel of those who have downloaded their toolbars, and Compete triangulates multiple input sources.

If you remember, the data from controlled experimentation in this fashion can help isolate the impact of each channel and combinations thereof. If available, it will make the work of statisticians much easier for developing marketing mix models.

Success Metrics for Brand Advertising

Finally, now that we've reviewed typical methods of measuring the impact of brand advertising on sales and brand equity, let's look at metrics that advertisers would want to calculate based on that data.

Operational Metrics

Although operational metrics such as reach and frequency are not success metrics, advertisers still depend on them to assess how far their advertising dollars are going. Various metrics are in use that you will encounter frequently in the brand advertising world.

Rating Points

Rating points are defined as the percentage of the potential, targeted audience that is reached by an advertisement. For example a *household rating point* of 10 would mean that 10 percent of all households in the population have been reached.

Gross Rating Points (GRP)

GRPs are a unique metric used for buying and selling brand advertising. They combine both reach and frequency-oriented aspects. Let's assume that an audience of 10 rating points is exposed to an advertisement twice. The GRP is defined as the sum of rating points. In this case, GRP = 10 + 10 = 20. Of course, some households will have seen the ad both times, so the 20 does not mean that 20 percent of the population has seen the ad. That is why the word "gross" is used in the name of the metric.

GRP is a useful yardstick for describing ad delivery. For example, an advertiser may buy commercial inventory with a TV channel planning to reach 50 GRPs. However, ahead of air time, it is not possible to know what the audience will be that will be watching each time the commercial is on air. Say it turns out that 10 percent of the potential audience is watching when the commercial is aired the first time. That means the advertiser has another 40 GRPs to go.

Ultimately, a GRP is a normalized measure of spending. As such it is helpful as an input into marketing mix models too. In Figures 5.4 and 5.5, the label of the *X*-axis, (ad volume reach and/or frequency) is typically expressed as a single value through GRPs. With that, Figure 5.4 indicates that there are diminishing returns when paying more to reach either larger audiences or the same audience more frequently.

Opportunities to See (OTS)

OTS refers to the number of times that typical members of the target audience can possibly view the advertisement in a given time period. Therefore, it is a frequency-oriented metric. Advertisers use it to help schedule their ads (for example, TV commercials) over time. As we will review in Chapter 8, it has been typical to seek an OTS of 2 to 3 with TV commercials in each buying period because that has been considered an *effective frequency*. In comparison, with print advertising it has been considered more advisable to plan for an OTS of 5 in order for the campaign to be effective.

Cost Metrics

If one publication offers to publish your ad to an audience of one million, whereas another quotes you a reach of only 100,000, you would pick the million. Right? But in truth, the answer also depends on the costs.

CPM A typical metric that combines reach and costs is CPM (Cost per Thousand). It refers to the costs of delivering an advertisement to 1,000 people or households.

Cost per Rating Point Because GRP is used for buying and selling ads, it makes sense to express costs in terms of GRPs as well. For that purpose, the total cost of ads scheduled in the time period is divided by the number of rating points.

Cost per OTS Advertisers may look at the cost per OTS as a measure for comparing campaigns within the same medium. It is defined as the total cost of ads scheduled in the time period divided by OTS.

If everything else were equal, you would pick the campaign with lower costs per rating points or costs per OTS to invest your budget. Then as you increase your budget on that channel and start to see diminishing returns eventually, you would begin shifting the rest of your budget onto more expensive channels.

Qualitative Performance Metrics

Getting a bargain for your ads is not enough. It doesn't say anything about the impact of the campaign on brand equity. We defined qualitative performance metrics as those that give us valuable hints for the performance of our marketing spending, but do not yield a complete picture of ROI yet. As discussed earlier, brand advertisers will look for improvements to various aspects of brand equity as a measure of success for their investments.

Lift in Recall Compared to the baseline, how many more in the targeted audience are able to recall the brand when prompted? Advertisers distinguish between aided and unaided recall because the measure will deliver significantly different results depending on how the survey question is posed.

Unaided recall may be prompted by asking for brands within a category. Aided recall, on the other hand, may provide the brand and ask respondents to assign it to a category.

Lift in Positive Sentiment Beyond just recalling the brand, are more members of the audience positively or negatively inclined toward the brand and its products?

Lift in Key Attributes or Benefits Associated Do more members of the target audience associate key benefits with the brand or its products, especially, the attributes that the advertiser has been looking to position?

Lift in Purchase Intent Recognition and familiarity are great, but do more members of the target audience intend to purchase the brand's offerings? Surveys look to measure by how much purchase intent has increased after ad campaigns are run.

Lift in Sales

As a busy person, you *intend* to do many things, but you probably never get around to doing all of them. That is why purchase intent is no longer considered a sufficient measure of brand equity. In his book *Marketing ROI*, Jim Lenskold writes very pointedly that "the short-term financial value of awareness = $0." The same is true for any other performance metric he underlines. Rather, the challenge is to demonstrate the actual sales that are attributable to brand advertisements.

Note: The good news is that short-term sales effects of advertising can be extrapolated from the behavior of panels or measured through controlled testing.

However, a big challenge remains. Namely, how can you estimate the future sales that will also still be realized thanks to the increased brand equity? If brand equity has been raised to unprecedented levels, the marketing mix models may be like ships that have been lifted out of water. The historical data that they were created from may no longer be able to serve as a yardstick in the new situation.

In the light of this problem, it may be necessary to restrict measurement to historical sales. At the end of the year, you may go back and use either single-source research or controlled testing methods to estimate what the medium term results of the campaigns have turned out to be.

Financial ROI Metrics

As with any other marketing discipline, ROI metrics are the ideal financial measure of campaign performance.

Lift in Customer Valuation (e.g., Life Time Values) The marketing mix models may be out of their element in predicting future sales if brand equity has been raised to levels for which no historical data is available in comparison. However, the customer valuation models may still be able to help. After all, they are oriented at the behavior of individual customers. The result of a successful brand ad campaign may simply be that more customers start behaving like high-value customers.

For example, more bank customers may open additional accounts and start interacting with the bank more frequently. This would typically raise the customer valuations predicted by the bank's models. Aggregating the total value across all customers, we could compare the before and after valuation of the customer pool. We could also compare that value to geographic regions that served as control groups in controlled tests for the brand ads. From that, we could uncover the lift achieved by the ad campaign.

 Note: Working together, brand and direct marketers can come closer to estimating the impact of brand advertisements by using the direct marketer's customer valuation models as basis.

However, even the customer valuation models may have become invalid if customers' impression of the brand has changed. For example, customers may not act differently but may turn out to be less likely to leave to the competition. The customer models would not indicate if current behavior has not changed.

ROI on Brand Advertising Short-term ROI on brand advertising can be calculated by comparing the lift in gross margins to the cost of the advertisement campaign. The short term lift in gross margin can be determined by taking the lift in sales results and combining it with the costs of goods sold. The ROI formula is the same as mentioned in earlier chapters. Namely, ROI is defined as returns (i.e., gross margin minus marketing investments) divided by marketing investments.

However, that ideal ROI formula also includes the net present value of all future returns if they would not have been realized without the brand ad campaign. Whether you go about predicting that number by estimating future sales or by calculating the lift in customer valuations, it is challenging to do accurately.

 Note: Brand advertising quite purposefully is game changing. As a result, ROI calculations for brand advertising probably have to restrict themselves to short-term results that can be measured rather than long-term results that need to be predicted.

The Uncertainty Principle of Brand Advertising

We walked through key methods that have been developed by brand advertisers over the years and that were originally used to measure offline media. Those methods included marketing mix modeling, reputation management, audience measurement, panels, scanner data, and surveys.

You were probably not surprised to see just how many elements of uncertainty remain in the measurement of brand advertising. Is it not reminiscent of Heisenberg's Uncertainty Principle that we learn about in physics class? As we saw for instance, you can get exact data on purchase behavior from retail scanners, but then your measurement of media exposure remains vague. You can nail down media exposure by going to panel based measurements, but then your extrapolation to the entire audience is somewhat uncertain.

As scholar Kevin Lane Keller put it during an interview with MarketingNPV, "It is practically impossible to make *definitive* statements about X causing Y — this ad campaign led to this consumer response — when there are so many things that went along with that campaign." It is also unreliable to project past results into the future because rarely is the ad creative the same, nor has the market remained unchanged.

What is striking is that marketers in the offline world are able to cope. In contrast to the discussion within the online world, they are more comfortable with the uncertainty and do not get as caught up as much on accuracy. At the end of the day, they are making the best out of the possibilities that they have. You can compare it to the fact that democracy is not perfect either, but it is the best form of government that there is.

Measurement and Metrics

II

Close your eyes. Visualize a multichannel analytics dashboard with charts, gauges, and funnels. We see the complete status of marketing initiatives. We see what customers desire of us next and where there is opportunity for greater efficiency. Meanwhile, leads and service alerts are distributed through the system to the right people at the right time for prompt action.

That is where we are trying to get eventually. But first we have to figure out how to collect measurements on customer behavior across channels and express them in form of actionable metrics. We can do it. We just have to fuse the multiple multichannel methods that online, direct, and brand marketers have developed so to build a bridge across channels.

Measure Lift Between Online and Offline

So, your company just branded the city's football stadium in your name and covered it with advertising posters and logos. Was the investment worthwhile? A portion of the answer depends on what the uplift is that you see via the company website.

Conversely, you just opened a virtual branch in Second Life. Was the investment a good idea? Typically, more than half of the answer depends on the windfall that the brick and mortar stores will see from the fun.

Let's see how you can go about measuring lift in either direction between online and offline.

Chapter Contents

Why Bother? I Am Busy Enough!

Measuring cross-channel lift does more for us than just helping to estimate marketing ROI better. Namely, it also helps us optimize outcomes over time through a continuous cycle of testing and improvement. In addition, the lessons learned can also be fed back to predictive marketing models for tuning their estimates. Moreover, you can observe how respondents interact with channels, offers, and messages to apply the insights back to future marketing communications across all channels.

In order to garner all these benefits for our companies, let's review how the multiple multichannel methods that are coming out of web analytics, response attribution, and brand measurement can be amalgamated to help us with measuring lift. Different techniques result, depending on whether we are measuring from online to offline or vice versa, so we will look at each direction separately. The measurement methods proposed in this chapter remain at the aggregate level, which is sufficient for measuring lift in most cases. Procedures for refining measurement at the customer level are explored in the next chapter.

Measure Online Lift from Offline Activity

Why did the chicken cross the road from offline to online? It could be that the chicken's curiosity was fed by a direct response offer. It could also be that the chicken needed additional information before committing a purchase decision. Heck, the chicken may simply have run out of time in the store. Maybe the chick started crying, and so she is fulfilling her purchase decision at home, online. Clearly, you cannot measure everything that would be worth knowing. But the more you can learn about customers' cross-channel behavior, the more you can do to support their wishes.

Picture the sport of curling as an analogy to your call to action as a multichannel marketer. From the point of view of the marketer, the customer is like the curling stone that is supposed to slide down the icy curling sheet as close to the target area, called the *house,* as possible. The job of the multichannel marketer is to operate the curling brooms, namely to aggressively sweep the ice surface in front of the curling stone in order to reduce friction and keep the stone sliding all the way to the house. (Check it out on YouTube, shortcut via multichannelmetrics.com/Curling)

Just as curling players do, multichannel marketers also want to keep track of their progress so that they know when and where to apply effort and how to get better with every shot. Let's fix our eyes on a real-life marketer as a role model in that regard.

Case Study on Customer Loyalty Marketing at Best Buy

Matt Smith, VP Financial Service and Loyalty Marketing Director at Best Buy, is one of the leaders spearheading the company's desire for building deeper relationships with its customers. Best Buy wants to hone its customer-centric skill set not just because it sees a very real avenue for growing business. Rather, the team at Best Buy is a true believer that deeper understanding of customers enables Best Buy to shape the business in a way that will hopefully appeal to those customers. As Best Buy is going global, Matt Smith says, "If the company did not work on building these skills in the local market first, it would be even more difficult to figure them out globally."

This endeavor is spawning an ever-growing number of studies at Best Buy, ranging from primary research with the help of customer panels through customer modeling to communication programs at the service of the customers. The mind-set transcends mere marketing campaigns and is aimed at providing two-way value: Better service as an investment for growing customer loyalty and business.

One tiny facet under this backdrop is an idea that Matt Smith and colleagues developed for saying Thank You to customers who make purchases in the Best Buy stores. Namely, registered customers may receive a postcard from Best Buy expressing gratitude for the recent purchase. The postcards are tailored to the buyer such that the backside proposes a discount for an item that Best Buy knows will enhance the buyer's experience with the product that they just purchased. Say, this may be a discount for DVDs for those who purchased a DVD player as can be seen in the sample in Figure 6.1.

Figure 6.1 Timely, tailored thank-you notes like the sample shown here are now sent to retail store buyers.

Besides the revenue opportunity, the program is aimed at providing real value to customers who may not have purchased certain accessories that are needed to get the most out of a product. Matt Smiths' team is seeing in the responses that the program is received well by customers. For this reason, Smith's team intends to refine the program further to put mechanisms in place for delivering the Thank You through the right channels beyond just postcards. For example, what if the recent customer calls in to the phone service line, shouldn't they receive their Thank You right there? What if a service engineer from the Geek Squad visits the customer in their home to resolve questions around the recent purchase? Wouldn't it be great if the engineer were equipped with a thank-you offer tailored to the customer's purchase?

Imagine Yourself in Shoe Steps Similar to Best Buy's

We will learn more from Smith's vision and experiences soon. For now, step back and imagine that you are a marketer at a fictitious retailer, Superco, and came up with a similar idea to Best Buy, namely a thank-you program for your customers. You work really hard to pull the program together, manage to get buy-in from the points of sale, bring the CRM team on board to make the purchase data available, get the marketing team to budget for the program, design the offers and creative, and finally get out the first wave of thank-you notes.

All of that was hard work. Tired, you go home for some much-needed rest, only to be called into your boss's office the next morning. Expecting a big Thank You yourself, you are confronted with a question instead: "So … how much lift did we get on the website because of all this time and money that you spent?" With all the overtime that it took to turn the program from mere vision into reality, you wouldn't be the only marketer who decided to leave cross-channel measurement as something to be figured out later. Now, you are put on the spot. What to do? The methods for answering the question that we will walk through can be generalized for measuring online lift from all the offline channels indicated in Table 6.1.

Methods for Measuring Online Lift

This is no time to fuss between web analysts, direct marketers, and brand advertisers. This is no time to stay within our silos. Methods from each of the disciplines are only stepping stones toward crossing the river. In order to reach a bridge that enables us to cross the river, we'll have to put our methods together.

Many of the following ideas should seem familiar because they are derived from techniques that we previously discussed for web analytics, response attribution, and brand measurement. For each method, the marketing disciplines that may most rightfully claim to be the originator are indicated.

► Table 6.1 Marketing Execution versus Response Channels Measured by Metrics and Methods in this Section

Campaign Channel \ Response Channel	ONLINE					OFFLINE				
	Website	E-mail	Mobile	Blog	Viral	Viral	Mail / Fax	Phone	Direct Sales	Store
Advertising (nonaddressable) — TV/Radio/Print, Out-of-home, Events, Product Placement, In Store	Lift?					Traditional Brand Marketers				
Direct Response (addressable) — Call Center, Direct Mail, Service Team, Mobile, Email, Web Ads, Search, Website	Traditional Online Marketers					Traditional Direct Marketers				

A common theme underlying all of the procedures will be to look for unique behavior among online visitors that reveals to which offline activity the site visit should be attributed. That is much easier to do if the marketing initiative was designed to trigger such unique behavior. If it was not, then there may still be a few angles that can be found.

CORRELATE TRENDS AND CAMPAIGN TIMING

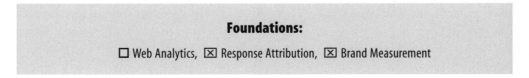

Foundations:

☐ Web Analytics, ☒ Response Attribution, ☒ Brand Measurement

Because Superco did not plan to include measurement, a thank-you recipient coming to the website will look no different than any other visitor. As such, traditional web analysts may feel like fish out of water with no tracking codes that can be used to identify campaign visitors. What can be done?

The first thing to try would be to borrow the general idea that marketing-mix modelers use when they build their models. (Direct marketers use essentially the same idea with inferred response attribution.) Namely, you can compare the trend of website activity with the launch dates of the campaign. Look for any spikes in traffic that coincide. If you remember though, marketing-mix models require historical data that permits isolating the contribution of one channel or campaign compared to others. Ideally, that is enabled through controlled testing in different markets or during different time frames. Because Superco did not think of measurement before launching the campaign, we are probably going to be out of luck here. A small company might be able to spot the impact of one campaign on the top line easily, but that would be out of question for larger corporations. Simply, there is too much going on in parallel that can influence the top-line.

REFINE CORRELATION WITH GEO CONTROL GROUPS

Foundations:

☒ Web Analytics, ☒ Response Attribution, ☒ Brand Measurement

All is not lost though. Did the campaign launch in selected geographic locations but not all? Say, in some states within the country, but not all? Or only in certain zip codes within a city? In that case, the situation is closer to meeting the requirements that marketing-mix modelers must meet to be able to isolate effects. Web analytics geo reporting, while not perfect, can indicate the geo locations from which website visitors browsed the Internet when they arrived on the website. See Figure 6.2 for examples of a geo report with A/B comparison of states that were included in the campaign compared to others that were not. Now, if a spike in visitation can be detected in states where the campaign hit, then the marketer is much closer to flying their flag of success on that hill.

The regions that were not targeted serve as our control group. Of course, in the next wave of our thank-you postcards, we should explicitly designate a region that will serve as the control group and prevent our postcards from going to this region.

To compare, Matt Smith's team at Best Buy is also drawing on control groups to measure their customer loyalty marketing initiatives. It would be unfortunate for the randomly selected control group members if they never received any of the extra service and offers. Best Buy makes sure to recycle the control groups periodically so that none of their customers are slighted. When a control group is rolled back into the program, there is another opportunity for measurement, namely to check how that group's behavior changes.

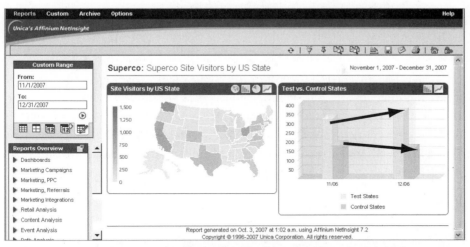

Figure 6.2 Superco site visitors by U.S. State and A/B comparison of states included versus excluded in the campaign

How Can Web Analytics Determine the Geo Location of Site Visitors?

The IP addresses (for example, 12.45.243.192) from which website visitors are browsing the Internet are used to derive their physical geo location. For this purpose web analytics solutions are equipped with geo location databases from specialist providers such as Quova, Digital Envoy, and others. Using complex methods, these providers triangulate the physical location to which an IP address is tied.

The techniques include using IP address registration databases, such as WHOIS, as well as associations with the ISP's proxy server through which a visitor appears on the Internet. Yet another approach is to *automatically crawl* website content for location information. For example, once a registration database reveals that 12.45.243.192 belongs to Unica Corporation, it would be possible to programmatically read Unica's website. The crawler would look for the corporate headquarters address and copy it out.

Limitations remain, however. Famously, AOL dial-up users cannot be located beyond the country level. More importantly today, if a visitor is dialed into the corporate VPN from her home office in Florida then she may appear to websites as if she were browsing the Internet from the IP address of her employer who may be located in Massachusetts. Aside from these kinds of issues, IP geo intelligence providers report up to 99 percent accuracy for those IP addresses that can be geo located.

REFINE CORRELATION WITH PRODUCT CONTROL GROUPS

Borrowing from the inferred response attribution technique used by direct marketers, we can refine the correlation a bit further. Our thank-you program provides suggestions and discounts for certain product groups at Superco. We shamelessly copy the team at Best Buy by offering DVDs to customers who purchased a DVD player from us. We expect traffic to the DVD section on our website to increase. In fact, if all other things are equal, the increase should be noticeable relative to other areas of the site. That is an effect for which we can query the web analytics solution. Figure 6.3 shows an example of that using date-comparison analysis by product category to show how category visitation and sales changed between time periods.

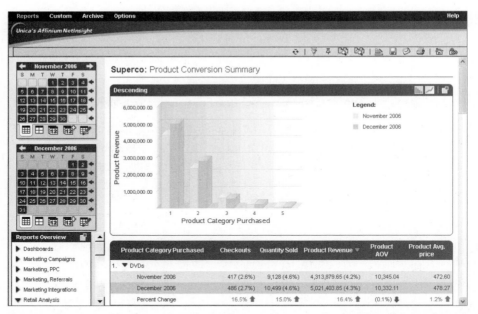

Figure 6.3 Date comparison analysis can be used to look for increased site visitation around DVDs relative to other product categories on the Superco site.

The spike in interest for those products that our program promoted can be interpreted to go to our credit if all else remained the same. Yet, in the example, the DVD category was not the only one that improved from one month to the next. The longer the time frame, the more factors are at work affecting change, making it difficult to attribute differences to any particular campaign.

This kind of report could not account for the halo effect of visitors coming to our site looking for DVDs but instead buying CDs for whatever reason. Still, we can query the web analytics solution to get a feeling for that halo behavior by running a report that tells us which products were purchased by visitors who browsed DVDs on our website. See Figure 6.4 for illustration. Retailers are looking for this halo effect when they advertise a loss leader to draw customers into the store.

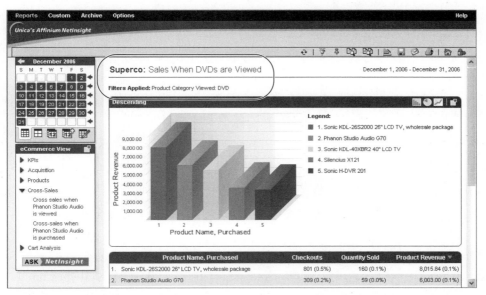

Figure 6.4 Looking for the halo effect of business resulting from visitors who browsed DVDs on the Superco site

INFER RESPONSE BY LOOKING FOR SIGNS OF THE BUZZ

Foundations:

☒ Web Analytics, ☐ Response Attribution, ☒ Brand Measurement

We already discussed how web analysts can measure buzz around their campaigns in order to infer their campaign's viral impact. This idea can help us in cross-channel measurement too. In the case of our thank-you program at Superco, we might search the blogosphere for any praise of the program. We could also run a web analytics report on related terms typed into our site's local search box to see if there is a spike of visitors looking for additional information on the program.

Some campaigns have it easier than others in this regard. If you can word your offline ads and messages such that they emphasize unique buzzwords or product names, their increased use online can be attributed back to the offline campaign. For example, Honda highlighted the term "environmentology" in their commercials on multiple channels in 2006 and 2007. That happens to be a fairly unique term. When you enter **environmentology** into Google or Yahoo! search, guess whose website appears first at the top of all organic search results? Yes, it is Honda's. As a result, any increased use of the term in blogs and search engines could be attributed to Honda's advertisements with some degree of confidence.

Trace the Handoff from Offline to Online

With the benefit of planning the next wave of our thank-you program at Superco in advance, we can render online responses much more directly addressable. Consider planting the following kinds of seeds for tracing the handoff from the offline activity to the website.

PROVIDE CONVENIENCE URLS

Foundations:

☒ Web Analytics, ☐ Response Attribution, ☐ Brand Measurement

Convenience URLs are mini destination URLs that can double as tracking codes. They are used everywhere. For example, in 2007, United Technologies ran broadcast and outdoor commercials that referenced more information available online at utc.com/curious. The offline ad campaign can receive credit for anyone entering the site on this unique URL. However, if you saw UTC's ad displayed while riding an Amtrak Acela train, by the time you got back to a web browser, you might have forgotten that you were supposed to type in the **/curious** URL to view the suggested content on the UTC site. You might have gone to utc.com to learn more, but you would be indistinguishable at that point from any regular visitor to the home page.

National Geographic Magazine uses *convenience URLs* for a purpose that makes it more likely that visitors will type in the whole URL. At the end of many articles in the magazine, the reader is referred to additional information that is available online with short URLs such as ngm.com/0706. This convenience URL takes readers straight to the content pertaining to the June 2007 magazine in their hands. Readers can order prints of photographs they saw in the magazine or other merchandise. *National Geographic* could attribute that business back to each edition of the magazine given that the visitors entered the site on the unique tracking URLs. The same kind of pointers that *National Geographic Magazine* is offering from print, PBS is offering on TV. For example, the short URL pbs.org/nature/andes is blended within the Nature program's edition on the Andes Mountains.

In the case of our thank-you program, we could suggest a location online such as superco.com/thankyou that lists all items on discount in one convenient location. Who could resist checking that? What if you are going to send your campaign to the printers in the coming morning but you forgot to ask your web team to create a short convenience URL that you could include? Is it too late now to utilize the ability to measure? Not necessarily! You can consider using URL shortening services such as snipurl, tinyurl, and many others. These services take any destination URL of choice and instantly provide a short URL that will redirect all visitors to the desired destination. For example, instead of:

```
multichanneltimes.com/?source=superco-thank-
yous&sourcecode=1212ABC&topic=shortURLs
```

a much shorter redirect link can be created on the spot as:

```
snipurl.com/manythanks
```

By using convenience URLs, the online effects of offline marketing are funneled into web analytics reports in the same ways that any online campaign is. The convenience URL leads to a campaign landing page. The campaign reports will attribute everyone entering the site on that landing page to the offline campaign. The web analyst is happy. Figure 6.5 shows an example of what a report might look like. Just as he does with online campaigns, the marketer can experiment with different landing pages to minimize bounces and draw more visitors into the site.

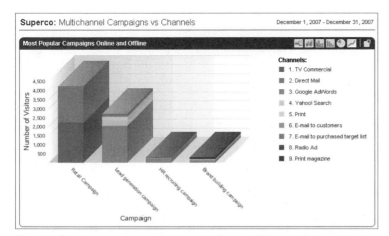

Figure 6.5 Sample web analytics campaign report including online and offline campaign results on the Superco site

Foundations:

☒ Web Analytics, ☐ Response Attribution, ☐ Brand Measurement

From the discussion of Doritos's Super Bowl campaign, you learned about using microsites, such as CrashTheSuperbowl.com. They are a great way to avoid the problem of respondents neglecting to type in the unique parts of a convenience URL, which suggests that they are campaign visitors. If you enter the microsite domain **CrashTheSuperbowl .com**, you are actually redirected to http://promotions.yahoo.com/doritos. The latter is a URL that respondents would be much less likely to type in compared to the inspiring microsite name. Yet, the Doritos campaign could still receive credit for everyone who is redirected to this Yahoo! page.

There are big benefits to marketers who redirect campaign respondents from the microsite domain name back to the advertiser's main domain. For example, in the case of Superco, we could list all items that we have on discount at the microsite www .SuperThankYou.com. That domain name is so easy to remember, even a surfer listening to our commercial on their iPod while waiting for the next crasher to come in under the Golden Gate Bridge would remember it—if they get back home alive. When visitors enter the domain name, we could redirect them to our main site, such as www.superco .com/thankyou/current_discounts.html.

First of all, we benefit from having the Superco brand name appear in the URL at the top of the web browser now. More importantly, the same first-party visitor cookies that are used on the rest of Superco.com will also automatically cover this microsite because it is on the same domain. That opens up all sorts of doors. Based on the cookie, we could connect the dots and tell who among Superco's registered online customers looked at the list of discounted items even if no purchase was made online. Based on customer data available about the registered users, we could report for example on the most frequent demographic makeup of those who responded. In addition, we could report what other content on the site this group of visitors viewed in sessions prior and subsequent to the campaign response. Based on that, we could technically target the individual visitors with additional display ads when they are browsing pages elsewhere on our site, as in "Hey, the toaster oven that you placed in your shopping cart recently feels all abandoned. Won't you call back to rescue it?"

Of course, it's the marketer's responsibility to put these tracking and targeting capabilities to good use and provide visitors with a more relevant experience while adhering to the stated privacy policy. After all, the goal is not to create more sneaky spam; it is to provide better service to customers so that they will gladly come back.

The web analytics techniques can be sharpened now with the help of the direct marketer's response attribution toolset. As direct marketers have always done, they can also use offer source codes to attribute online responses to offline activity. For our thank-you program, the Superco site could encourage customers to type in their discount codes to view the reduced items that are available for them or to apply the savings during checkout. All site visitors doing this would be directly attributed to the thank-you program. The response type would be set as either a completed cross-channel purchase or the consideration of items on discount.

Through that, we could create a web analytics funnel report similar to Figure 6.6 to show the drop off from those who arrive on the website by typing in the convenience URL compared to the subset who type in the offer code and the even smaller group that complete a purchase online.

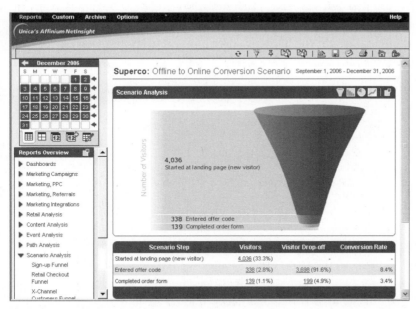

Figure 6.6 Sample web analytics funnel report on the Superco site from entry page to source code entry to conversion

As web analyst always do with funnel reports, we can look at the shape of this funnel to identify where the bottleneck is for persuading more customers to use the offers.

155

■

MEASURE ONLINE LIFT FROM OFFLINE ACTIVITY

Foundations:

☐ Web Analytics, ☐ Response Attribution, ☒ Brand Measurement

Web analysts already know that studying visitor behavior does not reveal why visitors behave the way they do. To determine that, web analysts are quite used to drawing on surveys and researching panel-based measurements. By corollary, the same is required for multichannel metrics.

For example, at Best Buy, Matt Smith says that customers continue to amaze his team with the way they use the multiple channels that Best Buy provides. When Best Buy introduced online customer reviews for instance, they studied the first couple thousand product reviews that were submitted. To their surprise, a majority of the reviewers had not purchased online but offline. This just goes to confirm that it would be wrong to assume one could know what customers are thinking until we ask them.

Consequently, Best Buy does not stop at measurement but is heavily invested in doing primary research using their own customer panels consisting of volunteer members. For example, the Best Buy team may interview their Online Community panel to learn how members perceive Best Buy's thank-you program, whether they find it helpful or detrimental, and why. On the backend, Best Buy can measure the behavior of the panel and compare that to what they expressed in the study. The lessons learned are fed back to refine the customer communication programs.

ANTICIPATE BUILD-UP AND DECAY OF MOMENTUM

Foundations:

☐ Web Analytics, ☐ Response Attribution, ☒ Brand Measurement

Taking a lesson from Advertising Adstock models, we can anticipate that the momentum built by Superco's thank-you card program will grow over time, but marginal returns will diminish as the reach and/or frequency are increased. With every wave of thank-you notes that goes out, we can also assume that their impact on online visitations will be relatively large at first and decay gradually going through a half-life time point at some point.

Web analyst can take this observation derived from Advertising Adstock models and turn it on its head. Instead of using it to build forward-looking, predictive models, web analysts can measure the trend of repeat visits from visitors who responded to the program. That information can then be used to time the next communication that may go out to this group of customers to rekindle their interest.

See Figure 6.7 for a chart put together by Daniel Waisberg, Web Analytics consultant at easynet search marketing and co-chair of the Web Analytics Association. The graph represents retention rates over time. Each line shows a group of users who registered on the website during a particular month. The lines follow the subsequent retention of each month's group of registrants. The points on each of the lines represent the percent of those who remained active on the site a month later, two months later, three months later... up to six months later. The dotted lines clearly reveal the trend of return visits to the site in the first and second month after the initial visit. Web analysts can use the chart to demonstrate how changes made to the site resulted in increased return visitation rates. Daniel Waisberg put the chart together taking data from a user-defined report in Google Analytics and applying additional analysis and visualization in Microsoft Excel.

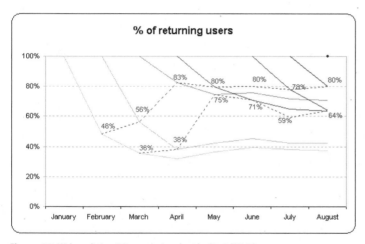

Figure 6.7 Web analytics visitor retention chart by Daniel Waisberg

CAUSE VERSUS CORRELATION AND CANNIBALIZATION

Foundations:

☐ Web Analytics, ☒ Response Attribution, ☒ Brand Measurement

Say a customer receives a discount for DVDs through the thank-you program and buys a DVD online. Can the thank-you program and the online channel in good conscience take the credit for this business? What if the customer was going to purchase the DVD anyway and was going to do so in the store? While in the store, the customer might have picked up additional items, say an impulse buy of candy bars at the register. If so, then the thank-you discount may have hurt Superco's business in the short term and the online channel may have cannibalized store business. Naturally, we want to know to what extent this is happening and what the long-term effect is. Matt Smith from Best Buy calls out the general challenge: "As the dialog of communications with customers gets more fluid, it gets harder to read any single element and determine the efficacy of a particular phrase within the dialog." So, what to do?

Note: In each of the marketing disciplines that we discussed, measurement ultimately required control groups in order to separate cause from mere correlation. Is it any wonder that the same will be a requirement for multichannel metrics?

USE CONTROL GROUPS TO SEPARATE CAUSE FROM CORRELATION

At Superco we should follow Best Buy's example and designate control groups of customers where we will suppress our marketing programs for a period of time. There are a number of options for selecting the control group, namely:

Geo Location-Based Control Group As already discussed, we can designate a geographic region as the control group. However, the control group region has to be representative of the test regions where we are conducting our campaign. For example, it might not make sense to use a high-income neighborhood as a control group for making observations on the behavior of a low-income neighborhood.

Panel-Based Study and Control Groups If like Best Buy we are able to draw on panels of volunteer customers, then a control group can be put together as a random selection of individuals within the panel. Their behavior can be compared against the rest of the panel. With this method, it is easier to ensure that the control group's makeup is representative of the makeup of the rest of the panel. If we can also assume that the panel is representative of the entire customer base, we can extrapolate the impact that we measure for the panel.

Identified Customer Control Groups Finally, the level of measurement can be brought down to the level of individual customers. In that case, the control group can be randomly selected as a number of individuals.

Let's say that 5 percent of the customers in the control group purchase a DVD following their purchase of a DVD player at Superco. Let's say that among those who also received a thank-you note, 10 percent turn out to purchase a DVD. As long as the size of the control group is statistically significant, we can derive with a good degree of confidence that the difference in conversion rates is caused by the thank-you program.

STUDY HISTORICAL BEHAVIOR TO IDENTIFY DEGREE OF CANNIBALIZATION

Now that we've accounted for cause and correlation, what about the cannibalization effect? Consider Table 6.2 for a simplistic view on the kind of data that we can collect through a controlled study. Neglecting the sales amounts, let alone margins, the table just looks at the number of transaction for sake of illustration. The controlled study may find that there was an overall lift of business and a minor amount of channel cannibalization.

▶ **Table 6.2** Channel Cannibalization Analysis Through Controlled Study

	Control Group	Test Group	Delta	Lift and Cannibalization vs. Control Group
Size of group	100	100		
No. of DVD purchases *online*	2	9	7	350%
No. of DVD purchases *offline*	3	1	−2	−67%
No. of candy purchases at checkout	2	1	−1	−50%
Total Lift	7	11	4	57%
DVD Lift	5	10	5	100%

Channel cannibalization is defined as the extent to which business on one channel comes at the expense of business on other channels. In the example, the cannibalization of two DVDs and one pack of candy were the expense for seven additional purchases of DVDs online. Oversimplifying, the degree of cannibalization was three out of seven, or 43 percent.

Measuring cannibalization is relatively easier if we are focused on only a single product, say DVDs, and only two channels. You would probably start by simply taking a quick look at the trend of DVD sales on the other channel to see whether the curve shows a downtick. With more channels and products, it can get very complex. See the sidebar for studies on the subject.

To summarize, correlation techniques help measure the impact of the offline on the online even when customers were not prompted to cross channels by the marketer but decided for themselves. Response attribution techniques can more directly credit offline triggers with online visits provided that the handoff is captured through some type of convenience URLs or source codes. Panels enable deeper observation, albeit on narrower samples. Control groups are fairly inevitable when correlations need to be separated from causal relationships. Finally, before true ROI can be declared, more work is needed to judge the degree of channel cannibalization that may be taking place.

Studying Cannibalization Between Channels

Cannibalization between channels (irrespective of marketing campaigns) has been the focus of numerous academic studies over the past years. For example, in 2002 authors Deleersnyder et al. studied the effect of the online editions of newspapers on their offline circulations in their paper: *How Cannibalistic Is the Internet Channel?* In their 2006 paper *Challenges and Opportunities in Multichannel Customer Management,* Neslin et al. presented an overview of many more recent studies. The common approach to most or all of these studies has been to use historical data on channel usage for creating statistical models. (shortcut via multichannelmetrics.com/cannibalization)

A typical finding has been that the degree of cannibalization will vary depending on the amount of overlap between channels. For example, the greater the redundancy between the online and offline versions of the newspapers studied by Deleersnyder et al., the more likely it was that the online edition had a negative correlation with offline business. However, with a differentiated channel offering, companies were able to add online business without negative impact on the offline.

Under that light, a brilliant method for understanding channel migration and cannibalization is proposed by author and practitioner Kevin Hillstrom with his book *Multichannel Forensics* published in 2007. A summary paper is available for download from www.minethatdata.com. Hillstrom's Multichannel Forensics method typically uses an extract from the customer data warehouse in order to observe channel migration at the hand of individual customers' behavior. This enables business leaders to understand, among many other things, whether a channel's customers are coming from new acquisition or migration via other channels. That insight helps marketers not only judge cannibalization but also devise multichannel strategy. For instance, Hillstrom cites Circuit City's "buy online, pick up in store" program as an example of a company that "must have figured out that the lion's share of online customers were already retail customers."

Measure Offline Lift from Online Activity

Say you were so fascinated with your experiences measuring online lift that you move camps and become an online marketer altogether. Let's assume you take a job in the website team at an automobile manufacturer such as Honda, Ford, or Volkswagen. Car sales are getting to the point where almost nobody purchases a car from you without first researching it online—yet, sales almost always close offline. So, as a web analyst you can measure online reach, engagement, and lead generation all day long. At the end of the day, the question is how much is sold offline. The cross-channel measurement question has followed you from the old job to the new one!

It is no wonder that automobile manufacturers have been at the forefront of measuring cross-channel effects from the online to the offline. The requirement also applies to other industries though, most notably CPG, pharma, healthcare, real estate, and of course B2B. Retailers too would be unwise to neglect the research shopper phenomenon as you will recall from the studies referenced in Chapter 1, "With Great Opportunity Come Great Challenges."

The methods in this section are meant for measuring offline lift from all the online marketing channels indicated in Table 6.3.

▶ **Table 6.3** Marketing Execution versus Response Channels Measured by Metrics and Methods in this Section

Response Channel / Campaign Channel	ONLINE					OFFLINE				
	Website	E-mail	Mobile	Blog	Viral	Viral	Mail / Fax	Phone	Direct Sales	Store
Advertising (nonaddressable): TV/Radio/Print, Out-of-home, Events, Product Placement, In Store	Lift?					Traditional Brand Marketers				
Direct Response (addressable): Call Center, Direct Mail, Service Team, Mobile, Email, Web Ads, Search, Website						Traditional Direct Marketers				
	Traditional Online Marketers					**Lift?**				

Methods for Measuring Offline Lift

Your first project working on the website team of the fictitious automobile manufacturer, CarCo, is to create a car accessories *configurator,* a virtual showroom. It takes you months of diligent work to get the design approved and the wireframe model usability tested. You get the artwork developed and finally one day the configurator goes live. Tired, you go home, only to be called into your boss's office the next morning.

You face the question: "Hey, young friend, how many extra cars are we selling because of all this effort and money that you are spending?" Nobody had mentioned anything about ROI measurement to you when you took the job, so you are in good company if you are taken by surprise. What can you do to answer the question?

The following tricks for measuring offline returns attributable to visitors' web activities are once again assembled from combining methods of online and offline marketers. Even though these procedures cannot produce 100 percent accurate results for calculating total offline impacts, the closer we get, the better we can manage the online efforts. For an automobile manufacturer, cross-channel measurement is in fact the only real way to assess, for example, whether the bid amount on individual pay-per-click keywords is justified. In fact, pay-per-click bid management without taking into account offline returns will most likely result in less-effective bid placement.

CORRELATE ONLINE VERSUS OFFLINE TRENDS

Foundations:

☐ Web Analytics, ☒ Response Attribution, ☒ Brand Measurement

Our first inclination for answering the boss's question would be to "take a look" at what happened offline since the car configurator has been launched. Indeed, for many years now, automobile manufacturers have compared historical volumes of site activity in one time period to the volume of offline sales in the following period. They have found a strong correlation, as we might suspect, because of the research shopper phenomenon. The manufacturers use this fact to forecast next periods' sales based on the current period's volume of site activity. Imagine how valuable such a forecast is, given the complex supply chain that goes into manufacturing automobiles!

Figure 6.8 suggests the kind of chart that can be put together by combining web analytics trends for the CarCo online product configurator with offline sales data within a business intelligence report. Intuitively, we would look for spikes in online usage to precede spikes in offline sales to suggest that the online activity is an indicator for the offline activity.

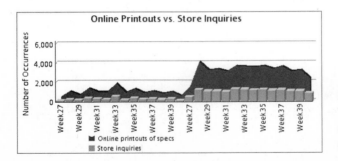

Figure 6.8
Trend of CarCo's online product configurator usage versus offline car sales combined into a Cognos business intelligence report

REFINE CORRELATION BY PRODUCTS AND FEATURES

Foundations:
☐ Web Analytics, ☒ Response Attribution, ☐ Brand Measurement

In Chapter 1, we likened direct marketers to crime scene investigators. When they infer who should get credit for a response, they like to consider all the evidence. Clues that help the direct marketer formulate a better correlation include information as to what products have been viewed vs. purchased. In the case of our accessories configurator for CarCo, the direct marketer would ask what the most common accessory packages were that visitors browsed online and which ones were most frequently purchased offline? In the experience of car manufacturers, the correlation between online and offline does hold true even at the feature option level.

REFINE CORRELATION WITH GEOGRAPHIC CONTROL GROUPS

Foundations:
☒ Web Analytics, ☒ Response Attribution, ☒ Brand Measurement

Let's say visitors favor a certain accessories package in our online configurator at CarCo. Wouldn't it be a career-enhancing move if that accessories package also became the most popular one purchased offline? Looking at the offline purchase data, let's say we can see that is in fact what has happened. The promotion should be almost guaranteed now—or is it?

Well, maybe. As always, we need to work harder to separate cause from correlation before we can sleep at night knowing that we are being fair. A good way to solve this puzzle would be to take our measurement a notch down to the customer level. We would compare those who used the configurator to others who didn't. However, in this chapter we are concerned with aggregate-level measurements. To answer the question here, geographic control groups could come back to our rescue. Yet, how could we exclude any geographic region from being exposed to the online configurator given that a website can be accessed from pretty much anywhere in the world?

Geo Target Site Content With advance planning, content on our site can indeed be geo targeted. The same IP address–based data technology that permits web analytics to report visitors by geographic location is used by many websites in real time to identify the geo location of live visitors while they are on the site. Sites can use this for targeting more relevant content to the visitor and also for fraud detection. Using this technology, we can focus the roll out of the product configurator to visitors from test states or cities.

We can compare how sales are impacted to other regions that serve as controls until we roll out the configurator nationally. Voilà!

Geo Targeting Display Ads Say CarCo is also running an online advertising campaign, maybe even one of those artful rich media ads that take over the screen when visitors mouse over a banner. Those take quite a bit of cost and effort to develop. Even if visitors do not click-through, we want to test how good the ad is at bringing people into the dealerships—i.e., we want to measure online to offline "view-throughs" to the dealership. Obviously, the cookie-based view-through measurement that we know from web analytics will not help here. But, geo control groups will. Namely, we can test online advertising in specific geo regions while suppressing them in others. Ad-serving companies such as Atlas and Doubleclick enable geo targeting ads, once again derived based on visitors' IP addresses. Of course, even without the fancy technology, we can simply publish the ad on a local city newspaper's website first instead of a national paper. That too has the effect that the ad's exposure will be focused primarily to a local audience. All that remains to do is to stand at the door of the dealerships with a counter in the hand.

Geo Targeting Paid Search Even paid-search advertising can be geo targeted. Some search engines enable geo targeting only at the country level, while others, for example Yahoo! Search Marketing, can target much finer geo regions down to the city and zip code level. Because countries are so different from each other, that level of geo targeting would probably not be refined enough to help us compare test and control groups.

Trace the Handoff from Website to the Offline

What is really nice about the correlation method is that it accounts for cross-channel behavior even if it is entirely buyer-driven. Nobody forces car buyers to research online. No marketer tells them when to go to the nearest dealership in order to take a test drive. Buyers decide for themselves. Yet, the correlation method still makes sense of their behavior.

Alas, the marketer whose job it is to attract more buyers to the site and into the dealerships has much reason to grieve nonetheless. Namely, the correlation method does not enable inferring whether or not one search keyword is better at driving offline sales than another—unless the search ads ran in different geographic regions or different time periods for controlled testing. But that is simply not practical in search advertising where many companies advertise on tens or hundreds of thousands of keywords. So, we need a more direct method for measurement.

Note: Although we can measure how much site traffic each online advertisement drives, we could be wrong if we assumed that the offline business that results should also be attributed to each ad in the same proportions.

After all, remember the wake-up call in Chapter 1: Research from Forrester (as cited by Brandweek) found that almost half of cross-channel shoppers said that they buy from a retailer other than the one they used to do research. We can try to gloss over this fact and take shortcuts. But as we learned from direct marketers, going with average numbers can kill our ability to discover nuggets of insight in the data. We would like to do better if possible. There are a number of techniques that can help capture the necessary data to enable more direct response attribution.

DISPLAY UNIQUE TELEPHONE NUMBERS

Foundations:

☒ Web Analytics, ☒ Response Attribution, ☐ Brand Measurement

What convenience URLs do for the Web, unique toll-free phone numbers can do for telesales. One established variant is pay-per-call advertising offered, for example, by online yellow pages. Another sophisticated variant available today is the idea of dynamically inserting unique phone numbers onto the website for visitors from different marketing sources (e.g., paid keywords). Solutions such as ClickPath from Who's Calling specialize in providing online marketers not just one but multiple unique phone numbers that the website can automatically display in a location and format defined by advertiser. With that, ClickPath can attribute the business that is generated back to the individual paid keywords that first brought the customer to the site.

For instance, if a visitor comes to the CarCo site searching for "family sedans," the site may display a specific phone number different from one that direct visitors would see. What happens though if on subsequent return visits the family sedan visitor types in the URL directly? No problem. A cookie-based mechanism can ensure that they always see the same phone number that they were originally provided—that is, as long as the same computer is used and cookies are not deleted of course.

BUY ONLINE, PICK-UP IN STORE

Foundations:

☒ Web Analytics, ☒ Response Attribution, ☐ Brand Measurement

Great for providing customers with convenience and enabling companies to secure a sale while the customer is researching online, the option of buying online and picking up in the store also facilitates measurement. Namely, as part of the customer's transaction record, it can be noted what the source of their visit to the website was, say an e-mail click-through or an organic keyword. That source (or multiple) can then be associated not only with the purchase but also additional cross-sales that the customer may pick up in the store along with the items purchased online.

INSTRUMENT WISH LISTS AND GIFT REGISTRIES WITH SOURCE CODES

Foundations:

☐ Web Analytics, ☒ Response Attribution, ☐ Brand Measurement

What if research buyers are not quite ready to purchase online yet? With our product configurator at CarCo, we can provide a Print function to enable site visitors to list out the accessories that they configure online. The visitors can then bring the printout with them into the dealership. The premise should be that this will enable the sales personnel to quickly lead the customer to the cars on the lot that are the best match. We can instrument the printout with a bar code, as is commonplace with movie tickets purchased online or flight check-in online. That bar code could be extended with just a couple extra bars to also capture the referring source of the online visitor (e.g., the search keyword). In the ideal case, the sales personnel in the dealership would simply scan the bar code to print a list of the most relevant cars along with their location on the lot. During that process, the source code can also be collected so that the event and any purchases that result can be attributed to the online marketing source.

A record in the sales force automation system could also be created in order to span measurement across multiple visits to the dealership. For example, whenever you consult a sales person at some car dealerships about cars on their lots, the first thing that the sales representative tends to do is to invite you into one of the offices and create a ticket that includes your requirements and information.

INCREASE RESPONSE ATTRIBUTION ACCURACY THROUGH PROMOTIONAL COUPONS

Foundations:

☐ Web Analytics, ☒ Response Attribution, ☐ Brand Measurement

With all that people have going on in their lives, how many are going to bother printing a wish list to take to the store? Of those, how many will leave it on the kitchen table and forget to take it? Quite a few—unless of course, there is something in it for them! For CarCo we could top up the incentive of convenience in the dealership with an additional value, such as a discount on the car's first maintenance service. Even visitors to CarCo's virtual dealership in Second Life could be given a special offer code that they can redeem at their local brick and mortar dealer.

As before, the coupon source code can be instrumented with the online referral source—for example, the referring keyword for a website visitor or a code indicating the Second Life virtual store. Even if the customer brings the coupon to the dealership only after the completed purchase of a car, the source code can still be noted in the customer's record in the CRM system, thereby establishing the link to the online referral.

Loyalty cards are examples proving that marketers are willing to provide value back to customers in return for the permission to learn from their behavior. Why not apply the same idea to multichannel metrics?

RESEARCH PANEL BEHAVIOR ACROSS ONLINE AND OFFLINE

Foundations:
☐ Web Analytics, ☐ Response Attribution, ☒ Brand Measurement

How many shoppers did you see running around with coupons and printouts of online wish lists the last time you went to a car dealership or store? You saw a few maybe, but not too many. We need other methods so that we can more completely judge the offline impact of online advertisements. The next chapter will discuss more response attribution methods when we review measurement at the level of individual customers. But before going down to that level of detail, we can turn to primary research and use a representative panel of volunteer customers.

We could follow the panel's behavior throughout the sales cycle, online, and offline. This may be a little more difficult to imagine for the automobile buying process that occurs only once every couple years and then may take many weeks to complete. It is easier to imagine in other industries—for example, a bank where customers interact with their accounts much more frequently. As an example, at the Net.Finance conference in 2005, Eskander Matta, senior vice president of the Internet Services Group at Wells Fargo, presented the process through which the bank arrived at their new website design. Part of this process included in-home studies with volunteer customers to observe how they actually used the website to achieve their goals.

To summarize, correlation techniques help measure the ability of online advertising and website engagement to drive offline business. For that to work though, the correlation needs to be refined with direct marketing staples such as inferred response attribution and control groups. Still, that would not be practical for attributing offline business to specific online ad variations, e-mail creative, or individual search keywords. There are a number of techniques for making the handoff from online to offline explicit. These methods work well for telesales but not so well for tracing the handoff all the way to store sales. For that reason, panel-based studies have been taken to surprising amounts of sophistication. Additional alternatives will become clear when we open up measurement to the level of individual customers in the next chapter. But first, we have earned a look at success metrics for lift that leverage all our hard work for measuring those chickens crossing the road between online and offline.

How to Connect the Dots Between the Panel's Behavior Online and Offline?

A clever idea for using panels to understand cross-channel behavior was introduced by Yahoo! and ACNielsen with the Consumer Direct service in 2003. Namely, the volunteers in Nielsen's Homescan panel were matched up against Yahoo!'s base of more than 100 million users. This enabled Consumer Direct to study the behavior of those volunteers from the Homescan panel across Yahoo!'s website. For any product that the Homescan panel purchased offline, Consumer Direct could report the most frequent areas within Yahoo! where the same consumers would linger. The thinking goes that in the online locations where the best customers are hanging out, more prospects of the same kind are likely to be found as well. For that reason, chartered members purchased ad space on the recommended sections on Yahoo! that were found to have a high concentration of visitors among their customer or target base. ACNielsen reports that one client experienced a lift of 70 percent in offline sales using Consumer Direct to target communications to consumers via the Yahoo! platform.

Offline lift from the online ads can be studied with the help of Nielsen's Homescan panel too and extrapolated to the rest of the market. Reversing the Consumer Direct process, the service can be used to observe the behavior of all panel volunteers who have been exposed to the advertiser's ads on Yahoo! The study can then show how many of the panel went on to purchase the advertised product. That behavior can be contrasted to the rest of the panel who have not been exposed to the ads and will serve as the control group.

Success Metrics for Lift Between Online and Offline Channels

Finally, we can address the questions with which we started the chapter. If we just branded the local football stadium in our company's name, how should we formulate metrics that indicate the degree of our success? If we opened a virtual store online, what metrics indicate whether we are satisfied with the impact on the offline?

Quantitative Performance Metrics

Foot traffic from online to offline or vice versa does not represent a business value in itself. It does, however, indicate how customers like to use the multiple channels provided by a company. These are the well-worn pathways stated in Jack Aaronson's analogy from Chapter 1. Marketers should watch and make these paths as convenient as possible. The metrics that express just how worn the paths are as follows:

Cross-Channel Referrals This most-basic metric counts how often a visit to the website or an offline inquiry in the store or call center was triggered by a preceding activity on another channel.

Cross-Channel Responses and Respondents If the activity on the other channel that prompted the cross-channel referral was a marketing campaign, we can speak of cross-channel responses and respondents. We can calculate this metric using any of the methods proposed in this chapter.

Incremental, Cross-Channel Campaign Respondents Before we can define *lift* in the true sense, we need to filter cross-channel respondents to only those who would not have crossed the road between online and offline if it had not been for the campaign. If the respondent would have visited via the other channel anyway, the campaign cannot take credit for the event.

Is there a way to tell without looking at the individual respondents one by one? Actually, there is a way, namely by using control groups. If we want to avoid resorting to control groups all the time, however, an alternative will be to go down to the data about each individual customer.

In the direction from offline to online, we can filter cross-channel respondents to just those where the absence of a preexisting cookie identifies the respondent as a first-time visitor to the site. Similarly, we can also count new registrations on the site by campaign respondents. However, with a site such as Best Buy, these definitions would be too restrictive. After all, you can count the people on one hand that have never been to the Best Buy website. So, if we were in the shoes of Matt Smith's team, we might loosen the requirement and decide to count anyone who had not visited the site in the current time period as an incremental respondent.

In the reverse direction from online to offline, we can follow a similar idea. Here, we could consider anyone who had not purchased in the store or via the call center in the current time period as an incremental respondent.

Lift in Channel Reach Attributable to a Cross-Channel Campaign *Lift in reach* is intuitively defined as a percent increase of reach that is attributable to a marketing effort. If 120 unique visitors checked the Superco website whereas normally only 100 would have visited if Superco had not branded the local football stadium in its name, then the lift amounts to 20 percent. The *metric* is defined as incremental respondents on the channel divided by baseline reach of the channel—in this example, 20 / 100.

This definition of lift conforms in spirit to the one provided for promotional lift in *Marketing Metrics: 50+ Metrics Every Executive Should Master* by Farris et al. The baseline that is used in this definition refers to the reach that we would have enjoyed without the campaign that is being measured. We can calculate the baseline by measuring total reach on the channel and subtracting the number of incremental, cross-channel campaign respondents. See Table 6.4 as an example.

▶ **Table 6.4** A Report Displaying Online Lift Triggered by Offline Campaigns

Week	Visitors Related to Offline Campaigns	Visitors Not Related to Offline Campaigns	% Lift in Reach
Week of Oct 6, 2007	437	564	77%
Week of Oct 13, 2007	545	369	148%

Qualitative Performance Metrics

Ah…those good old dotcom days when it was fine to just count eyeballs! Because those days are over now, we have to move further and get to the bottom line—the value that is generated. The following performance metrics get us closer to that goal step by step:

Incremental Channel Conversions (or Sales) Attributable to a Cross-Channel Campaign The number of conversions (or additional sales) in a channel by incremental, cross-channel campaign respondents. For example, 5 of the 20 additional visitors to the Superco website may have converted by completing a call-to-action, such as a purchase. We can measure that number with conventional web analytics once we have flagged the visitors as incremental, cross-channel campaign respondents.

Note the important fact, however, that some of these customers might have purchased anyway in the store if they had not visited the website. In other words, a portion of these conversions may be due to *cannibalization* of an offline channel. We can estimate the degree of cannibalization by following the methods of the studies that were described earlier. Granted, this will not be trivial. In the case of Hillstrom's Multichannel Forensics method, this typically will also require us to go down to data at the level of individual customers.

In the reverse direction from online to offline, we can sum up sales to those who call in to the unique phone number or make a purchase in our brick and mortar stores using an online coupon, wish list, etc. Cannibalization can play a role here too. Maybe the same visitors would have purchased online if the stores or call center had not been available. It seems though that a customer would not leave their comfortable couch to march to the store unless they perceived a significant value from doing so. They may have wanted to touch and feel the product or ask questions about it. They may not have wanted to wait for shipment or maybe the store is simply a fun place to be. In these cases, it would be inappropriate to speak of pure cannibalization. The store visit must be adding value and should get partial credit for the sale.

Lift in Channel Conversions/Sales Attributable to a Cross-Channel Campaign The number of incremental channel conversions (or additional sales) attributable to a cross-channel campaign divided by the baseline volume of conversions or sales on that channel. As with reach, we can calculate the baseline as total conversions (or sales) on the channel minus incremental conversions (or sales).

Costs of Incremental Sales Farris et al. defines the metric as costs of the cross-channel marketing campaign divided by the incremental sales revenue that is achieved.

Jargon Alert: Costs of Incremental Sales

The metric costs of incremental sales is simply the inverse of the ROAS metric that is common among Internet marketers, as discussed in Chapter 2. It is a small world, after all.

Costs of Cross-Channel Measurement By now it is obvious that cross-channel measurement comes with costs that are not negligible, especially when control groups and panels are involved. These costs should be added to the costs of the campaign. The ROI of measurement should be a succession of marketing investments that gradually become more successful. All other things being equal, an increase in overall marketing ROI should be expected.

ROI Metrics

If you are the person in charge of the budget, you will want to know whether an extra dollar invested is going to bear more fruit in one campaign or channel than in another. For that purpose, you will need to go beyond the incremental sales that the dollar can generate and get down to the ROI. In other words, you need to take into account the costs of goods sold to calculate gross margin. As before, the formula for ROI is gross margin minus marketing investments divided by marketing investments.

Gross margin here would be incremental channel sales minus costs of goods sold and overhead costs. Ideally, gross margin should also include the net present value of all future sales that would not have been realized if it were not for the cross-channel activity. Yet, in order to estimate those future sales, we would need a valid model that can predict them. No model can do that confidently unless there is data from comparable historical periods. Yet, given that multichannel strategies are still evolving today, no comparable situation may ever have existed before. In that case, we have to confine ourselves to measuring short-term ROI.

Note: To summarize our findings in this chapter, it appears that aggregate level measurements are helpful for assessing the cross-channel impacts of marketing initiatives down to individual ad variations and search keywords. The metrics can guide us in improving marketing campaigns over time and reducing drop offs of customers when they cross from one channel to another during their buying cycles. Yet, judging the degree of cannibalism that occurs between channels remains difficult. Measurement at the aggregate level cannot help us take a personalized look at each sales cycle. How can measurement at the level of individual customers help us with these challenges? Let's find out in the next chapter.

Measure 1:1 Interactions Between Online and Offline

Let's say a customer logs in to your website three weeks after his last online session. You want to display a promotional offer that has the best chance of matching this visitor's interests. Yet, the dialog that influences what this offer will be may have played out offline meanwhile. How can the website determine those phrases in the dialog?

There are never enough hours during the day for your sales team to reach every prospect offline. Who should be prioritized and how should they be addressed? Part of the answer depends on the prospect's most recent activities online. But how can you tell?

7

Chapter Contents

Why Bother with the One-to-One Level?

We already know that marketers can report campaign results across channels without needing to report the behavior of individual customers. So why bother with the extra grain of detail? Some voices in the online marketing industry have indeed suggested ignoring the one-to-one level, citing the difficulties and expenses of implementation as reasons. Yet, as we learned during the previous chapter, doing so would leave a number of challenges unsolved, namely:

We want to select better control groups.

Without the ability to distinguish individual prospects and customers, we had to define control groups either as distinct geographic regions or by falling back on panels. Neither method was perfect though. In different geographic regions, differing external factors skew results (for example, the weather will be different). With panel-based measurements, on the other hand, there is always the question of how representative the panel's makeup is of the rest of the population so that results can be extrapolated. There is also the danger of selection bias: volunteers willing to participate in panels might be a self-selected group behaving differently than others.

In contrast, by distinguishing between individuals, we can create control groups from randomly selected customers within the same geographic region as the test group. As a result, outcomes measured for control groups will not be skewed by regional differences.

We want to understand cannibalization.

With aggregate-level measurements, the study of cannibalization was quite tricky. It relied on correlating up ticks on one channel with down ticks on others. (See the "Studying Cannibalization Between Channels" sidebar in the previous chapter.) That correlation requires sophisticated statistical modeling at best, or it can be hopeless at worst if too many simultaneous factors make it impossible to isolate the effects of a particular impulse. In other words, the signal-to-noise ratio can be too high. By measuring at the level of individual customers, however, how far an individual's transactions have shifted from one channel to another becomes relatively easier to observe.

We want to infer responses to campaigns.

The most powerful method for measuring cross-channel marketing results, namely inferred response attribution, uses data at the level of the individual in order to match contact history with interaction and transaction history. As discussed in Chapter 4, "The Direct Marketer Digs into Multichannel Analytics," this can, for instance, be used to match store purchases by individuals back to catalogs that they had received.

We want to understand behavior by segment.

In order to refine marketing investments, messages, and offers such that they hit home with the various segments within the target audience, it helps to study and contrast the behavior of these segments. For example, which customers prefer to respond online instead of by phone or in the store? Who watches our commercials during the day and who watches in the evening? By measuring the cross-channel behavior of individual customers, it becomes easy for analytics solutions to roll up results to the segment level such as by available demographic attributes, customer tenure, life cycle stage, customer value, etc.

Additionally, we also want to analyze migration of customers from segment to segment. Most importantly, we want to work with our customer base to migrate lower value customers to become higher value customers. Well, how could we tell how successful we are with this goal if we do not measure the behavior (and valuation) of individuals?

We want to prioritize follow-up.

A website is built to serve an almost unlimited number of visitors in parallel; doing the same for offline sales and marketing would be cost prohibitive. There is always more than enough to do. As such, sales teams have to prioritize who they talk to in order to maximize their productivity. To achieve the biggest impact on customer satisfaction, customer service teams have to be selective with which individuals they apply their time. Finally, as we studied in Part I, "Building Blocks for Multichannel Metrics," direct marketing efforts have to be targeted carefully by discriminating between candidate recipients in order to have any chance of breaking even. It is easy to see how companies that know how to prioritize where they spend their time can pull ahead of their competition.

We want to personalize the dialog.

Finally, the benefit that is typically stated for going down to the level of the individual prospect and customer is one-to-one marketing (i.e., the goal of automating sales and marketing with personalized communications). For example, if an airline customer logs back into the website after purchasing a trip to Istanbul over the phone, she expects to find her travel itinerary online. She would probably welcome easy links to additional information for planning the rest of her trip. Likewise, if a marketer has sent an invitation to customers to go online to retrieve a personal offer, then the marketer is not satisfied with measuring overall lift from offline to online. Rather, it is necessary to poll which recipients have gone online in order to know to whom to send a follow-up reminder two weeks later.

It is worth repeating that one-to-one personalization is not everyone's cup of tea. Due to the complexities of accumulating and gathering the necessary data, some have suggested that it may make more sense to address marketing messaging to segments instead of individuals. Regardless of where you fall on this discussion, the points that we discussed above show that personalization is not the only benefit of measuring at the level of the individual.

Note: The discussion among most online marketers often stops at aggregate or segment-level measurements. There is nothing wrong with reaping as much value and insight out of the latter as possible. There are plenty of success stories where web marketers achieved dramatic improvements to their key performance indicators without knowing the personal circumstances of individual visitors. But the dawn of on-site behavioral targeting suggests that the online world too is beginning to open their eyes to the untapped opportunities of addressing individuals more directly.

Frankly, measurement at the individual customer level is hardly new, nor rare. In direct marketing, it is very common for the purposes of response attribution, event-based marketing, customer retention, next best offers, and customer valuation.

Let's find out what methods are available to marketers for attributing individuals' interactions online to their preceding activity offline and vice versa. Then we will combine both directions to illuminate the proverbial 360-degree profile of customers for the purpose of informing relevant communications.

Measure 1:1 Online Interactions Following Offline Activity

Among all those visitors browsing the website, some of them are there because of something that happened in the offline world recently. For example:

- Some visitors go online after trying or buying a product in the store.
- Some retail prospects or customers come online after receiving a catalog.
- Some bank prospects or customers visit the website after receiving a credit card offer or a bill.
- Some telco customers (i.e., those of either a mobile or landline company) check online after receiving a cross-sales, up-sales, or retention offer.

We would like to know when these visitors come online so that we can provide them with a more satisfactory and relevant experience (or present more relevant offers). Table 7.1 shows the map of offline campaign (or activity) channels for which we are looking to identify 1:1 online interactions that follow the offline activity by the same customers.

Response Channel / Campaign Channel	Online					Offline				
	Website	E-mail	Mobile	Blog	Viral	Viral	Mail/fax	Phone	Direct sales	Store
Advertising (nonaddressable) — TV/radio/print, Out-of-home, Events, Product placement, In store	Lift?					Traditional Brand Marketers				
Direct Response (addressable) — Call center, Direct mail, Service team, Mobile, E-mail, Web ads, Search, Website	1:1 Interactions? / Traditional Online Marketers					Traditional Direct Marketers / Lift?				

Two clarifications are necessary for the details in Table 7.1.

Blog Responses Say a number of customers have a really bad experience in a store and blog about it online. Wouldn't it be great if the marketers could tell which of their stores was the culprit so that they could fix the problem? Yet, we can't link an individual blogger's posting to her activity in the store as a customer. There simply is no connection to be made unless the blogger offers one by providing her name and geographic location.

Therefore, the blogs in Table 7.1 refer to blog posts added to the company's own blog by registered site visitors. (However, you may remember from Chapter 5, "The Brand Marketer's Take on Multichannel Analytics," that it is still possible to measure the lift of postings across the blogosphere in time with the launch of marketing events.)

In Store (or Branch or Dealership) Triggers The folks putting together all the beautiful artwork in stores would love to know if store visitors later went online because they remembered specific store displays. Yet, we can't know who did and did not pay attention to the store displays. So, we are simply looking to measure in-store activities that are addressable, namely purchases where the customer has identified themselves by using a credit card or loyalty card.

We can also look to measure inquiries without a purchase event if the sales, or service personnel has had the opportunity to retrieve the customer's record in the Customer Relationship Management (CRM) or Sales Force Automation (SFA) system. This lookup could occur, for example, when a bank customer inquires about a home equity line of credit or wants to know about IRA investment options.

Methods for Measuring 1:1 Online Interactions

Take another look at the previous chapter where we walked through methods for measuring lift online triggered by offline activities. Which of those methods can be extended now to help measure the behavior of individual customers? The only techniques that we can expand on are the methods where we traced the handoff from offline to online with some kind of unique convenience URL or source code. Let's see how we can pair those methods up with the power of response attribution used by direct marketers to create the tools we need.

Trace the Handoff from Offline to Online

As you might imagine, the use of offer source codes can be extended such that there will be tracking codes that identify an individual respondent. If you want to go this route, there are a variety of flavors with which you can spice it up.

PERSONAL OFFER CODES

Foundations:
☐ Web Analytics, ☒ Response Attribution, ☐ Customer Decisioning

Did you ever apply online for a pre-approved credit card offer that you received in the mail? Do you recall how you retrieved your personal offer online? No doubt you entered one or two reservation codes that identified you, something like this:

```
Apply Online Today at www.SampleBank.com/ApplyNow
Access Code: 55880
Reservation Number: 070771281
```

The application forms were probably pre-populated with your contact details for your convenience so that you would have little to do other than press Submit. This interaction likely established a record in the bank's CRM system. A note was made that you had responded online by considering your personal offer and then went on to complete the application. As a result, direct marketers and their campaign management systems have all the evidence they need to attribute your responses to the preceding offline offers.

What if you gave the zero-percent credit card offer to a friend? She would likely follow the same steps and then find a link on the website such as "Click here if you are not such and so" enabling her to enter her own application. As a result, the campaign management system would now find that the personal offer code is used by someone who is not in the database of targeted contacts. The response would, therefore, be marked as a viral response.

PERSONAL URLS (PURLS)

Foundations:

☒ Web Analytics, ☒ Response Attribution, ☐ Customer Decisioning

Personal URLs (PURLs) put the idea of personal offer codes on steroids. Instead of asking Jack Schmidt to apply at www.SampleBank.com/ApplyNow, marketers can provide a PURL that contains the offer recipient's name, such as www.SampleBank.com/JackSchmidt, or even a domain name, such as www.Jack.Schmidt.SampleBank.com. Vendors such as the Direct Marketing Alliance and others facilitate the generation of PURLs, their merging into direct mail pieces during the digital printing process, the production of microsites that are personalized to the offer recipient, and even the response reporting. See www.purldemo.com as a vivid sample of the potential with PURLs. The site, including all video productions, was created by DME (www.dmecorporate.com) in Florida, who together with CorporatePress, formed the Direct Marketing Alliance.

The goal is to make checking out his personal site irresistible to Jack Schmidt. There is also an implicit promise to Jack Schmidt that the vendor has worked hard to make the information directly relevant to him. In the vision of Alin Jacobs, vice president of Strategies and Partnerships at DME, marketers should think of PURLs not just as a one-time link from the direct response ad to the online. Rather, PURLs have the potential to be the online home of a company's relationship with the individual. Over time, the PURL site could grow to contain links to products and services consumed by the customer and the record of his interactions. It could replace the more impersonal self-service, customer account pages typical on sites today. In this vision, PURLs become a natural way to continue the dialog from the sales cycle into the customer relationship.

Saturated markets drive enterprises to be more creative at reaching their clients. Following the boom years, the real estate market has entered such a phase of saturation at the time of writing. As such, another sample of the Direct Marketing Alliance's work is a microsite created as a destination for the direct response marketing of real estate brokerage Prudential. A mirror of this impressive site is available at http://dme-finehomes.com. Respondents for buying or selling a home are virtually engaged into a conversation around their wishes. Along the way, respondents register and take a survey without minding.

LINK MOBILE TO ONLINE

There is a unique idea for linking people on the go to the online world through their camera-equipped mobile phones. Namely, software such as qode from NeoMedia (see www.qode.com) can be downloaded to a wide variety of mobile handsets to read barcodes of participating products with the help of the phone's camera facility. Nokia also offers phones that come with bar code scanning software by default. Upon reading the barcode, the software will automatically start the Internet-enabled mobile phone's browser and retrieve the manufacturer's related web page with more information about the item. An endless array of applications is imaginable across any industry. Marketers can make it easy to access customer reviews or dietary advice for food products or information on drugs. While the customer is online, there is opportunity to offer subscriptions to future communications. If you offer fish-food product, why not offer SMS (Short Message Service) or MMS (Multimedia Messaging Service) alerts warning of over-fished species? It would also be conceivable to send an SMS or MMS with a coupon.

The application has become very popular in Asia, especially in Korea. Adoption in the U.S. market has lagged behind. Still, the mobile web revolution has only just begun, and we have not even scratched the surface of user adoption to come.

Meanwhile, the spread of payment by mobile phone in Europe is a telltale. For example, in Edinburgh in the United Kingdom, on-street parkers are not stuck if they don't have sufficient coins in their wallet. They can simply pay at the ticket machine by calling a designated phone number from their mobile phones. During one of the payment steps, parkers can press 1# to also have an SMS message sent 10 minutes before the meter expires (see multichannelmetrics.com/paybymobile). That is essentially an opt-in to communicate.

Note: As long as communications to mobile devices are a service to which the recipient opts in, marketers have the opportunity to expand and capitalize on the technology. The mobile marketing industry self regulates to ensure that privacy rules are observed. This is facilitated through the Mobile Marketing Association (MMA) that has published a Code of Conduct, which you can view at www.mmaglobal.com.

Infer Response Attribution via Matchback

Do most catalogs that arrive in the mail contain a discount code or convenience URL? No they don't. Instead, they aim to whet the recipient's appetite with their stylish look and feel. Say a customer receives five catalogs from her favored fashion brand over time and one day goes to the online store starting at the home page. When she browses or makes purchases, she looks indistinguishable from other visitors arriving on the site after receiving fewer or no catalogs. Is the marketer out of luck for attributing her business to the catalogs that were mailed to her? Not so! The direct marketer's expertise for inferred response attribution through matchback comes to rescue.

INFER RESPONSE ATTRIBUTION FOR ONLINE BUYERS

Foundations:

☐ Web Analytics, ☒ Response Attribution, ☐ Customer Decisioning

When browsers complete a purchase online, their transaction information, including credit card, name, and billing address, is recorded. This transaction information can be accessed by the campaign management system through which the catalogs were mailed to recipients. To the campaign management system, the online transaction stream looks no different than purchases made in the store or through the call center. The inferred response attribution technique described in Chapter 4 will suffice to attribute the sale to the catalogs. For this purpose, the transaction and promotion history are matched up automatically by the campaign management system. Integration with web analytics is not even required because the transaction data comes directly from the eCommerce system.

INFER RESPONSE ATTRIBUTION FOR REGISTERED SITE VISITORS

Foundations:

☒ Web Analytics, ☒ Response Attribution, ☐ Customer Decisioning

What if no purchase is completed? Say a recent customer has received seven catalogs over time and she still has not made another purchase. Should the direct marketer mail an eighth catalog? Maybe the customer is really tired of receiving those catalogs and an eighth one could damage the brand. The answer can be based on general experience. You may have discovered that if people have not purchased anything after receiving five to seven catalogs, they never will. But, what if you knew that this customer browsed the website extensively after she received the last couple catalogs even though no purchases were completed? She might have even started a shopping cart and then abandoned it. That might suggest that the customer is on the verge of a buying decision and an eighth catalog could be welcome. Put in Recency Frequency Monetary (RFM) terms, even if monetary transactions have been zero lately, a customer's recency, frequency, and engagement online might suggest that she continues to be a hot prospect for the moment.

By feeding web analytics information into the traditional response attribution process, we can answer the need. If the web analyst and the direct marketer walk down the corridors and work on this together, the solution will be straightforward. Namely, for authenticated website visitors, the web analytics solution provides the data on their online visits keyed in the online username. The registration database can link that online username to the customer's account, name, e-mail address, mailing address or even historical payment information. That establishes a trail of information that the campaign management system can access to perform its usual matchback algorithms for attributing the online browsing activity to the preceding offline touch points. Instead of a purchase as the response type, we just have a website visit as the response type.

The cliché is that such registration information is not available readily or does not contain accurate names, addresses, and e-mail addresses. However, think of banking, insurance, stock brokerage, or telco websites. Think also of publishers with a subscription model such as *The Wall Street Journal*, or music subscription services. As a customer, you are almost always logged into your account when you visit these sites — and of course your account information is accurate even though your mailing address and phone number become out of date from time to time when you move.

Now, how about retail and travel websites which rightfully require a login or billing information only when the customer is ready to check out? This is where cookies can help bridge the gap between anonymous browsing activity and registration. As long as there is a persistent, preferably first-party cookie available, the web analytics solution can link the unauthenticated visit to previous visits where the customer may have made purchases. In fact, that cookie can be stored with the registration database along with the username.

Then again, what if the visitor has never purchased nor registered before? What if there is no cookie on the computer used to browse the site? If this is the case, we have reached the point where we truly cannot attribute the online activity to an individual offline customer. This would be the equivalent of someone walking into our retail store and walking back out with no purchases made. Remember that we can, however, fall back on the methods discussed in the previous chapter and measure at least the lift of such activity on an aggregate level.

ISOLATE CAUSE FROM CORRELATION

Foundations:

☒ Web Analytics, ☒ Response Attribution, ☐ Customer Decisioning

If you need to buy car insurance and go to GEICO online to obtain a quote, is it because of their TV commercials that you viewed and the direct mail that you received? Would you have asked GEICO for a quote anyway? You probably could not be quite sure about the answer to that yourself. If you don't even know, how then could marketers at a well-known brand such as GEICO possibly tell? Not even with measurement at the level of individual customers can marketers really isolate cause from correlation for an individual interaction or transaction. Marketers can only infer cause and correlation statistically at the aggregate level. We have already discussed using controlled testing (control groups) for this purpose.

That said, control groups without available data on individual customers had to rely on geographic segmentation or panels. Both of the latter have limitations as discussed in the beginning of this chapter. These limitations can be overcome now with the ability to measure the cross channel behavior of individual customers within control and test groups. How we use control groups remains the same, but how we put them together changes, namely, by choosing individual members. As discussed in Part I, campaign management systems can randomly subdivide customer segments into cells, some of which will serve as control groups during marketing campaigns. Additional selection criteria can also be specified to ensure that control group members will be representative of test group members. For example, in order to test the effect of three brochures compared to six brochures per quarter for driving customers to shop online, the segmentation process can ensure that control group members all receive three brochures while test group members will receive six of them.

In the end, we can use the methods from this chapter to measure how much control group members browse and shop online compared to test group members. As long as the size of the control group is statistically significant, and the makeup is representative, the difference can be causally attributed to the mailing of the additional brochures with good confidence.

Continue the Dialog from the Store or Call Center Online

Say you buy a DVD player in the store and then in the evening you shop for DVDs from the same vendor's online store. Should the online store get the credit for the DVDs or should the retail store? Well, if the website did not exist, would you have bought the DVDs in the store at the next available opportunity? Maybe yes, maybe no! The answer will differ from customer to customer, location to location, product to product, and even time to time. There is no easy way to run a test either. No wonder there is a large amount of fussing between offline and online store employees around this point, not to the least due to sales commissions.

This is a case where it may be fruitless to ask who deserves credit. A better question to ask is instead: who *should* get credit in order to foster more cross-sales? The consensus among marketers seems to be that both store and website employees need to be given credit so that they have incentives to support each other.

What can the website do to fuel cross-sales when the person who just purchased a DVD player in the store arrives on the home page? It is clear what the site would do if the DVD player had been purchased online, namely focus ads on cross-sales and maybe offer advice along the lines of: "people who bought this also bought XYZ." The same would be desirable now.

To prevent visitors from feeling as if they are being watched by Big Brother though, the site could make the capability explicit in the beginning and prompt the visitor to activate it if they wish. Namely, the site could offer an option for the visitor to retrieve special offers pertaining to her offline purchases. Especially, if the visitor is already logged into her account (as in "Welcome back, Mary"), this should easily find acceptance by customers. After all, in banks, telco, travel, websites, etc., it is fully expected that the site displays a complete record of the customer's multichannel purchases.

Regardless of how the site offers up the link to offline purchases, how can it retrieve the purchases pertaining to a website visitor? Well, in the same way that banking, travel, insurance, telco, and other websites do it millions of times every single day. Namely, by identifying the customer online and retrieving their information from their customer databases.

In the case of retail websites, this could be done based on loyalty or credit cards. Imagine your local supermarket opens an online store with delivery service. Wouldn't you love to be able to specify your loyalty or credit card number so that you could retrieve your most recent shopping carts from the brick and mortar store? Then you could mark in the list what you want to order online and submit the order very quickly.

This offline information can also flow into a customer decisioning process, the outcome of which suggests the most relevant promotions that should be offered to the individual while they are online. More about the latter will come in Part III.

Measure 1:1 Offline Interactions Following Online Activity

Like it or not, many sales cycles start online today and yet finish offline. This is true especially in the B2B sector, but it is increasingly true with B2C due to the research shopper phenomenon — that is, the tendency to use one channel for research and another for purchasing. As a result, there is not just a marketing optimization problem, but also a sales cycle optimization opportunity. Is your company making the most out of the chance to convert site visitors beyond just the website? You want to enhance your 1:1 communications across channels to shorten sales cycles, increase conversion rates, and drive up average order values.

For example, as presented by a speaker from a European automobile manufacturer at one of the eMetrics Marketing Optimization Summit conference series produced by Jim Sterne, website behavior data can be used and combined with offline behavior to predict where in the buying cycle individual prospects are at any time. Based on the individual's progress, timely and relevant communications (e.g., brochures) can be mailed. Likewise, a speaker from another automobile manufacturer explained how individuals' website behavior can be scored to predict the likelihood of making a purchase down the road. Based on the score, each individual can be prioritized for the appropriate level of follow-up throughout the sales cycle.

Imagine that you work at a fictitious car manufacturer, CarCo, and are inspired by the previous examples. You want to identify your best prospects on the website and mail them an invitation to their local dealership for a 24-hour test drive. That is an expensive offer that you could afford to make only for promising prospects. So, the question that you need to answer is who among the many website visitors should be targeted with this offer.

Notice how similar this question is to direct marketers' targeting questions that we discussed in Chapter 4. If you refer back to see how the direct marketer answered her question, what can you learn for CarCo's project? You probably want to have the customer life cycle model in mind that suggests looking for not just the right candidates, but the right candidates at the right moment within their buying cycle. You would run a test campaign to prove that the offer has merits. Then for formalizing the program, you would mine web behavior data to look for any patterns common among those who go on to have meaningful sales cycles offline. This insight can then be used to predict future prospects of value earlier in the sales process while they are still online.

What measurements would you put in place between online and offline to do all this? You need to correlate historical web behavior of individuals to their subsequent offline purchases and value. You would also want to know whether the offline experience is influenced for the better when you introduce the new treatment. Does it pay off or should you alter or scrap the program? Table 7.2 shows the map of online activity channels for which we are looking to identify 1:1 offline interactions that follow online activity by the same customers.

▶ **Table 7.2** Online Activities versus Offline Response Behavior of Individuals

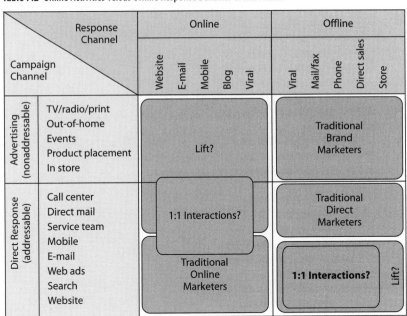

Methods for Measuring 1:1 Offline Interactions

Some of the ideas reviewed in the previous chapter for measuring aggregated lift, such as wish lists and coupons, can be refined for measurement at the 1:1 level. Whenever possible though, it would be preferable to add methods that will apply to broader audiences beyond just those who use wish lists or coupons. To that end, we can build on the idea of inferred response attribution by linking online registrations to the CRM and sales force automation (SFA) systems. More on both directions follows below.

> ## Foundations:
>
> ☐ Web Analytics, ☒ Response Attribution, ☐ Customer Decisioning

Printouts of wish lists could be extended with a code identifying the customer. Wouldn't it be much better though to avoid the hassles of having to print and bring along wish lists?

An exciting idea available today is to use mobile phone ticketing or voucher systems facilitated by vendors such as Mobiqa (see www.mobiqa.com). At the right point in time during the session on CarCo's website, the visitor could simply click to enter their mobile phone number. A registration is created under that phone number, the online wish list of car accessories or models is saved under that registration, and a ticket encoding the registration in a bar code is sent to the mobile phone. When the prospect arrives in the dealership, they could scan the code on their phone that identifies their registration (or simply retrieve their registration by their phone number). The wish list can be printed and the sales personnel can take it from there.

More than just enabling measurement, the greater value will probably come from providing additional incentive to online visitors for visiting the same vendor's offline store instead of taking a shortcut to competitors whose stores may happen to be located more closely nearby. Additionally, from the moment the prospect enters the store, the salesperson can be more helpful by knowing better who they are and what they are seeking.

LINK ONLINE REGISTRATIONS WITH THE CRM OR SFA SYSTEM

> ## Foundations:
>
> ☒ Web Analytics, ☒ Response Attribution, ☐ Customer Decisioning

A CRM system, or in the case of B2B, also a sales force automation (SFA) system, is inherently a multichannel tool. No matter which channel an interaction with a prospect or customer occurs through, and no matter the employee who serves the customer, the systems are meant to capture a record of the interaction. For that reason, CRM and SFA systems are natural tools to turn to for closing the loop on individuals' interactions between online and offline. To summarize the following recommendations in one sentence: the website needs to start updating the CRM or SFA system on its interactions with customers just as employees are doing for interactions offline.

Doing that requires some level of systems integration using, for example, available application programming interfaces (APIs) provided by many CRM or SFA systems. It is a project in which marketing and IT will need to cooperate, which has not always been an easy relationship.

We will walk through the necessary steps at the hand of the SuperCo example—i.e., the example from the B2C world. Yet, in B2B, the idea would be applied in the same fashion. The biggest difference with B2B is that multiple individuals from a company will be involved in the decision-making process. One colleague may initially find the website and evaluate the offering online. Yet, other colleagues may continue the evaluation and be the real decision makers. They may or may not ever visit the site.

STEP 1: EARN THE REGISTRATION ONLINE

The first step is to earn an accurate registration online, and it can be the hardest one. It is not enough to ask visitors to register whenever they are ready; they need to register with accurate e-mail and contact information. In a world laden with spam, that is only going to happen if visitors see adequate value in return. In the case of CarCo, this would have to be a promise to receive something of value that the prospect could not easily search for elsewhere (for example, a mailing with samples of car interior colors and upholstery textures).

Other businesses, especially those that work on a subscription basis, have it much easier here than CarCo. For example, for financial institutions it is natural that the online registration will identify exactly the corresponding customer account. Some publishers may reserve all or parts of their sites for paid access. Travel and transportation businesses can link to frequent traveler cards for special offers. Retailers can offer linking to customers' loyalty card accounts in return for retrieving online savings. Once customers make their first purchase, the site can register their contact information and link it to the visitors' persistent cookies.

A registration will likely not happen during the initial visit; therefore, it is necessary to cookie visitors so that delayed registrations can be attributed back to the original session. That enables web analytics best practices for attributing the business to the original site visit and preceding ad views or clicks.

STEP 2: FEED THE CRM OR SFA SYSTEM WITH ONLINE REGISTRATION AND INTERACTION HISTORY

Because we want to reunite the picture of a customer's online interactions with their offline transactions, we need to bring the data together somewhere. Therefore, at CarCo we will want to ensure that valid online registrations will also create a record for the prospect in the CRM system that is used by the sales personnel in the dealerships or call centers. Because many of the registrations online will be incomplete or contain fake data, a mechanism for filtering leads would be advisable to prevent the CRM system from getting cluttered. This could be done by using data purification services for validating mailing addresses that were specified before synchronizing the data across systems.

The CRM system would receive a pointer to the customer's online registration, such as their login name or cookie identifier. The sources of the original referral to the site can also be noted as could any flags indicating the customer's interests. With this pointer in place, subsequent online business events during return visits to the site can be automatically added to each customer's CRM record.

B2Bs can follow the same approach using their CRM and sales force automation systems. See Figure 7.1 for a sample record of a prospect including their online acquisition source and recent online business events of interest. Multiple web analytics solutions today facilitate integrations with SFA systems to make this happen. The additional step that needs to take place is to link contacts from the same target account together under that account. That can be done either by way of the registration information that each contact submits or by watching for the domain name from which the contacts are browsing the Internet. In the ideal case, that will be the target account's domain name. That is not always the case, though — e.g., if the contact is browsing from a Starbucks café. Therefore, manual data massage for keeping the records in synch and removing duplicate entries cannot be entirely avoided.

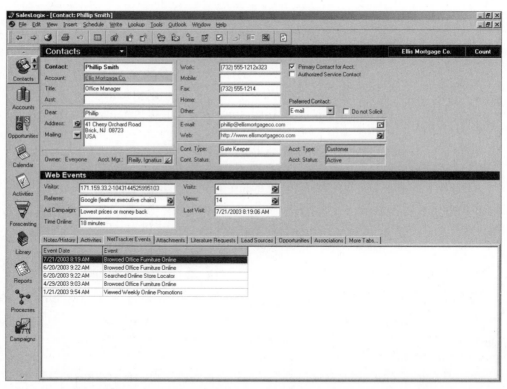

Figure 7.1 A sample record of a prospect in an SFA solution including online browsing activity

Finally, it would be business as usual to also hook up the campaign management system to the CRM or SFA database. This will enable direct marketers to prioritize prospects for various lead nurturing treatments and attribute responses using the standard direct marketing practices discussed in Chapter 4.

STEP 3: FEED THE CRM OR SFA SYSTEM WITH OFFLINE INTERACTIONS AND TRANSACTIONS

In the course of normal affairs, the CRM and SFA systems will eventually contain the transactions resulting from the sales cycles. At that point, we have both the business outcomes and the preceding online events tied together in one location. Using this data, we can measure what the sales results are that are attributable to each of the online marketing initiatives that attracted prospects to the site. These reports may typically be run through a reporting solution with access to the CRM or SFA database. This could be something that comes with the CRM or SFA solution or an external business intelligence tool.

Beyond measurement, however, the data can be mined for early indicators in the web behavior of prospects that can predict the sales outcome down the road. Such indicators may combine the frequency and recency of the prospect's visits, depth and length of visits, search keywords that are used, click-throughs from referring sites such as Edmunds.com or Consumer Reports, time spent on specific pages, geo location, etc.

We may, however, want to step back from predicting sales results and instead confine ourselves to predicting online prospects that will turn into offline prospects with serious buying intent. After all, during the direct sales process so much depends on circumstance and the skills of sales personnel that our predictions could be skewed easily.

What we need to do then is to ensure that the CRM and SFA systems will also be fed with the interaction history and not just the transaction history. Of course, that is what CRM and SFA systems are meant to do. But a well-known observation is that this typically does not happen with sufficient reliability unless there is an incentive for sales personnel and customers to keep the system updated.

What incentives could we provide at CarCo? For example, already during the first visit to the dealership the sales representative could offer to note the models that the prospect has viewed on the lot so that SMS alerts will be provided if similar new inventory arrives. Such alerts would be an example of providing two-way value in return for an accurate mobile phone number.

STEP 4: PRIORITIZE LEADS FOR SALES FOLLOW UP

> **Foundations:**
>
> ☐ Web Analytics, ☐ Response Attribution, ☒ Customer Decisioning

Even after filtering fake registrations online and preventing them from reaching the CRM system, there will probably still be more web inquiries than the sales team can follow up with in a proactive fashion. Typically, a need arises for prioritizing leads so that the sales team will focus on the most promising subset. The rest may be left for marketing treatments that nurture the leads until they reach a point where a call from a live sales representative is welcomed and warranted. Prospects further down the funnel may be nurtured with direct mail brochures while the less promising ones may only receive e-mail communications.

This kind of prioritization is the job of specialized lead management software solutions available from vendors such as Aprimo, Siebel, and Unica. These solutions prioritize leads, essentially by applying direct marketing principles. Business rules can be applied based on any available data to score each lead's likelihood to convert. At CarCo, for example, the process may be fed available data on prospects' past ownership of cars or intelligence on geo location. The only thing really new is that the prioritization process will now also have at its disposal rich information about each lead's website behavior harvested during steps 1 and 2.

STEP 5: CAUSE VERSUS CORRELATION

As always, we have to face the question whether the marketing and sales treatments are the cause for increased success or whether the same prospects would have turned into customers anyhow. We can verify the answer by randomly selecting promising prospects into a control group that will not be prioritized for sales and marketing treatments. The campaign management solution can then report what percent of control group members turn into customers compared to members of the test groups

For the example, in Table 7.3, assume that CarCo measured that 1,200 visitors have used the online car configurator and registered online with accurate contact information. Of these, 200 were set aside as a control group who did not receive follow-up communications. The remainder received a series of marketing treatments the effect of which was to be tested. After a while, conversion rates for the two groups were measured. The lift of the test group over the control group is calculated as the incremental conversion rate divided by the baseline conversion rate of the control group.

▶ **Table 7.3** Example of Test versus Control Group

	Number of Prospects in Group	Number of Conversions to Buyers	Conversion Rate	Lift Over Control Group
Test Group: have used online car configurator, registered online, and received marketing treatments	1,000	30	3.00%	500%
Control Group: same except have not been extended marketing treatments	200	1	0.50%	n/a

According to the example in Table 7.3, there was a 500-percent lift over the control group. Before running with this result, the marketer still needs to confirm whether the size of the control group was statistically significant for a given confidence interval, typically 90 or 95 percent. In other words, can it be said with an error probability of 5 to 10 percent that the results of the test conclude that the marketing treatments are more effective? Although the statistical significance analysis goes beyond our scope here, it should be noted that the answer depends on more than the sizes of the groups. Rather, the relative conversion rates in the control group compared to the test group flows into the significance calculation too. Namely, the narrower the gap in conversion rates between the groups, the larger the control group needs to be in order for the results to be statistically significant.

Create a Multichannel Marketing Customer Profile

Now, let us combine both directions between online and offline into a multichannel marketing profile of prospects and customers. If you have read anything about the notion of the "360-degree views of customers," i.e., a customer datawarehouse that contains all interactions with customers across all channels, you will know that the idea received a bit of a bad reputation in recent years. It has often been said to be technically difficult and expensive to build but also more challenging to turn into profits than anticipated. It was rightfully pointed out that there is much that can be done to improve the customer experience beyond the interactions that can be automated with the help of the 360-degree view. For instance, friendly, responsive customer service goes a long way.

Yet, if you look again, you will find that in actuality customer databases do exist all over the enterprise today. What are direct marketers everywhere using to help determine which customers will receive which marketing communications? A customer database, of course! What is the input into customer valuation models? The same! The campaign management system keeps a customer database of contacts and responses per customer. Online too, behavioral targeting is done by building a profile of each site visitor's behavior. In the front office, it can be taken for granted that the CRM system provides customer service representatives with immediate insight into customers' transactions or accounts. Just imagine calling your bank and hearing: "We are sorry, but we thought a CRM system was too expensive to implement and therefore we cannot currently allow you to change your address. Please send a letter to each of the branch offices where you hold accounts."

Note: The question today really is not whether to build a customer database, but whether to combine the multiple existing databases with 90 to 180 degree customer views into an integrated view across channels.

No matter which industry you are in, your customers expect to interact with you through all channels. Providing a consistent experience across these channels is both an opportunity and a challenge. As Kimberly L. Collins, Ph.D. (research director, CRM, Gartner) emphasizes: "Companies can no longer rely on channel-specific strategies that may create inconsistent customer experiences. Marketing is ideally positioned to 'know the customer' and deliver customer insight and intelligent interactions across a growing and diverse set of channels."

Collins' advice has become more pertinent today than ever as websites embrace real time, behavioral targeting for fine-tuning each site visitor's experience. The information base from which you derive targeted communications online should be completed with data about interactions across all channels. Otherwise, the relevance of the communications may be in question. For example, you may present a 20 percent discount offer for a TV to an online customer who just returns home from having bought the same item in your store for full price after exploring it on your website.

Elements of a Multichannel Marketing Profile

An implementation of multichannel marketing profiles can contain as few or as many data elements as you require to fine-tune your customers' experience online and offline. It makes sense to choose a bootstrapping approach beginning with a small number of profile elements before adding more over time after you have started generating profits from using the profiles. Don't try to complete all 360 degrees on day one. This way you avoid overinvesting before you have figured out how to turn profits. When you design the scope of the profiles, consider the categories in Figure 7.2 for guidance.

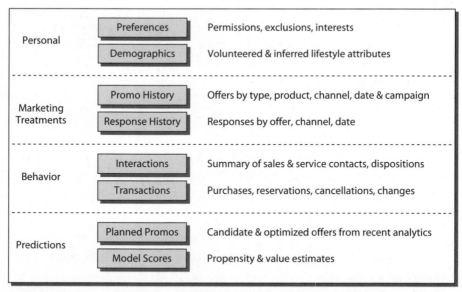

Figure 7.2 A proposed structure for multichannel marketing profiles (Source: Unica Corporation)

Personal attributes may be comprised of demographics, psychographic lifestyle attributes, and contact permissions. Treatments refer to the history of marketing promotions with which a person has been presented with or to which he has responded.

Behavioral attributes can be split into transactions and interactions. For example, in retail scenarios, transactions may consist of a series of purchases, whereas in financial services it could be more typical to think of a series of accounts or contracts. Nine out of ten interactions, however, may not include a monetary exchange but could be comprised of a website visit, a store visit, or a phone call to the customer service line. Predictive attributes finally refer to target segments and scores calculated for the individual's profile based on marketing models.

Maturity of Online-Offline Marketing Profiles

At the beginning of the customer life cycle, each customer's marketing profile is bare of information. Only over the course of the life cycle is the profile completed with insights as the relationship is deepened and widened across channels. We can distinguish levels of maturity through which each multichannel marketing profile evolves. Figure 7.3 proposes four levels.

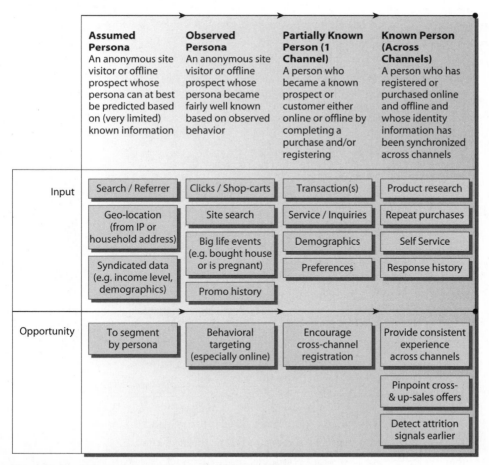

Figure 7.3 A model for the maturity of customers' multichannel marketing profiles

Even when an anonymous website visitor arrives for the first time, you can try to guess their persona using criteria such as their geo-location (as derived from their IP address), the referring site, and the search keyword they used. As you observe actual behavior, you can refine your assessment. When the prospect registers on one channel, try to entice cross registration on others. For example, you can offer an online customer a loyalty card by mail and include a $5 coupon for use in stores. The ultimate goal is to synchronize the information on a customer's interactions across channels so that you can listen to the customer's wishes and better assess your next best offers.

Building Multichannel Marketing Profiles

The first requirement for being able to build multichannel profiles is to conduct marketing activities in such a way that they are addressable. In other words, you need to be able to attribute interactions on any channel back to the related customer profile and preceding marketing touch points. We have already discussed all the groundwork. Namely, you can draw on the expertise of online and direct marketers. Then you can measure interactions across all the channels outlined in Table 7.4 by adding the techniques presented in this chapter.

▶ **Table 7.4** Campaign (or activity) and Response Channels Covered with Multichannel Marketing Profiles of Customers

Campaign Channel \ Response Channel		Online					Offline				
		Website	E-mail	Mobile	Blog	Viral	Viral	Mail/fax	Phone	Direct sales	Store
Advertising (nonaddressable)	TV/radio/print, Out-of-home, Events, Product placement, In store	Lift?					Traditional Brand Marketers				
Direct Response (addressable)	Call center, Direct mail, Service team, Mobile, E-mail, Web ads, Search, Website	**Multichannel Marketing Profile of Customers**									

Putting together the actual data mart of customers' multichannel marketing profiles requires bringing together the desired data points from each of the systems where they reside (Figure 7.4). Data about customers' contact information, status, and subscriptions may reside in the CRM system. Data about customer transactions come out of the ERP (enterprise resource planning) system but are typically fed into the CRM system so that they can be accessed there. Data on marketing treatments, responses, and scores of customers and prospects will typically reside in your campaign management or EMM (enterprise marketing management) solution. By tapping into the web analytics solution, the EMM system can also include interactions that occur through the online channel.

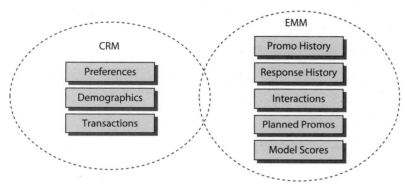

Figure 7.4 A typical situation where data sources about customers and prospects are distributed in multiple systems

Two implementation questions that require answers are the location that you choose for consolidating all data points into a single customer data mart and the mechanism by which you consolidate the data. There will be more questions to answer for reporting on the profiles or turning them into action, but those are left for Part III.

As for the location of your data mart, you could extend your CRM solution by completing it with information from EMM. However, when you think about the masses of anonymous prospects on your website who you would like to target based on their click behavior, you might decide that the CRM system does not seem to be the natural destination for all that anonymous profile data. Instead, it may make more sense to have the data mart reside within your EMM solution because it will also be your central, customer decisioning engine for turning the profiles into action — i.e., targeted treatments. Alternatively, you might decide to create the data mart as an independent database outside of all software systems or inside a standalone CDI (customer data integration) solution.

As for the mechanism for consolidating all data, you could build a central data mart using data warehouse ETL (extract, transform, load) processes. However, for enabling right-time marketing, it will be better to connect your disparate systems with real time APIs — for example, using EAI (enterprise application integration) connectors. Check with your vendor on available capabilities and shortcuts to facilitate the assembly of marketing profiles from disparate locations.

Challenges and Limitations

Not all customers interact with you often enough so that you could build a sufficiently detailed multichannel marketing profile for each. The stereotypical counter example is an online bookstore that may make futile book recommendations based on a customer's most recent purchase, which happened to be a gift for their mother. Don't let that stereotype discourage you, however. If you are like most businesses, you are deriving a proportionally larger amount of income from a minority of high-value, high-frequency customers. These are the customers who are the primary target group for multichannel marketing profiles. If you increased your revenue with just this segment of customers by 10 percent alone, what would that mean for your bottom line? Surely, it would make the effort pay off.

Measure Multi-Touch Conversions

8

It is far from happenstance that buyers are exposed to multiple ads during the buying cycle. Marketers are planning for frequency. For example, a cataloger may expect to send five to seven catalogs to an individual before making a sale. An advertiser buying online display ads will also expect that search click-throughs increase in their wake.

Therefore, if marketing accountability is the goal, then measuring multi-touch conversions is not a matter of "nice to have"—it is imperative. The time to tackle it is now! It is a mighty challenge for sure. Still there are a few methods that can help.

Chapter Contents
Put It into Perspective!
Study It!
Rule It!

Put It into Perspective!

Marketers are clear as to which channels their investments are going into and from which channels transactions are coming. Not so clear, however, is all that is happening in-between the two. Remember the wiggly line chart from Figure 1.1. Customers don't just see one ad and then go to the store to complete a transaction. They may stop by the website or may ask for references among their friends. They may ultimately pick up the phone and order that way. Seventy-year-old rural consumers may rely more on newspapers, while young urban professionals may instead rely on social networks or blogs.

Imagine that Mary and John are both in the market for a life insurance policy when they come into contact with a particular insurance company's products. Say they

1. Notice a few of the insurance company's TV commercials.

2. Also receive a number of direct mails and e-mail down the road.

3. Ask a consultant in the nearby branch to explain available options but do not yet begin an application.

4. Then, some time later, they read a blog that contrasts different insurance companies.

5. Complete an application on the insurer's website.

Now, which of these channels and touch points deserve credit for the transaction? This is a trick question. The answer is not really knowable, not even to Mary and John themselves probably. All of the steps will have helped move the buying cycle along. Yet, Mary and John might have bought even if they had not received as many offers in the mail, or if they hadn't seen the TV commercial, or if there wasn't a local branch nearby, or by going to the website directly instead of checking blogs. The truth may depend on the spur of a moment, on something that somebody said. The subconscious may play a role. The answer could very well be different for Mary and John. It could be different the next time they buy another policy.

So, if Mary and John don't even know themselves, how could the marketer ever hope to know the answer on their behalves? The marketer cannot hope to know it either. Yet, don't let this trick question throw you off track. Although the question cannot be answered for individual buyers, we can still make some sense out of it statistically, for groups of individuals. In other words, assessing the interdependency of multiple marketing touch points is something that we will have to judge at the group level and not at the level of individuals. Sounds like a paradox? But, it is not. The following sidebar compares the issue to the tricky business of weather reporting.

Emergence, as an Analogy

They say a butterfly flapping its wings could start a cascade of events that eventually adds up to a hurricane somewhere else in the world. When that happens, it would be futile to go backtracking for that one butterfly. Still, that doesn't mean that we don't do weather reporting. So, it is just a matter of finding the right perspective—i.e., the right level of reporting that suits the purpose.

Now, in the preceding paragraph, replace "butterfly" with "marketing communication" and "hurricane" with "a purchase event by a specific customer" and then read it again.

Weather reporting is neither easy nor exact. Compared to that, reporting the contribution of multiple touch points on business outcomes probably does not have quite as many unknown factors to reconcile. Yet, it is still going to require considerable amounts of effort. Therefore, the first thing to do is to figure out exactly when it is worth investing this much effort to get an answer.

Business Goals That Can Be Achieved without Tackling Multi-Touch Conversions

If you find that your marketing optimization problem can be achieved just as well without solving the multi-touch problem, that's awesome! Go after your business, and don't let anything else hold you up. Below are two examples where we will be fine without solving for the interdependencies between multiple touch points.

When It Comes to Sales Commissions, Prioritize Policy over Philosophy

Don't you feel bad when a sales clerk in the store or call center has been really helpful, yet the customer is not ready to purchase, and only later inks the deal online? Wouldn't you want the sales clerk to somehow get their commission anyway? For this purpose, it would indeed be great if we could attribute even a single purchase event precisely to one of multiple touch points that really deserves the credit. But the example stated earlier shows that we can't really hope to know this for individual buyers.

Incidentally, it may be less important to design sales commissioning schemes as a philosophy—i.e., based on the search for truth. Instead, it may be more important to design them as a good policy with the goal of enticing desired behavior. For example, the goal may be that employees happily guide customers to whichever channel happens to address their wishes most conveniently. The required behavior then is that employees from different channels will support and promote each other rather than compete. Consensus among successful multichannel marketers seems to be that this goal will more likely be achieved if credit for sales is shared among employees regardless of which channel the business ultimately came in through.

When It Comes to Optimization, Don't Neglect Tuning Step Conversion Rates Across Channels!

In the study by Bruhn cited in Chapter 1, "With Great Opportunity Come Great Challenges," many marketers who were surveyed commented that "Difficulties arise especially for measuring the interdependence of the coordinated use of marketing instruments." This was raised as one of the obstacles preventing marketers from adopting Integrated Marketing Communications (IMC). The objection is understandable when it comes to allocating marketing spending optimally between marketing vehicles. For that, you do need to be able to assess the impact of each allocation. Yet, there is more to marketing optimization than allocation.

Note: Marketing optimization, in contrast to equity investing for instance, is not just about assembling the right portfolio. Rather, it is just as much about optimizing each of the chosen marketing vehicles to increase their individual response and conversion rates. In the stock investing analogy, it is as if you were not only picking the right stocks but then also running the companies in which you invested.

In cross-channel scenarios, the optimization exercise requires eying, especially the moments within buying cycles, when prospects are switching from one channel to another. The goal is to minimize the loss of potential customers from conversion step to conversion step.

Case Study: Conversion Paths from TV to Website

When a financial services company recently introduced a new product they concentrated nearly 99 percent of their marketing spending on TV commercials. The marketing team initially crafted the TV commercials with a relatively older, more traditional target audience in mind.

Yet, to their surprise, the marketing team measured that roughly 40 percent of the responses came in through the Internet, by relatively younger customers, and often even during night time hours. The marketers also used a reputation management service to monitor online *buzz metrics* (consumer-generated content). The report found that in the week of the campaign launch, online chatter about the brand quadrupled.

Once you gain this kind of insight, it becomes clear what needs to be done to capitalize on it. In this case, the advertising and website teams need to coordinate their efforts. They will smooth the conversion process from TV to the web channel so that visitors find a consistent theme and tone across both.

The case study in the sidebar shows that smoothing conversion processes is highly meaningful for business results. Yet for this purpose, it is not as vital to solve the multi-touch attribution puzzle. Getting marketers from different channels to work together for making the experience consistent is more urgent. Equally pressing is to measure channel transitions to confirm that drop-off rates along the conversion paths are minimized over time. The methods presented in the previous chapters suffice for measuring this.

> **Note:** To those marketers in the Bruhn study who were taken aback by the difficulty of measuring interdependence between multiple marketing vehicles, the case exemplifies that there is really no time to lose for embracing multichannel marketing analytics. They are crucial for tuning conversion paths, step by step.

Business Goals That Do Require Studying Multi-Touch Conversions

Marketing accountability and portfolio optimization are two business goals that do demand an answer to the multi-touch-point question.

Calculate ROI of Individual Marketing Initiatives

Accountability refers to the task of proving the value produced by marketing investments. For this goal, it is necessary to understand the incremental contribution that each investment in the marketing mix is adding toward sales results. Otherwise, you may double-count business results across marketing channels or campaigns. Looking at the sum of all sales claimed by marketing initiatives you might then think to yourself: "Gee, we ought to be making a lot more money if all these claims are true!" Giving marketing investments more credit than they deserve can lead to suboptimal spending that could be cut in favor of better marketing avenues.

Optimize the Marketing Mix for ROI

How should you split your marketing budget between TV advertising and online display ads to maximize outcomes? What about direct mail and paid search? Or paid keyword advertising and search engine optimization for organic referrals? An informed answer to these types of questions does require assessing the interdependence of multiple touch points. It requires proving, for example, that a seemingly fruitless radio advertising campaign leads to valuable synergy effects when it is paired up with a direct mail campaign.

Pick a Practical Compromise

Just as with weather reporting, there are practical limits to the degree of accuracy with which multi-touch ROI and optimal media mix can be calculated. Customers encounter advertisements and messaging over many channels and media, including word of mouth. It is not possible to capture data on every touch point. Therefore, it is not possible to fully isolate the effect of every "phrase in the dialog."

In the end, marketers need to find a medium ground somewhere between always ignoring the multi-touch problem at one extreme and always investing in deep studies at the other extreme. Such a compromise is recommended here. Namely, don't ignore the problem but conduct a minimum number of focused studies to get a feeling for interdependencies. Based on these lessons learned, you can formulate rules of thumb for spreading credit to multiple marketing touch points. The rules of thumb can then be automated to varying degrees in different marketing software applications. Granted, the results will not be perfect, but neither are weather reports, yet we check them every day.

Study It!

A number of fascinating studies have probed deep into the interdependencies among marketing touch points. These works can serve as models when it is time to investigate your own projects. We will review various studies covering the following questions:

Reach versus Frequency? How frequently should I schedule advertisements on TV and other channels to build my brand and drive sales? Does it work better to pile frequent exposures within a short period in order to make a big splash? Or is it more advantageous to spread the advertising budget so that it can cover the entire year while increasing reach to additional audiences?

How Does One Marketing Message Impact Another? If one display ad gets more click-throughs than another, should I drop the latter and only use the former going forward? What if the seemingly weaker ad played a role in making the other one strong? That is exactly what is expected when one ad creative focuses on brand perception while the other stimulates a direct response.

How Does Marketing on One Channel Impact Another? Specifically, do search engines really deserve sole credit for everyone coming to a website after clicking on a search listing? What if some of those browsers were exposed to display ads in the run up? How should the credit be shared between search and display ads?

How Should Spending Be Shifted Between Online and Offline? Is the next dollar invested in advertising going to be more effective on TV, radio, in print magazines, direct mail, or via Internet display ads?

As we will see, the studies that investigated these questions brought together data from numerous silos. Significant amounts of data acrobatics were involved too. For that reason, many of the works have been produced in academia or by marketing agencies. No "out of box" report in any marketing application would be able to deliver these study results upon button click today.

The goods news, on the other hand, is that these agencies are available for hire to implement their methods for your company's marketing mix. The marketer's job now is to understand the various types of methods that are available—not to mention that the marketer also needs to pay for the costs of the study and bring that money back by turning the lessons learned into action.

One way to bring an order to these studies is to realize that they fall into one of multiple types. Namely, they may rely on controlled testing, uncontrolled testing, or marketing mix modeling. Let's contrast these three types to each other, before we review the specific studies that have employed them.

Controlled versus Uncontrolled Testing and Modeling

What does a marketer experimenting with new avenues in her marketing mix have in common with a parent introducing new foods into a baby's diet? Both want to be able to attribute the resulting impacts back to the additional item that was introduced into the mix. So then, what does the parent do with the baby? She proceeds in a controlled fashion—i.e., she may only introduce a new food every four to seven days to ensure that any allergic reactions can be clearly linked to the source. That is an example of controlled testing, and multichannel marketers may use a similar approach for their own purposes.

Namely, for marketing channels where marketers are holding the reigns in the hand, they can control which customers will or will not receive a particular test message. Channels where this works include direct mail, e-mail, and any of the other ones listed in the first column of Table 8.1. Controlled studies are neither cheap nor easy, especially not for offline marketing. We discussed the limitations of time, geography, and panel-based control groups. For that reason, we studied the workaround of applying controlled testing down at the level of individual customers.

▶ **Table 8.1** Channel Suitability for Controlled Testing

Channels That Marketers Can Control in Testing	Channels That Cannot Be Controlled in Testing
TV/Radio/Print	Traffic to the brick and mortar outlets
Out-of-home	Calls to the call center
Product placements	Direct website visits
Marketing events	Organic search
In store displays	Referring links to the website
Call center	Affiliate network referrals
Direct mail	Blogs and social networks
Sales or service personnel	
Mobile	
E-mail	
Web ads	
Paid search keyword advertising	
On-site promotions	

Although many marketing channels enable controlled testing, there are others that do not. Why? Because with these channels (e.g., the ones in the second column in Table 8.1), the customers are dealing the cards and marketers have to take them as they fall. For example, with traffic to brick and mortar stores, customers choose whether and when they will show up. Studies for these channels, therefore, need an alternative method. Such a substitute *is uncontrolled testing*—i.e., the analysis of historical behavior for identifying common patterns. What can the data tell us about typical customer behavior? Are there combinations of exposures to ads or channels that *correlate* with high value purchases?

Unfortunately, a common limitation of uncontrolled testing is that there is no guarantee that any correlation found in the data is also a causal relationship. Say, a retailer may find that most high-value customers use both the brick and mortar stores as well as the website. That does not prove that driving offline-only customers to the online channel, and vice versa, will turn either into more valuable customers. Nevertheless, the marketer can try doing it in a controlled study to see if it actually does make a difference. To summarize, the uncontrolled study can lead to a hypothesis that a subsequent, controlled study can dismiss or confirm.

Marketing-mix modeling, finally, can build on data from either controlled or uncontrolled testing. The models do not just merely correlate marketing investments and sales, but aim to infer causality. Statisticians can arrive at a probability level with which a regression suggests that a correlation found in the data is in fact a causal link.

Now, let's see how clever marketing analysts have placed controlled, uncontrolled, and modeling-based studies into practice.

Would You Like Reach or Frequency with That?

Let's start our investigation into multiple touch points with a single ad and a single channel—a TV commercial, an online display ad, or a direct mailing. What could be a simpler place to start?

> **Reader:** Is there even anything left to analyze in terms of multiple touch points?
>
> **Advertiser:** Yes, namely, how frequently should we schedule the ad to maximize its impact?
>
> **Reader:** Oh, that answer is easy! Just push it out as often as possible, at least until people start complaining.
>
> **Advertiser:** Not so, alas. Frequency comes at an expense. Namely, given that my marketing budget is fixed, the tradeoff is the duration over which I can afford to stretch the ad campaign and hence the total audience that I will reach.

Should the advertiser spend a fixed marketing budget to reach as many prospects as possible or limit reach so that he can touch a smaller group of prospects more frequently? Will effects be maximized if he concentrates the advertisement over a short burst period? Or, should he spread the budget throughout the year with low intensity advertising week by week?

Traditional View Point

Traditional brand marketers are of the opinion that a minimum frequency of exposures to an advertisement is needed before its message will become effective. Repetition is crucial! A psychological theory proposed by Herbert Krugman in 1965 suggested that the first impression of an unfamiliar product or brand may still be confusing to the audience. It may fizzle like noise in the wind. Only the second impression can bring clarity and be noticed in order to have a positive effect on purchase behavior. Starting with the third or fourth impression already, the additional impact may be diminished or zero.

The idea is often represented by refining the Advertising Adstock curve of diminishing returns from Figure 5.4 into an S-curve–shaped model as shown in Figure 8.1. The threshold point in the curve represents the minimum level of frequency to which a brand advertising campaign should be scaled up before it becomes effective.

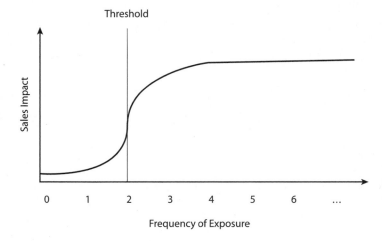

Figure 8.1
S-curve shaped diminishing returns with a threshold value that represents the minimum recommended scale for the campaign

As author John Philip Jones explains in *The Advertising Business*, marketers' consensus was hardened by Michael Naples' book *Effective Frequency* (published in 1979). For the following decades, almost all advertisers concentrated their spending on commercials with the goal of reaching at least three ad exposures within short time periods. This can be referred to as a *frequency strategy*.

Note: "Short time period" means the duration of a single buying cycle. For example, in the case of a breakfast cereal, the buying cycle may be seven days assuming that shoppers go to the store once a week.

Note: Note that the word "frequency" is sometimes used differently, namely more in the sense of repetition over longer periods of time. Our cereal marketer should repeat his advertisements every week, year over year in order to build his brand in face of competition. But that is not what is meant here by a frequency strategy that refers to a single buying cycle.

Narrowing of the Case for a Frequency Strategy

All the while that brand advertisers were indoctrinated with the frequency strategy, flaws in the reasoning started to become apparent to researchers. Namely, Krugman's theory did suggest that the first exposure to an advertisement may indeed not be effective if the product, brand, or ad is unfamiliar. But in cases of existing familiarity—for example, with a consumer packaged good—even the initial ad exposure within each time period can act as an effective reminder.

This was confirmed when author Colin McDonald recomputed an empirical study that he had conducted in 1966. McDonald used single-source research (discussed in Chapter 5, "The Brand Marketer's Take on Multichannel Analytics") to collect behavioral data on the effects of ad exposures. When recomputed, the study showed that the first impression did in fact achieve considerable impact on market share. The behavior looked more like Figure 5.4 and not like the S-shape in Figure 8.1. So, could it be that the advertising industry had been wrong for decades and that concentrating spending was not necessarily the most efficient schedule?

VALUE OF SINGLE AD EXPOSURE IS CONFIRMED IN ONLINE MARKETING

Foundations:

☒ Web Analytics, ☐ Response Attribution, ☐ Brand Measurement

Whether or not the industry had been wrong was a question that the Atlas Institute sought to answer for online display advertising. The institute is the research and education arm of Atlas, now part of Microsoft. Vast amounts of anonymous data collected from online ad display campaigns running on Atlas' ad-serving platform were analyzed in this study. The institute published their surprising results in the paper: "Optimal Frequency—The Impact of Frequency on Conversion Rates." The document is available for download from the Atlas website (shortcut via multichannelmetrics .com/Atlas).

Data from 38 online display advertisers in 2003 were analyzed with a method that falls into the uncontrolled testing bucket by our definition. The researchers measured conversions for these advertisers grouped by how many ad impressions each prospective respondent was exposed to. Atlas emphasizes that the count only included ad exposures up until the conversion events and not later in time. In effect, the calculation determined what the ad campaign's resulting conversion rate would have been if it had been frequency capped at specific numbers of ad impressions per individual.

On average, Atlas found that the ratio of conversions to ad impressions would have been maximized if the campaigns had been frequency capped to allow no more than a single ad exposure per person (i.e., per cookie). Granted, doing so would also have limited the returns from the campaigns, because the data showed that many visitors only clicked through on subsequent ad exposures to complete their conversions. Yet the ratio of conversions to impressions was diminishing with every additional exposure.

To illustrate, imagine that 10 people received only a single ad impression and two of them made a purchase. That would be a conversion rate of 20 percent. Ten others may have received two ad impressions. Even if three of these latter folks made a purchase that would only bring us to a total of five conversions among a total of 30 ad impressions—i.e., a conversion rate of $5/30 = 16.67$ percent.

The Atlas study attributed this result to the thought that "At any given moment there are only a fraction of users who will immediately respond to your ads." In other words, whenever the ad reaches a prospect at the right time, a single exposure to an ad can be enough to entice a click-through to the website for evaluating the offer.

The good news is that multiple ad-serving platforms are providing features for configuring a frequency cap. Individuals will not be served further exposures of an advertiser's ad after they have already been exposed to the maximum number of impressions. It should be disclosed that frequency capping is something that Atlas is positioning as one of the capabilities that its platform implements particularly well. In the study, Atlas hints that a loose frequency cap of 10 exposures can be a good way to start experimenting with the effects.

OFFLINE MEDIA PLANNING IDENTIFIES THE VALUE OF REACH AND RECENCY BEYOND FREQUENCY

Foundations:

☐ Web Analytics, ☐ Response Attribution, ☒ Brand Measurement

Interestingly, the result of the Atlas study had been heralded by media-planning guru Erwin Ephron and Melissa Heath in 2001, in their paper "Teaching Tap to the Elephant" (available via ephrononmedia.com). The study was based on the example of TV commercials. Their conclusion was in line with the results that Atlas would later reach. Increased frequency also increases waste because some heavy users of the media (i.e., frequent TV watchers) will see the commercial over and over again with no additional value that is generated. Others will continue seeing the ads even after they have already completed a purchase.

John Philip Jones finds another way to bring it to the point in an interview with rediff.com from May 2005: "In simple terms, what this means is that short-term media concentration produces sales that are more and more expensive to achieve. It is therefore uneconomic." Think of spinning wheels when you press too hard on the accelerator in a Mustang.

The worst is if that concentrated spending depletes the marketing budget such that advertising has to be discontinued during other parts of the year. Then the buyers that happened to be close to their buying decisions during those parts of the year and could have been won over with just a single ad exposure are lost. In the final result, Ephron and Heath predict a lower total return for a frequency-based strategy when measured over the course of the entire year.

That prediction is consistent with data analyzed in a study, "Single-Source Research Begins to Fulfill Its Promise," already published by John Philip Jones in the *Journal of Advertising Research* in 1995. By analyzing the effects of advertising for 78 American brands, Jones found that: "In the period before purchase, an average of 73% of sales came from households exposed to one advertisement, with the remaining 27% coming from those seeing more than one." Once again, single-source research was used to correlate panelists' media consumption with their short term purchase behavior. The study is the offline equivalent of the Atlas Institute study.

Note: The conclusion that all these researchers agree on is that there is "narrowing of the circumstances in which advertisers should plan to run their messages according to the original pattern of three exposures before purchase," as John Philip Jones sums up in *The Advertising Business*. Though, there are cases when short-term frequency can still be the right strategy. For example, when unfamiliar technology companies run commercials to debut their unique products or when small and medium businesses run advertising.

How Does One Ad Impact Another?

OK, so now we have looked into scheduling a single ad over the course of the year. But surely, we have to deal with several ad variations that we are running in parallel. That would be the case even in any single campaign that we are running. Traditional thinking, especially online, attributes all business to the last touch point. Under that light we would simply measure which ad variation gets better responses and drop the other ones that are getting fewer. Yet, that would ignore the interdependencies that may be at play between the ads when prospects see several of them over time. Could it be that one ad can make another stronger?

CASE STUDY BY AVENUE A | RAZORFISH

Foundations:

☒ Web Analytics, ☐ Response Attribution, ☐ Brand Measurement

Innovative analyses by Avenue A | Razorfish lead the way for illuminating questions of this nature for digital marketing. The interactive services firm released a report,

"Actionable Analytics," at the end of 2006 summarizing the methods that were used for a number of studies they ran on behalf of clients. The paper can be requested from the Avenue A | Razorfish website (shortcut via multichannelmetrics.com/AvenueARazorfish).

Among these clients, one prompted Avenue A | Razorfish to deliver an answer to a question similar to ours posed in this section: "Where should I spend my next advertising dollar — on brand or direct response advertising?" The client was from the travel and hospitality industry. They have been running a large display ad campaign that included both direct response oriented creative and brand oriented creative. Clearly, the aim of the brand ads was to create awareness and trust which should translate into higher rates of click-throughs and site conversion rates for the direct response ads. Given that goal, what split of the budget between brand and direct response ads is advisable for improving returns?

Flip open your web analytics solution to ponder how you would go about answering this question. What information might you need that is unfortunately typically not going to be found in a web analytics solution?

It is difficult to get data on ad views by unique visitors. As we saw in Chapter 2, "The Web Analyst Tackles Multichannel Metrics Online," the web analytics solution does not normally load up with ad impressions to individual visitors unless there is a click-through to the website.

It is difficult to report on multi-touch ad impressions. Even when data on ad impressions was loaded, reporting on interdependencies between ad types is still not easy. It requires counting how many brand and direct response ad impressions each visitor is exposed to before they visit the advertiser's website to complete a call to action. Any subsequent ad impressions that may follow must not be counted to avoid skewing results. Yet, this type of algorithm is not part of typical web analytics solutions.

The Avenue A | Razorfish study overcame these obstacles by creating a database of ad views directly from ad server data. All unique visitors (i.e., ad server cookies) were grouped based on the combination of brand and direct response creatives to which the visitor had been exposed. Exposures after a conversion event, in this case a purchase, were not included in the count. Conversion events on the client's website were tracked in the usual manner for ad serving, namely through adding an ad server page tag to the conversion pages.

The analysts queried their database repeatedly in order to produce the innovative report in Figure 8.2. The X-axis in this chart lists the number of brand ad exposures by visitor. Direct response ad exposures are plotted in the Y-axis. Therefore each cell represents visitors that were exposed to a particular combination of brand and direct response ads. The value in each cell is an indexed number indicating the probability for completing a conversion while on the advertiser's website. The score of 100 represents a baseline, namely the average conversion rate for all site visitors who were exposed to at least one ad impression but no more than 10.

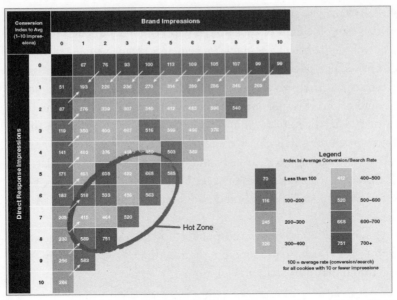

Figure 8.2 Avenue A | Razorfish visualization for frequency of conversions © Avenue A | Razorfish 2007

The most obvious result that jumps out is that conversion rates are highly variable depending on the mix of brand and direct response ads in each cell. For example, for visitors exposed to 10 direct response ads and no brand ads, the index for their probability to convert was a mere 99. Yet when visitors were exposed to a mix of five direct and five brand ads their score jumped up to 588.

For this particular advertiser, there is a "hot zone" with the highest conversion probabilities when visitors were exposed to a combination of one to five brand ad impressions and five to eight direct response ad impressions. But surely, the shape of such hot zones will differ from advertiser to advertiser, and campaign to campaign and the number of impressions of each type that will be served to each prospect can't be controlled. For these reasons, Actionable Analytics advises marketers to perform this type of analysis for their own display advertising campaigns to "identify a hot zone as the target, then monitor and optimize the mix towards that zone over the course of a campaign."

This work by Avenue A | Razorfish can serve multichannel marketers as a template for transferring to other channels too. For example:

- Mix of direct-mail catalogs and direct mail discount coupons
- Mix of e-mail offers and personalized offers on the website
- Mix of direct-mail offers and call-center cross-sales offers

The key requirement is that there needs to be a common identifier for a recipient so that data on exposure to messages across channels can be attributed back to the same individual. While the Avenue A | Razorfish study used ad server data and cookies to accomplish this, the channels mentioned previously would require other criteria. Namely, in this case the promotion and response history for each prospect or customer would be required. Chapter 4, "The Direct Marketer Digs into Multichannel Analytics," and Chapter 7, "Measure 1:1 Interactions Between Online and Offline," shed light on how that link can be established.

How Does Marketing on One Channel Impact Another?

Great, now we know how to measure and tweak the frequency with which prospects are exposed to our ads. We can also evaluate the interdependencies between two different ad types. The trouble is, some of the respondents to our ads will take detours on the way to reaching us—and that can make a terrible mess out of our measurements if we don't account for it.

Say, a customer rents a car using a discount code that arrived in the mail. Measuring that is so easy for campaign management solutions that it is tempting to attribute all credit for the rental to the direct mail. In reality though, TV or Internet commercials that have run in parallel may have enticed the customer to use this company's coupon instead of using that of another company. In fact, it is a recommended strategy to improve brand perception through advertising in order to render direct mail programs more successful.

The same situation is just as relevant in online marketing. It has been studied there extensively when it comes to the interdependence of display advertising and paid search.

The Impact of Display Advertising on Paid Search

When people are exposed to a display ad, some will click through to the website directly. Others will not do so, but instead perform a search at a later point in time. These visitors may then click-through to the site via paid search listings.

On the search engine, they may likely type in queries that include brand or product names. But they may instead also use category keywords, such as "life insurance." Alas when they do so, it has been typical practice in web analytics to attribute all credit for the resulting business to the most recent click-through—i.e., the search engine. The preceding ad views go underappreciated.

Naturally, display advertising professionals have great interest in setting the record straight. It comes as no surprise, therefore, that there are numerous studies on the subject, many of which have been sponsored and conducted by publishers and ad-serving companies.

Starting in 2006, several projects set out with the goal of proving the impact of Internet display advertising on search marketing. Each of the studies took a slightly different route—yet they all arrived at similar conclusions, namely that strong synergies are possible.

Why Has Traditional Web Analytics Ignored the Impact of Ad Views on Search?

It is probably because web analytics solutions can easily measure click-throughs from search engines, whereas measuring view-throughs from display ads is much more involved. There is the difficulty of getting data about ad impressions for each visitor. But as discussed in Chapter 2, there is also the need to use controlled testing to distinguish a mere exposure to an ad from an actual viewing of the ad.

Even if reliable data on ad views by a unique visitor become available, the web analytics solutions today are essentially asking the analyst how they think that credit should be split between touch points. Should both, the most recent click-through from search and the preceding ad view, be credited to the same degree? Or only the more recent search click-through? Or only the preceding ad view? There is nothing "out of box" in web analytics solutions that suggests what split is deserved. That leaves the responsibility with the marketer to research an answer.

Because most web marketers still have many lower hanging fruit to harvest, such as campaign landing page optimization, they have been taking a shortcut by giving all credit to search.

Some of the studies used controlled testing, whereas others relied on uncontrolled. One study by Atlas used data from its digital media platform to compare the behavior of visitors exposed to ads to others who weren't. Another study by Avenue A | Razorfish worked with the ad server to expose test and control display ads to audiences. Yet another study, this time by comScore Networks, relied on their panel to compare the behavior of users exposed only to display ads, only to search ads, or to both. Refer to multichannelmetrics.com/DisplayVsSearch for shortcuts to these individual studies.

There is a simpler even if less perfect approach to testing that is, however, much more practical to adopt for everyone who does not have access to raw data from ad servers or panels. Namely, that idea is to perform controlled testing over time. See the case study by Covario that employed this method next.

CASE STUDY BY COVARIO

Foundations:

☒ Web Analytics, ☐ Response Attribution, ☒ Brand Measurement

Covario is a search-marketing automation solutions company and has been analyzing synergies between display and search ad campaigns on behalf of a large client from the consumer electronics industry. Craig Macdonald, vice president of Product

Management at Covario, explained that the firm had originally been retained for the client's paid search campaigns. Covario was able to improve the performance of those campaigns to a degree that further tuning by adjusting keyword and engine selections would not easily increase the results. So the question arose as to what else could be done to break the ceiling to the next level. Could the flighting of display advertising campaigns in parallel do that trick?

Covario ran controlled tests through sequential period analysis. Search and display ads were run in parallel for a month and then display ads were switched off for the following three-week period. Covario found that click-through rates from search to the site decreased by 36 percent and conversion rates decreased by 33 percent. The firm's interpretation is that display advertising drives a lot of traffic to search that is better qualified.

To maintain the same revenue throughput with search advertising by itself required the advertiser to pay more for higher rankings. They also had to put up with lower conversion rates in that case. In Covario's results, costs per click had to be raised by 16 percent in order to achieve the same revenue throughput when no display advertising was running.

As Macdonald says, "Sequential period testing is not ideal since circumstances can change from period to period. However, it is a very practical method for getting critical answers." Multichannel marketers can use the idea for any other channels too as long as one of the two can be controlled.

Advertisers should run this kind of test for their own campaigns because results can differ. For instance, Atlas highlighted that for some of the advertisers in their study, display ads yielded no lift in conversion rates to search. Atlas attributed that to the possibility that those brands were running extensive offline advertising campaigns so that additional online ads may not have moved the needle any further.

How Does Marketing on Multiple Channels Impact Each Other?

We started with a single ad and then compared two. We began with a single channel and then reviewed the impact of one channel on another. If we continue at this pace, is there any hope of ever understanding a marketing mix that is overlapping TV, radio, print, direct mail, and online advertising? It turns out that several measurement methods have already been developed to accomplish just that. How were these analysts able to make the seemingly impossible possible?

Cross Media Optimization Studies

Back in 2001, the effectiveness of Internet advertising for brand building was still unproven. Most brand advertisers spent no more than 1 or 2 percent of their budgets online. So an extensive measurement project dubbed "Cross Media Optimization Study" was launched to understand whether this low amount of spending was really justified. Also referred to under the acronym XMOS, the project set out to answer the question of how online display advertising fits into a marketing mix otherwise consisting of above the line media, such as TV and magazines.

Advertising campaigns analyzed in the study over the years were from leading brands such as Ford, McDonalds, ING Direct, Unilever, Colgate, and Kleenex. Running these studies was a collaboration including Marketing Evolution, a firm that is specialized in cross media measurement. Other contributors were ad networks and agencies, as well as various industry associations such as the Interactive Advertising Bureau (IAB). The IAB partially sponsored the case studies. To be fair, it needs to be disclosed that the IAB's declared mission is to "help online, Interactive broadcasting, e-mail, wireless and Interactive television media companies increase their revenues."

XMOS combined many of the techniques that we have previously discussed in creative ways to tease out the effectiveness of various media. A research paper by Marketing Evolution available from their website (shortcut via multichannelmetrics .com/ME) details the method that was used and contrasts it to other techniques.

ONLINE AD EXPOSURE AND SURVEY COLLECTION

The base metrics that the study sought to measure were improvements in brand awareness, positive brand image, and intent to take action. Typical for these kinds of metrics, the technique that was used for measurement was surveys. Yet, they were employed in a very clever fashion. Namely, the surveys were taken online with the help of technology from measurement partners such as InsightExpress and Dynamic Logic, both marketing research companies themselves.

Dynamic Logic, for instance, has productized a measurement technique under the trademarks CrossMedia Research and Media Synergy Study. A document detailing these can be downloaded from the Dynamic Logic website (shortcut via multichannelmetrics .com/DL). Namely, whenever a website visitor is exposed to a participating advertiser's creative, Dynamic Logic registers the event and sets an anonymous cookie. Survey participants are simultaneously recruited on the publisher website where these ads are running. When a visitor accepts participation in the online survey, Dynamic Logic can glean from any existing cookie whether the visitor had an opportunity to see the test ads or not. Based on that, the survey response will be filed in the appropriate ad exposure bucket.

So far so good, but how can this method measure the change from before and after exposure to the display ad? Surely, participants are not taking the survey twice? Dynamic Logic employs controlled testing for this purpose. A control group was formed by randomly displaying an alternative control ad from a charity to a percentage of visitors who would normally be exposed to the test ad.

OFFLINE AD EXPOSURE

So far we have described how XMOS measures the online ad's effect on branding. But in order to solve the multi-touch-point puzzle, XMOS also needs to measure simultaneous exposure to ads on traditional media. How is that done, given that survey participants are a random group of anonymous website visitors? For magazine ads, the online survey simply shows thumbnails of magazine covers and asks survey participants to identify which ones they recall browsing recently. For direct mail or e-mail that the participant may have received, the same approach would be conceivable.

For broadcast media on the other hand, XMOS can resort to controlled testing over time periods. Namely, a portion of surveys are taken before the commercials begin airing, others during the campaign, and yet others after the campaigns have ended. This is referred to as *continuous tracking*. Participants can also be asked how often they have been watching programming on various broadcast channels where the ads are running. Depending on how many Gross Rating Points (GRPs) the advertiser has purchased, the researchers can make assumptions as to the percentage of survey participants that have been exposed to the commercials.

BRANDING EFFECTS AND COST EFFICICENCY

Ultimately, XMOS sorts survey participants into a number of buckets depending on the combination of channels on which they had an opportunity to see the advertiser's ads. In this fashion, XMOS can calculate the number of branding effects that each of the channels caused. The exact definition of what branding effects will be counted (e.g., lift in brand awareness) depends on the objectives that the advertisers set for their campaigns.

It would be one thing to compare alternative channels by the volume of branding effects that they are able to achieve, but Rex Briggs from Marketing Evolution makes it clear that the real key metric is the cost efficiency of each channel. Namely, by dividing the marketing cost per channel by the number of branding effects, XMOS arrives at the average cost per branding effect. The channel that has lower average costs should be funded until the incremental effects diminish so much that another channel becomes the most cost efficient investment for additional investment.

SAMPLE RESULTS

A number of case studies detailing XMOS's results for various advertisers can be downloaded either from the Marketing Evolution website or from the IAB site (shortcut via multichannelmetrics.com/IAB). A typical finding was that TV excelled at reaching the largest channel-specific audience quickly. Yet, the relatively high costs of air time and commercial production resulted in a cost per branding effect that exceeded other channels. Both print and especially online display ads proved more cost efficient.

For example, the case study for Unilever's Dove Nutrium Bar campaign found in 2002 that an increase of Unilever's online advertising budget from a 2 percent share of total budget to 15 percent of budget would have yielded Unilever an 8 percent increase in overall branding metrics and a 14 percent increase in purchase intent. Likewise, marketers at McDonalds and Ford also received the recommendation that shifting their budget further from offline media to online media would increase their returns for the same total marketing investment.

Single-Source Research with Arbitron's Portable People Meter

Another clever technology for measuring cross media effects is offered by Arbitron, a media and marketing research firm. Designed for measuring the effectiveness of audible advertising, the Portable People Meter (PPM) is a mobile device carried by volunteering panel members. The PPM is able to detect encoded audio signals that can be embedded in broadcasts by participating radio or TV stations. While the signals are inaudible to human ears, the PPM can record when panelists are listening to encoded advertisements whether through radio, TV, online streaming media, theaters, or really anywhere. Of particular interest may be the PPM's suitability for measuring even time-shifted consumption of media such as the playback of podcast recordings.

Yet, the story does not end with audience measurement. Namely, advertisers can also place inaudible codes in the sound systems at their brick and mortar outlets. The PPM will then be able to record when panelists enter these venues. It can be noted when and how long the volunteers have been there. Thus, both media exposure and action can be captured within the PPM, as a single-source of data for research. Arbitron reported in 2005 that numerous retail and entertainment locations were encoded in an ongoing trial project in Houston, Texas. Venues included stores from Best Buy, Gap, Old Navy, and others.

PPM studies can build on the foundation of everything else that is possible with panels. For instance, behavior can be segmented by demographic criteria, given that panelists are registered volunteers. Store purchases of panelists can also be captured by enlisting the volunteers to use a home scan mechanism. That is precisely what Arbitron and AC Nielsen have been trialing in a research project named Apollo. The study combines PPM with Nielsen's Homescan technology. Arbitron reported that a pilot panel of 10,000 individuals from 5,000 households was participating by 2006. Advertisers that joined the pilot project included Kraft, Pepsi, Pfizer, Procter & Gamble, Wal-Mart and others (see www.project-apollo.com). A compendium with case studies from the pilot project is available for download. It details various types of analyses that are becoming possible similar to what we have discussed here:

Assess Incremental Sales Contribution by Ad Channel Similar to Figure 5.2 for marketing mix modeling, the incremental revenue from delivering an additional ad impression by channel can be predicted.

Assess Incremental Sales Contribution by Ad Frequency Similar to the studies by John Philip Jones and Colin McDonald, one of project Apollo's studies suggests how the method will be able to forecast incremental revenues that can be achieved with additional ad impressions.

From the point of view of illuminating multi-touch conversions, PPM would probably fall under uncontrolled testing, by our definition. Analysts would likely segment panelists' behavior into different buckets depending on the media through which each individual has come into contact with the advertiser's commercials. Then they would compare behavior from bucket to bucket.

Marketing Mix Modeling Across Online and Offline Media

It seems that nothing should be better suited for measuring interdependencies between online and offline channels than marketing mix modeling. After all, cross channel measurement is precisely what the modeling approach is designed to do, even for media that are not addressable.

Sadly, specialists have observed that there are caveats that can come in-between. Namely, when a company's ad spending online is minuscule compared to its spending offline, the effects on total sales volume also remain small as a result. That impact may in fact be so small that it gets drowned out by larger campaigns running in parallel—or the effect may remain smaller than natural variances in daily sales.

The problem becomes even more pronounced if you want to isolate the value of different online marketing channels from each other—i.e., display ads, search, e-mails, affiliates, etc.—let alone try to assess the impact of individual paid keyword ads!

However, other specialists point out that there are ways to overcome some of these limitations. John Nardone from Marketing Management Analytics recommended in his whitepaper "Getting a seat at the big table," available from the MMA website (shortcut via multichannelmetrics.com/MMA), that advertisers can address the challenges if they

Spend enough to be meaningful. "If you only spend one half of a percent of your marketing budget on interactive, don't expect it to register in the model."

Concentrate spending in short periods. By focusing the efforts on the smaller channels to burst periods, their effects will become more pronounced. They also become more noticeable to the model.

Model the medium rather than individual campaigns. Instead of trying to model every ad vehicle online, modeling the channel in its entirety will also make it easier to see cause and effect.

Finally, MMA recommends using data from controlled testing as input into the modeling process for these relatively smaller programs. If spending online is varied at different levels or isolated by market, it increases the likelihood that statistical modeling can pick up the impact.

Rule It!

If it was not obvious before, it surely is so by now that studies into multi-touch conversions cannot be afforded for each and every campaign. Neither the costs nor the time that it would take will make investment sense on every occasion. We need a compromise that will do a pretty good job on a daily basis—at least, a better job than just assigning all credit to the most recent touch point. This will be more like wearing sweat pants rather than a business suit. It is much less handsome and surely not appropriate for grander occasions, but it will fit more comfortably for everyday use.

The following attribution schemes apply to addressable channels. For that reason they are destined for online and direct marketing more than brand advertising. They can be automated to varying degrees. Different solutions go to different lengths with enabling some or any of them.

The biggest functionality gaps today remain around automating rules for touch points from different marketing disciplines—say, the exposure to a TV commercial campaign while simultaneously receiving a direct mail offer and performing an organic search. The problem is that the analytics for each of these areas is still silo'd in different software applications. So far, no centralized solution has visibility into all of them —not out-of-box anyway.

Multi-touch attribution is probably one of the least standardized areas in marketing analytics. For that reason you will encounter the following concepts referred to under many different names in different places:

- Last touch point
- First touch point
- Fractional match
- Multiple match
- Weighted match
- Best match

While these are far from perfect, they are as close as it gets to a scalable "lights out" process for multi-touch measurement.

Most Recent Touch Point

Giving all credit to the most recent touch point is the de facto standard used in online marketing today. Complaints about its shortcomings have been becoming louder lately. Still, most web analytics solutions default to this scheme. The analytics solutions that are used do not always facilitate alternatives.

Direct marketers often resort to this method even though they tend to see its limitations more clearly and have access to better concepts. But, especially if it was your team that was responsible for sending out the last campaign, it can be irresistible to take all the credit for business that ensues! In other cases, marketers may be skeptical of their ability to estimate the impact of multiple touch points correctly. So, it may seem like a cost efficient compromise to give all credit to the last touch point.

First Touch Point

Imagine you are a marketer for an airplane manufacturer. A sales cycle may take two years to close. In the last week before closing a new sale, a prospective buyer might receive a weekly follow up e-mail. Should that e-mail be credited with the sale because it was the most recent one? That would be ridiculous, would it not?

For that reason, popular in B2B (business to business) more than B2C (business to consumer) companies, an alternative scheme is to give all credit to the original touch point that first brought a lead in. As a symptom, most sales force automation implementations contain a data field that denotes the marketing source that should be credited with acquiring a B2B prospect.

Fractional Match

Now, remember when you last bought airplane tickets. Maybe you have traveled hundreds of times over the years. Should the credit for your most recent trip still go to whichever marketing touch point first introduced you to the airline that you used? That would be silly too, wouldn't it?

Indeed, attributing business to the first touch point is not typical in B2C because recent customer campaigns and ads impact repeat business far more directly. So an alternative is to split credit between the most recent number of touch points that have been recorded for a customer—for example, a search, an e-mail, and a direct mail catalog. Each of the latter may get credit for a third of the sale if business is shared equally.

The concept of fractional match can make sense with a multi-wave campaign. A sequence of touches may be designed to promote awareness of an offer. Maybe a teaser SMS says "Check your mail for an exciting program just for you," and then the actual offer is sent as multiple follow-ups in case there is no initial response. Fractional match can also make sense when there are competing offers that occur relatively close (in a temporal sense) to a response. Especially, if there is no source code that is captured during the purchase, via a coupon for instance.

Fractional match can be automated within direct marketing channels with the help of campaign management systems. For online marketing channels, the method can be automated with some web analytics solutions. Best of all, by connecting the web analytics solution into the campaign management system, fractional match can be automated across online and offline touch points.

Multiple Match

One extreme method of fractional match is to assign full credit to all touch points leading up to a sale. Obviously, if you summed results across all campaigns, you would then arrive at a nonsense number. The idea is simply meant for a "What If" analysis with the purpose of identifying the campaigns that may have influenced the greatest amount of buyers.

Weighted Match

As an alternative to sharing credit evenly among the most recent touch points, it would be desirable to split weight in more refined ways. The following concepts are desirable. Unfortunately, few of these are supported by marketing software applications out of box for the moment.

More Recent Touch Points Get More Credit

Credit could be shared as 60 percent, 30 percent, 10 percent, or similar, between the most recent three touch points. The exact percentages that you would like to assign to each touch point could be derived from the results of deeper probes into multi-touch conversions that you conduct.

"Rock, Paper, Scissors" Schemes

After studying historical campaigns in depth, a marketer may find that a high-gloss direct mail catalog has typically triggered more activity for their company than a coupon or an e-mail. So, business rules could be set to always assign catalogs more weight than coupons or e-mails. Similarly, a branded search term triggering a website visit could always be given less credit than a category search term.

Custom Weights

Jim Lenskold points out the greatest shortcoming of all fractional match schemes in his article, "Measuring the Impact of Multi-Touch Marketing," published on the CMO Council website (shortcut via multichannelmetrics.com/CMOCouncil). Namely, the greater the reach of a campaign, the more credit it will ultimately receive even if the campaign had no real influence in closing business. Say, an e-mail that is blasted to everyone in the customer file would show up as a huge success because it correlates with all purchases that coincide in time. This would still be the case even if nobody even opened this e-mail.

Therefore, in my opinion, an attribution scheme is desirable where marketers can adjust the weights that should be assigned to specific campaigns within the mix. For example, if single touch-point analysis showed that by itself a particular e-mail had little impact, then the e-mail could be weighted down manually. As a mechanism, it would be conceivable that marketers will assign stars to campaigns, say between 1 and 10. Marketing software could then adjust how credit for each purchase event is split between multiple touch points relative to the number of stars that were aligned around each event.

Even more sophisticated would be a scheme where credit is adjusted automatically based on the actual engagement that can be measured. For example, an e-mail could receive relatively more weight for those recipients who clicked through and engaged with relevant content on the website for a lengthy duration of time. At the same time, the e-mail could receive a lower weight for others who also clicked through but then bounced.

Online, the necessary click data for measuring this engagement would be readily available to web analytics solutions. Offline, on the other hand, the same would not be true. There is no way of telling how long each recipient has spent reading over a catalog at home. At best, a panel can be used to get an average assessment.

Best Match

Think of all the marketing messages that you receive from financial institutions. One month you may receive not only balance transfer checks, but also an offer for a home equity line of credit, and a message promoting an investment account. Imagine that you now proceed to open that investment account. Should the balance transfer checks and home equity offers also receive partial credit just because they were among the last few touch points?

Sometimes, it may just be better to identify the best matching campaign and give it all the credit. This can be automated today in campaign management solutions based on information surrounding transactions. In this example, the product that was purchased reveals which preceding offer is the best match. In other cases when a coupon number has been used, the best match may be the direct match based on the coupon's source code.

Remember though that this is called *best* match, not *perfect* match. It is understood that other offers have played some role in keeping the brand on the mind of the buyer. But the best match method compromises on neglecting those effects.

Splitting Credit

As can be seen, direct response marketers have a number of concepts for splitting credit between touch points in a rule-based manner. Granted, not all of these concepts are offered by software solutions, off the shelf.

Something else that is not automated today are mechanisms for giving partial credit to brand advertising campaigns that may run in parallel to direct response marketing. To the least, the systems could be enhanced to let marketers provide data on the GRPs invested into geographic region, for various product lines, in each time period. Then the purchase events occurring from those geographic regions could automatically share part of the credit with those advertisement campaigns.

The biggest bottleneck today, however, may not be in the ability to configure more rules, but rather to make marketers more comfortable with using the existing ones. After all, the rules leave the burden on the marketer to determine what split is deserved. Therefore, in practice today response attribution for larger campaigns is often still completed manually. In those cases, it may take weeks or months and will require someone who knows their marketing campaigns just as well as the available data.

Conclusions

If you only took away a single recommendation from this chapter, it should be that the complexity of multi-touch attribution should not keep you from investing in multi-channel analytics. Even if you neglected the multi-touch problem, the analytics are still imperative for improving cross-channel conversion paths to reduce drop-offs of prospects.

For your most significant marketing investments, however, do not ignore the multi-touch reality. Do invest in deeper studies to get a feeling for their true impact on your business. You also want to understand how to create synergy effects by combining different campaigns. A number of specialized marketing agencies are available to assist by applying the methods that they have developed across online and offline channels.

Such studies take time, however, and typically cost hundreds of thousands of dollars. Therefore, take a more pragmatic approach to multi-touch-point analytics for the rest of your campaigns that are not of a sufficient size to justify such investment. For this purpose, use rule-based multi-touch attribution schemes provided by your online and direct marketing analytics applications. These rules still require you to tell the marketing applications how credit should be split. Therefore, you should draw on the results of the deeper studies to make your selections.

Multichannel Marketing Methods

III

All hands on deck now! Come together, marketers from online and offline, direct and brand disciplines, the visionaries, the business minded, and the technologists. All report to the CMO at once! No more silos, no more solo escapades, no more pointing fingers are permitted. Let's put the Team back in Marketing Team and bring together what belongs together. Let's see how to conduct integrated marketing across the disciplines with the help of the metrics and measurement techniques that we have developed.

Attract and Acquire

For the purposes of raising awareness and acquiring new customers, integrated marketing goes to work at three distinct levels. At the most basic level, we are all ears and eyes so we can sense changes in demand and organize our firm to respond. Next, we seek to measure marketing results on all channels and across all channels, to make methodic decisions for allocating our advertising spending. Finally, we seek to integrate our communications with individuals during acquisition campaigns across channels so that buyers will perceive us more like a chorus than a karaoke shop.

9

Chapter Contents

Sense Demand

Being customer-centric is not just about customer communications and service. It is also about being attentive to demand and providing the products, features, and services that customers are seeking. In other words, a more "pull"-oriented approach to business is required in addition to the standard, inevitable "push" of "what's on the truck."

Marketers can observe inquiries on all channels to see what customers are looking for—i.e., to sense the directions into which the market wishes to pull the company. This can be done by taking notice of feedback from call centers, customer surveys, e-mails, and employees. But if there is one channel that is ideally suited for the purpose, it is the web channel. Marketers can sit back and derive the market's preferences from the choices that visitors are making on the website. Jim Sterne calls this the "insight machine into the hearts and minds of the market."

Case Study: 2nd Byte Provides Demand Intelligence for Automobiles

Automobile companies might have been the first to recognize the value of the online channel for illuminating market preferences. For instance, in order to understand which combinations of accessories are popular together, they have been observing how their prospects interact with online car accessory configurators. If visitors to the car manufacturer's website from the United Kingdom (U.K.) keep flocking to a green exterior with light colored leather interior, and a sunroof, then maybe this is the image that should also be used in the brochure. An accessory package could be offered that combines these features, and there may be room to charge a premium price. If visitors from France are seen to prefer a different combination, then a different package can be crafted for that market.

2nd Byte out of the U.K. has taken demand intelligence a great leap forward. They are a wholly owned subsidiary of the Trader Media Group, which publishes over 70 weekly titles including *Auto Trader*. The firm provides products and services to the automotive used car industry to help consumers locate their perfect used vehicle. Its clients include Jaguar, Land Rover, and Hyundai among many others.

2nd Byte offers their clients a wide variety of services one of which is a "Used Vehicle Locator." Through the dealerships' own branded websites, their customers are able to search for their perfect vehicle by criteria including model, color, engine size, and mileage. Visitors to the website register their interest for vehicles in an online form or over the phone.

2nd Byte was very forward thinking in its approach to web analytics, moving away from tallying up visits and page views. Instead, they packaged the data in a way that was easy to digest and attractive for its clients, such as Land Rover.

As 2nd Byte's Cameron-Heslop explained in an interview with SCL Analytics: "Being able to tell a dealer that black Ford Focuses are in great demand in, for example, Birmingham may help them decide to pay a higher price for a used vehicle in that area, as they know they will be able to sell it quickly and with a healthy profit in their dealership." As a result, 2nd Byte clients can make more informed decisions as to the relevant inventory of cars to stock in each dealership.

Case Study: AIRMILES Senses Travel Trends and Responds Swiftly

The travel industry holds a surprising amount of pitfalls for the uninitiated. As an example, inventory is not only seasonal, but also just as perishable as strawberries on the shelves of a grocer. A seat on a flight cannot be sold a day later than its "expiration date." It's no wonder that marketers in the travel industry need to be very nimble.

With over 20 years in the market, AIRMILES Travel Promotions Ltd. is the U.K.'s most popular travel loyalty scheme. Members can collect points on anything from groceries and petrol to Christmas presents. The more miles they collect, the more they can spend on worldwide travel options that AIRMILES offers. Deals range from flights to hotels, cruises, and many specialist vacation types.

Jukka Kamarainen, who is a technology architect at AIRMILES, explains how the web channel does its part to help the company meet the challenge of matching supply and demand. As you might imagine, the most frequent way in which members search and book travel is through the AIRMILES website at airmiles.co.uk. But in addition to this key role for AIRMILES' operations, the website also provides demand intelligence. Namely, web analytics can, of course, be instrumented to capture the search options that are popular. Reports can detail the desired travel dates, origins, and destinations. This behavior can be observed and aggregated in a completely anonymous fashion without invading any client's privacy.

Marketers obtain the equivalent of early detection radar for upcoming spikes in travel trends. They can simply compare the most recent search data to the data from the day before, the last week, the last year, etc. Jukka Kamarainen's colleagues on the purchasing side who are responsible for arranging travel options from travel providers can then scout the market for attractive deals. Once arranged, deals are promoted back to AIRMILES clients via the website. What an ingenious way of turning a travel business into an agile market for buying and selling vacations!

The examples provided by AIRMILES and 2nd Byte convey beautifully the benefits of establishing a central nervous system for business. The market's preferences can be observed through all senses of the business and then translated into action through all applicable channels.

Allocate Advertising Dollars

Monday morning, eight o'clock, you are the Chief Marketing Officer (CMO) sitting in the boardroom with all your marketing managers from the various disciplines. Each of your staff is equipped with the historical results from past campaigns. Based on these results, the marketing managers have also formulated an expectation on campaign candidates that have been lined up for the coming year. The goal of the meeting is to distribute the marketing budget between the various campaign candidates so that returns for the company will be maximized, as much as possible. That is when the confusion begins:

Online Marketers

- The online marketing guys are equipped with metrics for Costs per Acquisition, Average Order Values, Returns, and ROI.

- However, they also brought with them a proposal for a viral marketing campaign that has never been tried at this company so that the results forecast is uncertain and relatively low.

Direct Marketers

- The direct marketers brought the same metrics as the online marketers because they have been coordinating with each other throughout the past year. How commendable!

- Yet, the direct marketers also brought designs for completely changed promotional offers for the company's direct mail program. This is in response to competition that also changed theirs recently.

Brand Marketers

- The brand marketers brought their marketing mix models that explain how much of the past year's sales were attributable to their efforts on various channels. Because they too have coordinated with their direct and online colleagues, they have already reached agreement how historical results should be split between the disciplines so that credit will not be double counted. (Your staff is as skilled as it is cooperative!)

- Finally, since brand marketers' efforts are not completely described by same-year sales results, they also brought the results of their brand equity surveys.

Over to you now, Mr. or Ms. CMO, go make a decision! After reviewing the data from each of your marketing managers you may encounter some of the following questions:

- Quite likely, your TV commercial campaigns are showing relatively lower ROI but a larger volume of total returns compared to your online keyword advertising. Which should you maximize, ROI or total returns or both? (See Table 9.1.)

▶ **Table 9.1** Tradeoff Between ROI and Returns

	ROI	Total Returns
TV Commercials	Low	High
Paid Keywords Campaigns	High	Lower

- What should you do with the online marketers' viral marketing campaign? Should it be eliminated given that it is predicted to result in lower ROI than other campaign candidates?

- What should you make of the fact that the direct marketer's offers and creative will be completely different from previous years?

- How should you incorporate the nonfinancial brand equity metrics into your decision-making process?

  Let's review answers to these questions.

Maximize Total Returns, Not ROI!

Even though we speak of "maximizing ROI" colloquially, what we really mean by that is the maximization of returns—i.e., gross margin minus marketing investments. In his book *Marketing and the Bottom Line,* Tim Ambler describes it as the maximization of "payback."

Think of it: maximizing ROI (i.e., the percent metric defined as returns divided by marketing investments) would be easy. Just cut almost all marketing and instead go hang out in the golf club all year long. You will probably meet somebody eventually who will buy your product. As a result, your percent ROI would be very high. But your sales and returns would be just that one customer. Clearly, that is not what we mean to do.

Yet, ROI must have something to do with maximizing returns. After all it describes the effectiveness of a dollar invested into marketing efforts. Where is the catch? The idea is to maximize total returns by way of rank ordering marketing campaign candidates by ROI potential. So, as a general concept:

1. You would start by funding the campaign that promises the highest ROI.

2. The more you increase investments into this campaign, however, the more likely you will reach a point where further investments only yield diminishing marginal returns. How quickly you reach that point will depend on the details of each campaign.

3. One way or other, at some point the marginal ROI of increasing investments into a campaign further would become lower than funding the next best campaign. So instead you should fund that other campaign and continue with the same algorithm.

How long would you continue down this conceptual algorithm? As explained in Chapter 4, "The Direct Marketer Digs into Multichannel Analytics," under the Marketing Allowable metric, use the concept of an ROI threshold. Also known as the "hurdle rate," this is the minimum ROI that a campaign needs to hit in order for it to be worthwhile compared to its opportunity costs. Jim Lenskold in his book *Marketing*

ROI describes that you would continue funding the list of campaign candidates until you reach a point where there is no more candidate left that is forecasted to achieve at least the ROI threshold.

In the case of our example, you would start by funding the online channel and then at some point switch to funding the TV commercials. But how can you know in advance when the ROI from the online advertisements will cross below that of TV? Ideally, your marketing mix models will tell you. But as described in the previous chapter, it is not always easy for marketing mix models to compare online and offline channels. So most likely, you will reach an opinion by experimenting with different levels of funding in each channel over the years.

Weigh Additional Factors

Is maximizing short-term returns the whole story to marketing spending allocation? No, it is not, as all the authors mentioned before will also emphasize. There are further considerations and judgment calls that need to be made besides returns. Some examples follow.

Set Aside Funds for Experimentation

The algorithm for funding campaigns applies only to known candidates. But there is an infinite space of marketing ideas that you have not tried yet. Applying the Champion Challenger concept from direct marketing, you want to make sure that part of the marketing budget is reserved for experimenting with new ideas even if their first year ROI is low. It may take multiple tries before you get it right and craft a high ROI design.

In the boardroom example, we probably should fund the viral campaign, at least enough to try the concept. If the trial results are promising, the funding can be increased in the next round.

Consider Strategic Goals

There often are strategic goals that will override short-term optimization of returns. Your company may be looking to enter new markets, counter new competitors, establish new differentiators, or launch new products. In these cases, you may decide to overinvest in related campaigns regardless of short-term returns. Deciding how much budget to set aside for strategic investments is difficult. The answer requires balancing short-term cash flow needs with the investment into long-term competitive advantage.

Use Your Judgment

How much value should be ascribed to nonfinancial brand equity effects achieved by brand advertising? That remains a judgment call that every company and marketer will have to make for themselves. Likely you will form an opinion over the years through trial and error.

Play It Safe

Given the changes planned for the direct marketing program in our example, a safe strategy could be to prepare for the possibility that the new program may prove less effective than the previous one. In addition, the competition is also changing their messaging. So you may want to reserve extra funds that can be committed during the year if you need to compensate for weaker results.

There may be more methodic ways to approach these latter judgment calls. But in the end, it is always going to be tough to answer questions such as: "Should I spend $10 million on this ad campaign?" According to Kevin Lane Keller in his interview with MarketingNPV available from their website (shortcut via multichannelmetrics .com/KLK), "The answer is always 'maybe,' because the payback ultimately depends a great deal on a number of different factors." Yet, the better you get with multichannel metrics, the more accurately you can learn from historical outcomes to refine your decisions over time."

Marketing Optimization: Human versus Machine

Is marketing optimization a matter of configuring a piece of software and letting it run by itself? No, the role of marketing optimization software is like the autopilot within a jet airplane. Nobody would step on a jet airplane that was flown entirely by the autopilot during takeoff and landing. At the same time, nobody would step on an airliner that was not computerized to at least some degree. Pilots and autopilots work together each contributing what they do best.

Likewise, in search advertising, for example, bid management software solutions automate bidding on paid keywords. But best practice is to have an experienced search marketer oversee the work of the software. The reasons for this are some of the same factors explained in the previous section.

Similarly, marketing-mix modeling predicts optimal allocation of brand marketing investments and contact optimization predicts optimal direct marketing contact plans. In both cases, experienced marketers look over the results and pair them up using their own judgment.

Integrate Multichannel Acquisition Campaigns

What would a fully integrated, multichannel acquisition campaign look like? What would the "perfect storm" of acquisition campaigning entail? Imagine that you are responsible for growing business at an insurance company called MultiSure Co. A typical insurance company, this multichannel business includes online, call center, and agency outlets. You have been hired to take its marketing strategy to the next level.

After much deliberation, you are in the boardroom to present your campaign plan for the coming year. In attendance with you are colleagues from brand, direct, and online marketing disciplines. They already know everything that you are going to present to management though. After all, as multichannel-minded marketers, you have been working out the plan of attack jointly.

Act 1: The Advertising Campaign

To raise awareness, you are going to run ads on TV, radio, newspapers, magazines, online, and outdoors. You are splitting the budget between these channels as recommended by your marketing mix model. In lieu of a frequency strategy, you are stretching the campaign budget to schedule ads over the course of the entire year. As discussed in the last chapter, this is because you wish to reach as many people as possible at a moment when they happen to be thinking about their need for an insurance policy.

However, instead of creating traditional commercials you will try a viral campaign. The theme of the ads is going to be personal accounts of people who thought they would not need insurance but somehow ended up signing a policy anyway. Then disaster struck and worse came to worse. Insurance could not undo all losses, but what would these folks have done had they not been insured with MultiSure?

At the end of all these ads, there will be a consistent call to action for a direct response—namely, to go to the microsite WorseCameToWorse.com, where people can forward the story in the ad to a friend or submit their own story for a chance to appear in a commercial.

Act 2: Initial Response

Many prospects may enter the URL of the microsite directly. Others may not remember the URL correctly and may instead perform a search for it. Therefore, the online marketing team is going to perform search engine optimization to make sure the site ranks highly for relevant keywords. They will employ paid keyword advertising for keywords for which they cannot achieve high organic rankings.

When visitors eventually reach the microsite WorseCameToWorse.com, they will be instantly redirected to MultiSureCO.com/WorseCameToWorse. As explained in Chapter 2, "The Web Analyst Tackles Multichannel Metrics Online," this is done so that the same first party cookie that is used throughout MultiSureCo.com will apply to microsite visitors too.

Act 3: Engagement and Viral Referrals

Starting with the landing page of the website, visitors' experiences will be consistent with the tone and theme of the broadcast commercials. In fact, the same actor who narrates the personal accounts in the ad campaign will also be featured on the microsite. The actor will address visitors directly, similar to the PURL example at dme-finehomes.com that we discussed in Chapter 7, "Measure 1:1 Interactions Between Online and Offline."

The dialog will provide visitors with options. Do they want to replay one of the commercials and forward it to a friend? Do they want to register and submit their own story? Finally, would they like to find out more about MultiSure's insurance products and get an instant quote by e-mail?

Especially in the latter case, our actor will walk visitors through an interactive questionnaire where they explore the types of insurance in which they are interested. For example, for life insurance the dialog will eventually determine the prospect's age, health history, and desired coverage details.

Act 4: Lead Conversion

At the end of the interview, the narrator will ask the prospect to enter her e-mail address to receive the resulting quote. As an alternative, the actor will display a toll-free phone number along with a reservation code. With the help of click-to-call technology, the number can also be automatically dialed with a click of a mouse. Friendly phone consultants can then instantly retrieve the details of the online dialog via that reservation code to address remaining questions. While the consultants have the prospect on the phone, they can ask for additional contact information to complete the data in the CRM system.

At this point, the lead may receive their own PURL, such as akin.arikan.MultiSureCO .com, which will provide a home for their relationship with the insurance company going forward. We now have a multichannel customer profile established for the prospect. Their online registration is synchronized with their record in the CRM system. Browsing behavior can be retrieved via web analytics thanks to the cookie on the website. This interaction history can then be linked with prospect's records in the CRM system if the company's privacy policy permits doing so and only for those prospects who have not opted out from measurement. The multichannel customer profiles will be used for behavioral targeting during the lead nurturing phase.

Act 5: Lead Nurturing

As the dialog with prospects deepens, they will be offered additional information through e-mail, newsletters, and direct mail. These materials will all be linked automatically to each prospect's PURL so that the prospect can quickly reference them there.

Other hints and links may be added to the PURL based on behavioral targeting. The particular content will depend on prospects' behavior on the MultiSure website as well as their call center interactions. The behavioral targeting solution may serve up cross-sell and up-sell promotions on the website that the company thinks may interest the leads. When prospects call in with a question, for example, about term versus whole life insurance, the phone consultant may add a link to a related FAQ to these prospect's PURLs.

Act 6: The Finale

Whenever buyers are ready, they can complete an application online by going to their PURL, activating the quote of their choice, and executing payment. Of course, they can do the same by phone or through their agent.

Insurance applications often require a sequence of additional events before they become effective. For instance, with life insurance there will be medical exams to complete and many more documents to receive by mail, sign, and return. The PURL can track the degree of completion of the entire process, as in "You have completed steps 1 through 3 of 5. Step 4 is to do XYZ within the next week please." Should the client fall behind schedule, helpful reminders can be automated to avoid attrition. Whether the reminders are sent through SMS, e-mail, direct mail, or phone service will depend on the business value and preferences of the client.

Measurement

Just about every step within this acquisition campaign lends itself to measurement. Doing so enables you to experiment and improve the conversion rates from step to step within the conversion process over the course of time.

Brand Reputation and Equity

Using the methods described in Chapter 5, "The Brand Marketer's Take on Multichannel Analytics," MultiSure will measure the baseline of brand equity and media coverage before beginning the ad campaign. The baseline will then be compared to the results during and after the ad campaign.

Advertising Success

When visitors arrive at the microsite, you know that they are there because of the ads. With some controlled testing as described in Chapter 6, "Measure Lift Between Online and Offline," you can figure out which ad channels are most effective in getting prospects to visit the microsite. With the cross-media optimization method described in Chapter 8, you can even investigate how far each of the ad channels contribute to raising brand equity.

Viral Referrals

When prospects forward a story to a friend via the microsite, the e-mail will contain a hyperlink that is instrumented with tracking codes. As discussed in Chapter 2, this will help you know which visitors are arriving on the microsite due to a viral referral. Using the methods for tracking delayed conversions, you can then measure how much business results from these viral referrals over time.

Lead Nurturing and Conversion

For measuring the impact of e-mails, direct mails, and call center calls that are extended to leads, we can use the methods for response attribution via matchback as proposed in Chapter 4.

We can tie online and offline interactions of individual clients back together with the help of the methods explained in Chapter 7. Specifically, the fact that the prospects are registered online so that they can securely access the sensitive data available in their PURL helps us follow the dialog across online and offline.

Lead to Sale Conversion

Throughout the sequence of events leading toward a completed insurance policy purchase, every action is tied back to the individual client's account. The status is displayed online within the PURL. This is reminiscent of a CRM or SFA system in reverse. Instead of the sales personnel, the prospect can follow along where things are standing with the buying process. Hence, you can measure status and process completion rates from this data. More about that will follow in the next chapter, where we will discuss the "multi-channel funnel report."

ROI Analysis

Ultimately, credit for resulting business from this acquisition campaign would probably be split evenly between all the touch points involved in attracting and acquiring each customer.

Is the integrated multichannel acquisition campaign worthwhile compared to the traditional siloed approach? The case studies that we have discussed throughout the book surely suggest so. Yet there is no other way to tell but to try and compare overall ROI for both approaches.

Engage and Convert

Marketers employ a number of staple practices for engaging prospects into sales cycles and driving as many to bear fruit as possible. One of these practices is funnel reporting. It is revered for its help with improving conversion processes. Another staple is remarketing that helps reengage lost prospects for another shot at the goal. Cross-sales offers on the other hand are a pitch for increasing customer values. Yet, most businesses use these old staples as if we still lived in a single-channel world. It is time to upgrade them to today's multichannel reality.

10

Chapter Contents
Funnel Reporting
Remarketing
Cross-Sales Offers

Funnel Reporting

Sales managers of all kinds swear by their funnel reports and have done so for a very long time. Sales funnels are used to measure the progression of burgeoning sales opportunities into engaged sales cycles and eventually closed business. Beyond measurement, sales organizations also use funnels to forecast expected revenues. More importantly, they look to them for identifying holes in the sales process suggesting specific areas for improvement to practices.

However, the funnel report has really met its true community of fans in web analysts. Here, it is the queen of all web analytics reports. Thanks to the superior measurability of the medium, web analytics funnel reports can pinpoint the step-by-step progression of website visitors through a conversion process up to the point where they drop off.

Jargon Alert: Funnels

What sales managers know as the *sales funnel,* online marketers may call scenario, drop-off, fall-out, or funnel reporting.

Historically, stages in the web analytics funnel have been defined as specific web pages or groups thereof. But steps can also represent events such as, "Visitor stayed at least 5 minutes on the website," as seen in Figure 10.1. Similar to sales funnels, some web analytics funnel reports can measure process completion over the course of the sales cycle (i.e., across multiple subsequent visits).

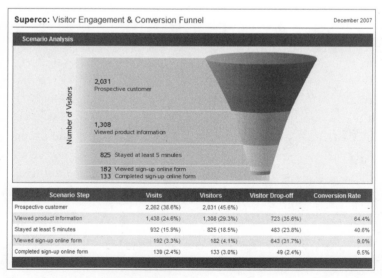

Superco: Visitor Engagement & Conversion Funnel — December 2007

Scenario Analysis

Number of Visitors

- 2,031 Prospective customer
- 1,308 Viewed product information
- 825 Stayed at least 5 minutes
- 182 Viewed sign-up online form
- 133 Completed sign-up online form

Scenario Step	Visits	Visitors	Visitor Drop-off	Conversion Rate
Prospective customer	2,262 (38.6%)	2,031 (45.6%)	-	-
Viewed product information	1,438 (24.6%)	1,308 (29.3%)	723 (35.6%)	64.4%
Stayed at least 5 minutes	932 (15.9%)	825 (18.5%)	483 (23.8%)	40.6%
Viewed sign-up online form	192 (3.3%)	182 (4.1%)	643 (31.7%)	9.0%
Completed sign-up online form	139 (2.4%)	133 (3.0%)	49 (2.4%)	6.5%

Figure 10.1 A sample web analytics funnel report.

Online marketers use funnel reports to manage and optimize website processes. For example, Jim Sterne, who was quoted earlier, explains that a funnel shaped similar to the form of a martini glass suggests that a website is able to attract visitors but has its bottleneck in engaging those visitors. Likewise, a funnel shaped more like a champagne glass suggests that the bottleneck may be in attracting visitors to the website in the first place. The marketer can address the bottleneck and continue measuring to verify whether the shape of the funnel has improved.

Alas, in a multichannel world, neither sales funnels nor web analytics funnels capture the cross-channel behavior of customers within the buying cycle. That is a serious measurement gap for online marketers, given that the majority of sales following online research are actually closing offline, as discussed in Chapter 1, "With Great Opportunity Come Great Challenges." It is also a serious measurement gap for offline marketers because a significant portion of the response to brand and direct marketing occurs online via the website.

There really is a need for multichannel funnel reports that extend the benefits of this management tool to today's cross-channel world. Using the measurement techniques that we have honed, especially in Chapter 6, "Measure Lift Between Online and Offline," and Chapter 7, "Measure 1:1 Interactions Between Online and Offline," we can now put that kind of report together.

Define the Multichannel Funnel Report

Your first step in defining a funnel is to name the process you are looking to measure, manage, and improve. For example, this could be our integrated multichannel acquisition campaign from the previous chapter. For that process, now identify the critical conversion steps along the conversion path. These are probably the stages that you will want to measure within your multichannel funnel report. In our acquisition campaign example, these steps would likely be the six acts ranging from the advertising campaign all the way to the sales conversion.

In defining the funnel report, online marketers need to loosen their definition of a funnel a little bit and think more of a sales funnel. In web analytics, funnel reports typically measure progression from one defined step to the next. Yet, in a multichannel world it is very difficult to predict in which order customers decide to interact through which channel. For multichannel funnels to be meaningful, they need to be broad enough to allow for this ambiguity of step orders. In our example, we expect most prospects who watch our TV commercials to flock to the microsite before they call the toll free phone number. But a number of prospects will reverse this order, and that should not cause them to drop out of our funnel report.

Therefore, instead of defining steps too narrowly (e.g., Visited microsite), it will be better to define them broadly such that they can be fulfilled via any channel (e.g., Engagement). What specifically qualifies as engagement can then be defined differently for each channel. For example, all prospects calling the phone center and inquiring about a particular offering may qualify as being engaged. Yet, on the website, engagement may be defined to mean the subset of visitors who spend at least a minimum amount of minutes browsing relevant content.

Create the Funnel Report

The funnel process in our example crosses brand, direct, and online marketing activities. So that you can create this report, you will need to bring together the numbers from the various related systems into a single location. That location may be a marketing data mart in conjunction with a marketing dashboard or business intelligence solution, such as those offered by Business Objects (acquired by SAP), Cognos (acquired by IBM), MicroStrategy, Oracle, or Unica—or you may fall back on Microsoft Excel.

In order to make the funnel stages comparable to each other, we need to use the same metric in each stage despite the fact that different channels are involved. The metric that suggests itself is the number of unique people who have reached each stage. Figure 10.2 shows a sample funnel report based on this metric. In this chart, the number of unique prospects within each funnel stage is further broken out by the channels through which their interaction has been measured.

The key question is where to find the necessary data from each channel for filling this funnel with life. Let's see the answers for the multichannel acquisition campaign from the previous chapter.

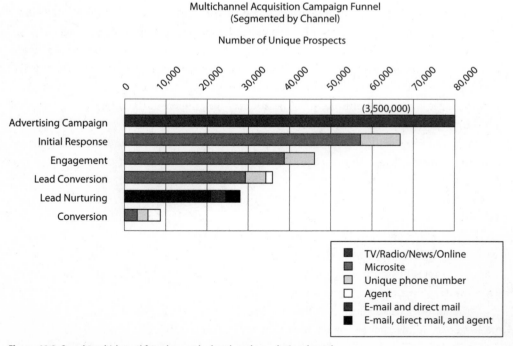

Figure 10.2 Sample multichannel funnel report, broken down by marketing channel

Act 1: Advertising Campaign

For the ads on TV, radio, newspapers, magazines, and outdoors, we can obtain publishers' estimates on reach—i.e., the unduplicated number of individuals who have been exposed to ads. For online ads we can also obtain the reach metric—i.e., the number of unique visitors who were exposed to an ad. We will get this number from the ad-serving platform.

The data in this step needs to be taken with a grain of salt though. The offline advertising data may be more readily available at a household level rather than at the individual level. On the other hand, the online unique visitor numbers are inferred to be unique people but two visitors are sometimes the same person if this person has been using two computers each of which will have a different cookie. Finally, there is no easy way to de-duplicate the audience data from different advertising channels—i.e., to know how many people viewed both the TV commercial and the newspaper ads. You can guesstimate overlap, or if you really want to know, you can resort to the panel-based audience measurement methods that we discussed in Chapter 8, "Measure Multi-Touch Conversions."

Act 2: Initial Response

If the initial response occurs as planned via the microsite WorseCameToWorse.com, we can simply count the unique visitors to this site by way of their cookies. However, the initial response may also occur by phone. If we have listed a unique toll free number in the ad campaign, then reports on the number of calls will be available from the phone line provider.

Yet, some responses will also come in through the company's regular channels, such as through a conversation with an insurance agent. In the latter case, the conversation might not get logged as a campaign response if there is no customer record in the CRM (Customer Relationship Management) system yet. Therefore, these prospects will likely be missing from our funnel report.

Act 3: Engagement and Viral Referrals

Web analytics for the microsite can report the number of visitors that we want to define as being engaged with the content. We may choose to define engaged visitors as those who have replayed commercials and referred friends to the site. We will also include those who have begun exploring the company's products and have gone at least part way down the interactive dialog with the actor on the microsite.

Likewise, call center and insurance agents can have engaged conversations that go beyond mere inquiries. However, these activities may or may not get logged in the CRM system if no lead record is yet created.

Act 4: Lead Conversion

Regardless of whether sales leads register online, via phone, or with insurance agents, all leads should flow into the CRM or SFA (Sales Force Automation) system eventually. Whether the leads are entered programmatically or manually, we need to ensure that they are flagged with our acquisition campaign as the lead source. That is easy for leads coming through the microsite or unique phone number. But the leads coming in from direct sales personnel may not always carry the desired flags.

Act 5: Lead Nurturing

From here on, it is business as usual for direct marketers. Leads can be prioritized for different kinds of nurturing treatments based on available information. For example, by bringing web analytics data into the CRM or SFA system along with online registrations, we can draw on a metric for the degree to which each prospect was engaged with content about the products online. Those that were more engaged are likely better leads and can be scored with the highest priority for follow up by an agent. Others can be enrolled in a series of informative e-mail or direct mail communications until they return to the website and exhibit behavior suggesting that they are ripe for a call too.

The response to live calls and e-mail communications can be assessed with the response attribution technique discussed in Chapter 4, "Direct Marketer Digs into Multichannel Analytics." For the purpose of our funnel, all we need is a count of the number of people who are within the lead nurturing state but have not yet signed a policy.

Act 6: The Finale

Finally, the CRM or SFA system should also contain the number of resulting opportunities that have been closed. This is the number that we need for the last stage of the funnel. Hopefully, the CRM system will include the channel through which the transactions came.

Use the Funnel for Multichannel Process Improvement

Visualize how you would put a multichannel funnel report into action for improving conversion rates. The funnel will pinpoint the breakdowns in the conversion process that cause the largest number of prospects to drop out. Study especially the transition points within the funnel where the dialog is switching from one channel to another (for example, before and after the lead nurturing phase in Figure 10.2). Can the fall out be reduced here by designing more consistent experiences across the channels or providing better incentives? Only experimentation and further measurement can tell.

Compared to web analytics funnels, the data in the multichannel funnel is less certain. Some of the measurement gaps that are to blame for this were mentioned in the previous paragraphs. However, you probably know that the data behind sales funnels is notoriously inaccurate too. Nonetheless, they remain a mandatory management tool in sales organizations. Soon, so I hope, no serious marketer will want to get caught without having their multichannel funnel report handy either.

Remarketing

When direct marketers contemplate funnel reports, they do appreciate them as a management tool for process optimization. However, they also notice that this point of view ignores an entire dimension that remains invisible in the funnel report. Namely, this is the dimension of the actual prospects that are in the funnel. Direct marketers emphasize that another way of using funnel reports is to drill down to the actual people within the funnel and target communications to them based on where they are within the funnel. Most notably, this is applied to prospects who seem to be falling out of the funnel without completing the process. Direct marketers seek to rekindle their interest for another chance to earn their business. This is called remarketing, or retargeting.

Jargon Alert: Remarketing

Remarketing is also a typical practice in the online world even though it may be known under different names there. For example, retailers speak of "abandoned shopping cart programs." These typically involve personalized e-mails that are sent to prospects who started but did not check out a shopping cart. A week later the site may send an e-mail to entice the prospect to return to the site. Typically, the e-mail content and images will be personalized to relate to the category of products that the visitor left behind in the abandoned shopping carts.

Case Study: Event-Driven Remarketing at an Online Bank

Our case study is about one of the leading online financial institutions in the United States. Although the online channel is far from being the only channel at this enterprise, it is the most critical one. New and existing customers can open accounts online without ever visiting a branch or talking to a banker. That convenience for customers also puts a lot of responsibility on the institution's online marketers. They need to ensure that the account opening and usage experience is as intuitive as possible from start to finish.

This is why the online bank is, of course, working tirelessly to improve web pages, functionality, and customer service. However, they are also striving to regain the interest of customers who begin but do not complete an account opening process. The marketers designed a multiwave customer dialog strategy for this goal. A communication stream is triggered when an account application on the website is abandoned. Once such a website event is detected, an e-mail is sent to the prospect emphasizing the unique value proposition that the institution brings to the consumer. The hope is to encourage the individual to return to the site and complete the account application. If within one week the application is still not completed, a direct mail piece is sent. In cases where there is an existing relationship with the customer, a customer relationship manager may be scheduled to place a call to the individual.

The contact history is automatically populated into the sales force automation system so that there is a complete view of the promotions that have been given to each customer. Figure 10.3 highlights this event-driven process. The bankers reported open rates above 50 percent for the remarketing e-mails and a large amount of additional account openings that were completed thanks to the effort.

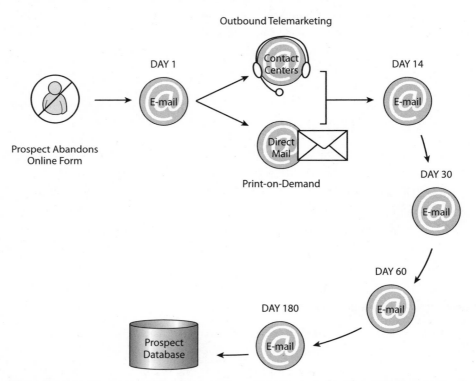

Figure 10.3 Event-driven remarketing process at a leading online banking institution (Source: Unica Corporation)

Remarketing in a Multichannel World

There is more to a successful remarketing program than what meets the eye. For instance, the prospects who abandon the account opening process on the website of the online bank institution in our case study may later complete the process over the phone instead. A remarketing program that did not take this into account would cause these customers to look down on a bank's practices.

A marketer from one of the major hotel properties in Las Vegas explained a similar problem that they had: Remarketing offers with room discounts were sent to everyone in the customer file, including those who had already reserved a hotel room for a higher price. As a result, these customers simply canceled their reservations and rebooked at the lower price.

Clearly, there is a need to tie something equivalent to a multichannel marketing profile of customers into remarketing programs for intelligent customer decisioning. This way, remarketing communications can be suppressed for those who have already completed the process through another channel. Doing this requires relating both the completed transaction and the incomplete transactions back to the same individual's marketing profile. The techniques from Chapters 7 are designed to help with that as much as possible using the partial data that is available from customers' incomplete transactions.

However, as we know from our review of direct marketing practices, the question is not just "to retarget or not." Rather, the direct marketer will ask what the most relevant offer is that should be extended to the individual under the circumstances. This too is a decision for which the multichannel marketing profile of each individual is indispensable.

Campaign management solutions are built to automate the execution of such remarketing programs in a multichannel world. Figure 10.4 shows a simplistic execution plan as an example. Here is how to read the plan. Website visitors who complete the online application process will receive a confirmation e-mail. On the other hand, visitors who begin the online form but abandon it before completion are routed into the remarketing branch of the execution plan. At that point, the campaign management system matches the online credentials against known prospects and customers. If there is a match, the prospect's value score is retrieved. If the prospect is in the high value segment the event is routed to the company's branch office to be followed up by an agent. Otherwise, if the prospect's value score is too low to afford a live call a remarketing e-mail is generated instead.

To wrap up this section, here are a few examples for remarketing programs:

Online Process Abandonment A visitor to a travel website saves a travel itinerary that he is considering and checks an option that is offered for receiving alerts when the price of the itinerary changes. As the days go by and the prices start going up, the prospect is alerted.

> **Multichannel Aspects** The alert is suppressed if the customer has meanwhile purchased the itinerary by phone. The match between site and phone purchases is done as discussed in Chapter 7 (e.g., simply by using the reservation ID).
>
> **Multichannel Profile Aspects** Now imagine that the customer is a tour operator and the itinerary is for a sizable group trip. This situation would warrant more than just an e-mail. It would be worth a phone call by the travel provider to deliver the alert in person and make the booking if possible.

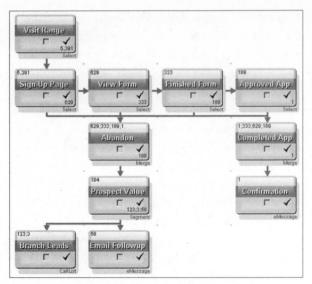

Figure 10.4 A sample execution plan for a multichannel remarketing program within a campaign management solution

Offline Product Return A customer returns a product to the store.

> **Multichannel Aspects** At the register, the customer agrees to receive a confirmation e-mail. The confirmation e-mail may also include a sidebar with related, alternative products. Most importantly, these products are displayed along with their rating by other customers so that they appear as peer recommendation.
>
> **Multichannel Profile Aspects** If the customer is in the high-value segment according to his multichannel marketing profile, the company should make sure that the product return does not leave a bad taste. Therefore, the confirmation e-mail could also include a discount coupon for this customer's next purchase.

Direct Mail Offer Expired A fashion store customer receives a direct mail with a discount coupon.

> **Multichannel Aspects** When the customer goes online where she is a registered site visitor, the website may welcome her back as usual, as in "Welcome back, Mary!" In addition, the site may alert her to the expiration date of the unused coupons in her promotion history. The coupon status can be determined using standard response attribution techniques as discussed in Chapter 4 (unless the customer paid cash or passed the coupon to someone else).
>
> **Multichannel Profile Aspects** If the customer is in the high-value segments and her coupons have expired meanwhile, the site could offer a feature for checking on available "VIP" promotions for her account. If granted, these could extend the validity of her coupons, "just because she is a valued customer."

Privacy Policy

With great power of multichannel measurement comes great responsibility to guard your customers' wishes for privacy. Every time you ask yourself "What is good for my company?" you should also ask "What would I want if I was the customer here?" Document the rules that govern your use of customer data in a transparent privacy policy. Abide by that policy and provide customers with the ability to opt out. This is the law.

While "opt out" is the minimum privacy option that you must offer, you will be well advised to reserve some marketing programs for only those customers who opt in to receive them. For instance, Chapter 7 recommended that retail websites offer their customers the option to retrieve their offline transaction history if and only if desired. The more unexpected or novel a measurement is, the greater the danger that your customers may perceive it as "big brother" watching over their shoulder. When that happens, you could lose your customer's trust and good will. Avoid the risk by being extra conservative and transparent.

The cliché is that customers never want their behavior to be known to others. But is that really true? Many family secrets are happily discussed at the barber shop or with the friendly shopkeeper at the corner store, aren't they? Yes, but only if a relationship of trust has been established. Trust is the key to unlocking permission for marketing, which is one of the central ideas in Seth Godin's well-known work, *Permission Marketing*.

It goes without saying that it is much more difficult for large enterprises to build the kind of trust relationship that customers sometimes establish with the proverbial, small-store shopkeeper. So while a customer may, for example, not discuss family secrets with a personal shopping consultant at a fashionable department store, the customer may come to trust her advice. Thanks to that trust the customer may keep going back to the store and may become more likely to open direct marketing offers sent in the name of the shopping consultant.

As Seth Godin's book continues, most important for building trust is to provide a good customer experience during direct interactions with employees and products. When it comes to the role of marketing in the equation, the well-known recommendation is to strive for customer-centricity and relevancy with communications. In other words, stay away from spam and unwelcome interruptions as much as possible.

Cross-Sales Offers

Cross-sales offers are a standard practice in virtually all businesses from retailers to restaurants and from corner stores to global enterprises. Depending on the circumstances, their goal is to increase order values beyond the customer's original intent, to increase wallet share of the customer, and to gain repeat business. The art behind cross-sales is to know what to offer, when and where. There are multiple ways in which marketers go about deciding that.

Rule Based

Rule-based cross-sales offers are usually complementary products or services that go with a purchase. For example, as a typical rule, extended warranty services are offered along with a digital camera purchase.

Market Basket Analysis

Market basket analysis involves deep number crunching to determine the items that buyers most frequently purchase together. The premise is that more buyers can be enticed to purchase these high affinity items if they are displayed prominently and in close proximity. The folk tale among friends of analytics is that the practice originated at Wal-Mart, where analysis of transactions showed that buyers of diapers frequently also picked up a six pack of beer along with it. That's quite plausible, isn't it?

Today the analytics reach beyond purchases within a single shopping basket and also include subsequent purchases the same customers make later. Table 10.1 shows an example of a typical market basket analysis report. This one shows the attachment rate of affinity products compared to a selected study product, in this case diapers. For example, 46 percent of customers who purchased diapers also purchased an affinity product from the beer category.

▶ **Table 10.1** Market Basket Analysis Report for a Selected Study Product in Diapers

Product	Customers Who Bought the Affinity Product	Customers Who Bought Both the Study and the Affinity Product	Attachment Rate
Diapers	10,121	10,121	100%
Wipes	7,392	6,543	65%
Beer	20,218	4,653	46%
Lotions	6,321	2,023	20%
Baby Food	12.211	1.721	17%

For instance, data analysis at an electronics retailer showed that one of the most frequently purchased items following the acquisition of a flat-screen TV is higher-end audio equipment. Beyond mere affinity with TV purchases, audio equipment is also a large revenue and profit driver. This insight was translated into targeted cross-sales programs such as direct mail sent to recent flat-screen TV customers featuring audio equipment front and center.

Social Intelligence

Cross-sales offers of the nature "People who bought this product also bought ..." have been a welcome addition to eCommerce websites. These offers rely on market basket analysis, but what is different is that the offers are proposed with every item that the visitor is browsing. In contrast, market basket analysis has been something that a couple of people in white coats would study in the back office. The way the offer is presented is also different. Namely, it is presented as peer advice instead of a suggestion by the vendor.

Cross-Sales Offers in a Multichannel World

It is time for the age old cross-sales practice to catch up with today's multichannel world. This applies to both the input side that informs cross-selling and the output side of delivering the offers.

Input: Combine Transaction History from All Channels

The data basis about what individual customers are buying together and over time should be extended beyond just a single channel and include all channels. In other words, this data basis should be the transaction history of customers that we discussed for multichannel marketing profiles in Chapter 7.

Without connecting customer purchases from store, phone, and online points of sale, we may lose significant insights. For example, customers who purchase a computer monitor in the store may only purchase a monitor stand later in time but do so by ordering it online.

Input: Don't Stop at Transactions!

In the example of a monitor stand, customers may perform a site search on the vendor's website but ultimately purchase the item elsewhere for a better price. If the marketer only looks at the transaction stream they may fail to realize this. Therefore, another type of question to ask is: "What searches have been performed on the website by customers who have purchased computer monitors in the store in the past?"

Alas, this is not a question that most web analytics solutions at retail websites are configured to answer today. The answer requires integrating customers' online profiles with their offline transaction history. It is technically possible though. The techniques from Chapter 7 enable it for the subset of customers with an online registration, if they have been completing online purchases at some point in time. See Figure 10.5 as an example.

While this integration may sound futuristic for retail websites today, think of other industries such as banks, telcos, and insurances. Do you think the marketers at a mobile phone service provider can run a report on the site searches performed by customers who own a BlackBerry? You betcha! Under this light, it becomes easier to imagine that retailers will also connect their websites to their registered online customers' loyalty card accounts. This is no longer a matter of technical limitations. Rather, it is a matter of finding a way to make it desirable to customers and proving ROI for the retailer.

Figure 10.5 Web analytics report on local site searches performed by offline store customers

Output: Integrate Channels for Extending Offers

When customers purchase a flat-screen TV in the store, it would be silly to wait until their next store visit to hand them cross sales offers, if meanwhile the customers are visiting the website multiple times. Likewise, while these customers are online, it could be a lost opportunity if the website featured memory cards as a cross-sales offer because some months ago the customers purchased a digital camera online. Instead, the website should be able to draw on registered customers' recent offline transaction history and feature audio equipment, assuming that the privacy policy of the firm permits this. The same applies to the call center and direct marketing channels.

In other words, the flat-screen TV purchase should register in customers' multi-channel marketing profiles. Based on that, a next-best offer of audio equipment may be calculated to complement the TV purchase. Website, call center, and direct marketing programs would ideally all tap into customers' multichannel marketing profiles to retrieve the next-best offer for each individual.

The latter is actually already standard practice with cross-sales offers in call centers, for instance at some banks and telcos. The next best offers for the client on the phone will pop up within the CRM system so that the call center agent can choose to extend any of the offers that seem relevant. What we will likely see is a widening of the practice to other channels and other industries that invest in the opportunity. To wrap up, here are further examples of cross-sales offers in a multi-channel marketing world:

AFTER PURCHASE ONLINE, CROSS-SELL IN THE STORE

A customer purchases a kayak online and chooses to pick it up in the store to save on shipment costs. Such an option is offered by the REI website for example, and free of charge to their customers. When the customer arrives in the store there is a good chance that she may purchase a few additional items, as seems to be the general observation with "buy online, pick up in store" programs. This behavior can also be encouraged at the pick-up window by issuing the customer a small gift card as a thank you. The size of the gift card may depend on the customer's value score that is retrieved from her multichannel marketing profile.

AFTER BROWSING ONLINE, CROSS-SELL BY DIRECT MAIL AND DIRECT SALES

Web analytics reports at a B2B services vendor may show that somebody from an existing enterprise customer spent more than 10 minutes on the website the previous day. What's more is that this person browsed information on a product that this enterprise customer does not yet own. In the end, the person dropped off the website without registering to reveal their identity.

This event can trigger multiple automated actions. The primary account contacts may be sent information relating to this product by direct mail. The account manager may also receive an alert to give his contacts a call to offer his assistance.

AFTER LARGE BANK DEPOSIT EVENT, CROSS-SELL CUSTOMER

A checking account customer at a bank may one day deposit $20,000. For some bank customers, this will not be an out of ordinary event but for this customer it is an amount that exceeds his average deposits by more than a standard deviation. In addition, the customer browses mortgage products on the bank's website that he has not been browsing before. These two events taken together may prompt the customer decisioning process to prioritize the customer for receiving a mortgage offer. The offer may be delivered by any channel, even by phone if the customer has given permission to be contacted. The latter makes sense for reaching prospects before it is too late and their business has already gone elsewhere.

Figure 10.6 shows a simplified campaign execution plan. On a nightly basis, customers with significant deposits are considered for a cross-sales offer. Regular exclusion rules are run, however, to suppress offers to customers who have opted out from receiving promotions. During the last step of the process, remaining prospects are segmented by the channel through which they will receive the offer. Some will receive the offer via e-mail while others are prioritized for an offer delivered by direct mail.

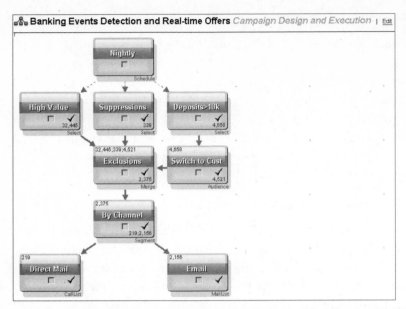

Figure 10.6 Simplified campaign execution plan for a cross-sales program to banking customers with significant deposit events

Grow Lifetime Value

Once businesses have taken the slack out of the growth path through new customer acquisition, the next opportunity for growth is to make more out of existing relationships. Efforts to grow customer lifetime value start when customers first come on board. Customer marketing programs span the entire customer life cycle and continue even after the customer has left in the hopes of winning the customer back. Naturally, these endeavors ought to cross all marketing channels and draw on every marketing discipline and metric in the book.

11

Chapter Contents

Why Focus on Lifetime Value?

As Peppers and Rogers, the renowned authors and customer-centric business experts, put it: "increasing the lifetime value of a customer (or at least not allowing it to decline) should be one of the principal value-creating activities of any business focused on building a financially successful company." While a younger business has plenty of growth opportunity through new customer acquisition, the same is increasingly difficult and expensive for larger companies operating in more mature markets. For example, Best Buy already has stores in virtually all metropolitan areas in the U.S. and could hardly reach additional customers by adding further stores.

It is under this light that in their book *Return on Customer*, Peppers and Rogers stress that customers are the scarcest resource in business today: "even scarcer than capital." The "optimization" problem that most firms wrestle with has to do with customer scarcity—there aren't an unlimited number of customers, so creating the maximum lifetime value for each customer is necessary for maximizing total returns in the long term.

Note: As a reminder, customer *lifetime value* is defined as the net present value of all the margins that the company expects to earn from a customer over time through their repeated transactions conducted over any channel. Peppers and Rogers describe the essence of the metric as "value that you have already 'earned' through your past actions; you just haven't collected the cash yet."

Following this observation, many businesses are working to change their traditionally product-centric organizations to a customer-centric order. They aim to provide a better experience to customers and create two-way value as we discussed in Chapter 1, "With Great Opportunity Come Great Challenges."

Yet, in *Return on Customer* Peppers and Rogers also emphasize a more specific application of the lifetime value metric that is often overlooked. Namely, increases and decreases in lifetime value that occur as the result of how a customer is treated by a company are every bit as important to the company's success as the near-term sales or costs generated by the customer. Still, too often the success of sales and marketing activities is measured by short term sales and profits only. In reality, the effect on customer lifetime valuation needs to be taken into account too. For example, forcing a customer to solve their customer service inquiries through the website or IVR (Interactive Voice Response) channels saves costs in the short term. But it could turn out that it actually destroys value if it causes customers to defect to alternative vendors earlier in the relationship.

Indeed, Peppers and Rogers coined the metric *Return on Customer* (ROC)[1] specifically to acknowledge the importance of changes in lifetime value for understanding how a customer creates value for a business. ROC is defined as a firm's current period cash flow from its customers plus any changes in the underlying customer equity (i.e., sum of all customer lifetime values), divided by the total customer equity at the beginning of the period. ROC therefore quantifies "how well a company creates value from its customers." We will refer back to this metric as we walk through the various efforts for growing customer value in this chapter.

On-Boarding New Customers

On-boarding refers to marketing programs that systematically introduce a company's range of products and services to their new customers. The purpose is to increase the expected lifetime value of new customer relationships. Get those new customers started off right, and you will be rewarded with longer relationships and higher lifetime values. That has been the observation, most notably researched in retail banking.

A study by the Bank Administration Institute (BAI) from 2003 found that 73 percent of cross-sales to banking customers take place during the first 90 days of their relationship with the bank (90-Day Window of Opportunity: shortcut via multichannelmetrics .com/90days). That may be because new customers are still in "switching mode" and, therefore, receptive to recommendations as Dove Consulting suggest in their article "Onboarding New Customers" (shortcut via multichannelmetrics.com/Dove). They are also more likely to speak live with a consultant in the branch, or at least via the phone.

Therefore, instead of catering cross-sales offers solely to established customers, the BAI paper advises that it makes sense to refocus some of that attention to the window of the first 90 days. Due to the "switching mode" phenomenon, this advice seems to be worth reviewing for industries beyond banking too (e.g., telco, utilities, insurances, and similar businesses).

However, the early days also hold risk. If something goes wrong or does not conform to expectations, customers may "snap-back," as it is called. That is to say, they may terminate the new service early to return to their previous provider. In the case of banks, it would be typical for the old account to be closed only months after the new relationship is established, after all.

According to Dove Consulting, the majority of U.S. banks report triple the average attrition rate for customers who are within their first year. This is why the BAI study notes that some U.S. banks pay employees only half their commission when a new account has been opened. The second half is paid out after sixty to ninety days if the account still exists and shows increased use (i.e., funding). Obviously, this problem does not apply

1. Return on Customer and ROC are both service marks of the Peppers & Rogers Group, a division of Carlson Marketing Worldwide.

as much to services such as mobile phones, where customers are usually locked in for a year or two.

Designed to take these risks and opportunities by their horns, on-boarding is accomplished in part through a specially designed, multichannel, event-based marketing program (EBM). This is the aspect of on-boarding that we will discuss here. However, a successful on-boarding experience depends on much more. As an example, the BAI study also recommends packaging products in an easy-to-comprehend fashion and training employees to match the right ones to each new customer from the get-go.

Event-Based, Direct Marketing Programs for On-Boarding

The ideal direct marketing program for on-boarding is a combination of rule-based communications with others that are event-based. What's the difference between the two? To use an analogy, as a *rule*, a good host might ask every newly arriving guest what they would like to drink. But, the host would also keep a watchful eye that new guests are able to make connections and enjoy themselves. In the *unexpected event* that a guest seems to be standing by themself, the host may jump into action in order to weave the guest into a conversation with others.

Likewise, on-boarding processes are here to ensure that new clients get all the connections to service options that they need to reach their fullest satisfaction. Some communications may be sent to every customer, as a rule, following a protocol of expected customer touch points throughout a relationship. Such a touch point event is, for example, the beginning of a new customer relationship with an account opening. Other communications are launched in the event that there are signs of unexpected dissatisfaction or accidental service failures. The business wants to know about these signs as soon as possible so that the situation can be saved before it is too late. From a multichannel marketing perspective, let's see how the puzzle pieces come together for a successful on-boarding program.

Baseline: Rule-Based Communications

If you have ever signed up online for a stock trading account or a retirement savings account, you may remember receiving a large envelope in the mail with account materials. In fact, you may have been surprised at the impressive size of the format. Well, if so, what you experienced was probably a well-taken effort by the bank's on-boarding marketers to get you excited about your new banking relationship. Not only did they want to put something substantial into your hands, but they also wanted you to notice the deposit slips that were likely included in the package so you might fund the account generously.

There can be further rule-based touch points that follow. For instance, the marketers may segment their new client base using the limited information that is available at this early stage in the relationship. Clients with the largest expected lifetime value scores may be prioritized for a phone check-in by their account manager. For others, the expected margin may justify only a friendly e-mail.

How can the impact of these communications be measured across multiple channels? For the deposit slips, we can use response attribution, as discussed in Chapter 4, "The Direct Marketer Digs into Multichannel Analytics." In other words, we know we sent deposit slips to the owner of account 01234567, so did that account receive a deposit in a few weeks time? For e-mails on the other hand, we can use standard web analytics to measure click-throughs and subsequent business events leading to conversions on the website.

However, part of the impact of our communications should be a lift in customer satisfaction. How can we measure that? We can do what brand advertisers also do, namely survey customers. We can ask selected customers: "Do you recall receiving this communication and did you find it helpful? If not, why not?"

EBM: Detect Service Usage Events

It is more important for a customer to exhibit the signs of a budding, healthy relationship than it is for them to directly respond to the welcome communications. That may mean, for example, that the customer completes their self-service registration online, automates bill payment, sets up alerts, etc. These convenience features allow the customer to let the account run on autopilot without needing to think about it again.

The next most important thing to measure is customer usage levels. A telco, for instance, can measure account usage activity in terms of phone usage minutes. A bank might measure the level of account funding and RFM (recency, frequency, monetary value) of deposits and withdrawals. For online publishing, on the other hand, we can use standard web analytics to measure recency, frequency, and depth of online sessions.

In addition to looking for positive usage events, companies also want to watch for possible service failures. For instance, when using the website's local search engine, a customer may attempt to search for keyword phrases that return no results. A website that is built to detect this event could highlight an offer to help the customer with live chat. Web analytics can also detect when search results do come up but the visitor drops off the website without clicking any of them. In that case, an e-mail with an offer to help could be prioritized later that day or next. If the client appears to be in the highest value segment, the event could be routed to other channels, even to an account manager who can reach out with a phone call.

EBM: Detect Missing Events

Monitoring for events that you expect from a successful client relationship but that fail to take place is just as important as watching for events that do take place. If a client opens a bank account but fails to fund it or does not register their payroll deposit or their monthly housing payment, the bank wants to know about this. These may be telltales that the relationship is superficial or a fulfillment error occurred, and the relationship could be undone easily.

Similarly, in retail, a customer who buys a digital camera may not purchase the extended memory card that you know they are going to need for a satisfactory experience. Granted, there could be many valid reasons for this, but why not prioritize a cross-sales offer just in case.

Likewise, a social networking website, such as LinkedIn, will watch for situations where a customer registers an account but does not use critical functions such as completing their profile. The website may rally customers by indicating the benefits of completing their profile.

Finally, it will also help to compare a customer's response rate in regards to on-boarding communications to the average response rates for typical customers. If a new customer deviates from the typical response rates, it can be an early indicator that the relationship is not off to a good start.

EBM: Translate Events and Nonevents into Action for On-Boarding

Events and nonevents alike can suggest opportunities to increase cross-sell and up-sell rates, reduce attrition, and increase loyalty. For instance, an online stock trading customer may read up on information for stock options but not pursue an authorization of his account for trading them. This could be an opportunity for the bank to engage the customer with an e-mail that includes pointers to educational materials on the art of options trading.

Similarly, a telco may observe that a customer keeps exceeding their monthly plan minutes and could make a recommendation to upgrade the plan in the interest of a more satisfied customer. Right-sizing the account could also go in the other direction if the current contract is more expensive than necessary. If less than six months are left on the plan and the customer is likely to switch to a competitor instead of renewing, it may make good business sense to propose downsizing the account.

Monitor Satisfaction, Lifetime Values, and Churn Rates

The ultimate measure of success for the on-boarding program is to compare vital metrics for the group of customers served by the program and a control group for which the communications are suppressed. The most important metrics to look for are probably lifetime values, conversion rates for add-on offers, churn rates (a.k.a. "attrition rates"), and customer satisfaction. The program should not just yield short term cross-sales revenues, but the ROC metric that we discussed earlier should also indicate long term value generation. To be more precise, customers served by the program should yield higher ROC compared to control groups that are excluded.

As with any marketing program, this one will not be perfect from inception either. You can experiment with various triggers and actions to arrive at a better and better program over time.

> ### AIRMILES Case Study: Scavenger Hunting for Online Quality Control
>
> Fulfillment errors are not limited to offline transactions; they can also occur during website trans-actions. They are especially difficult to track down online because the website can seem like a black box. "When customers experience an unexpected problem on the website, they may simply leave and you may never hear a word from them," says Jukka Kamarainen from AIRMILES, who was introduced in Chapter 9, "Attract and Acquire." Using web analytics, the AIRMILES team found that some customers who experience an error condition during a travel booking process may not only drop off the website at that point but may never return. Therefore, at AIRMILES, quality con-trol is one of the top priorities for ensuring customer satisfaction. Kamarainen continues, "You have invested so much in attracting and converting these customers in the first place, so how could you not do your best to keep them as satisfied customers?"
>
> An alert can be set to trigger an investigation if more than a threshold percentage of customers experience failures when completing a particular website process. In the case of the online travel industry, troubleshooting problems may be performed through investigative analysis to identify common denominators in the incidents. For example, if there had been issues with car rental reservations, you would investigate further to see if they pertained to a particular page or supplier and refine your analysis to identify the exact cause.
>
> Kamarainen recalls customers describing issues on the website that the team thought impossible, but web analytics proved the customers right. The opposite could also happen, where a customer was adamant that they made a booking for May not March, yet a web analytics investigation on the customer's request would prove otherwise.

Right-Channeling Customers

Growing customer lifetime values also requires serving customers' needs as cost efficiently and profitably as possible. That is where a right-channeling strategy for customer service comes into play. In its broadest sense, a right-channeling strategy is understood as the availability of all channels desired by customers in order to access customer services (e.g., phone, e-mail, and self-help website). Clients can pick the channel that is the *right* one for them to accomplish their customer service tasks. For example, Sento (who have registered the term *Right Channeling* as a services mark) enables companies to outsource their multichannel customer service operations.

From a company's point of view, there is a right channel for customer service too. Namely, assuming all things are equal for clients, a company prefers to encourage each customer to use, not the cheapest, but the most profitable channel. For instance, monthly statements are most profitably delivered through e-mail rather than paper billing. For basic account services, such as address changes and account balance checks, the most profitable channel would usually be the self-service website.

Yet, for more complex questions, some companies find that the website may not be the most profitable channel even though it is the cheapest. This is the case when a conversation with a live services representative results in increased value. For example, a retailer may find that questions about some products and catalogs are better answered live because they result in higher conversion rates and average order values. A bank may find that questions about a mortgage may be better answered live if they result in higher application rates for refinancing. At least one multichannel retailer of fashionable women's footwear found that it was most profitable for them to encourage their customers to visit their brick and mortar stores rather than pushing them to the website. The richer experience in the stores simply drove more sales than the website could.

One additional caveat is that the answer as to which channel is the most profitable will differ from customer to customer. For example, bank customers who have questions about mortgages but who ultimately are not going to refinance should ideally use the website to answer their questions themselves at lowest cost. So, encouraging each customer to use the most profitable channel is dependent on predicting what that channel will be for each customer. We find ourselves entangled in a typical direct marketing thought process for predicting customer value and response. The targeting and measurement methods that we reviewed in Chapters 4 and 7 will be helpful for addressing this challenge.

Matching the Right Channel with the Right Customer

The cost of the average customer service call compared to a self-service website visit is easy to calculate. Yet, the value that is generated through each channel is a lot harder to assess. We need to estimate that value, however, so that we can make an informed prediction as to what the most profitable channel will be in each case.

Saving Costs versus Increasing Short Term Revenue

In the simplest case, a self-service website visit where a customer registers their own address changes generates value in terms of cost savings. Namely, the company saves the $30 to $50 that a customer service phone call may cost the business on average. What if the business happens to be an insurance company and the phone agent manages to cross sell a home insurance policy while registering the new address? That would change the picture dramatically. The value generated by the phone call would be relatively easy to measure simply by summing the volume of cross-sales that the call center logs or CRM system list in conjunction with address changes.

It is easy to conceive that some customers will decline the offer on the phone but may mull it over and return to the website a week later to buy a policy. No problem for us! As long as the offer has been logged into the customer's promotion history, we can use the method of inferred response attribution from Chapter 4 to credit the call center for this business instead of the website.

Increasing Lifetime Value

What, however, if the value that is generated through the more expensive channel is even more long-term oriented, namely greater customer satisfaction and a decreased churn rate? The long term view is likely the one that Peppers and Rogers would encourage when deciding on right-channeling customers. Short term cost savings are great. But what if they are reducing lifetime value due to lower satisfaction rates overall? Then we would be destroying value while thinking that we are doing well. Our ROC (and likewise the incremental long term ROI) would be negative despite positive short term cash flows.

As explained in Chapter 8, "Measure Multi-Touch Conversions," we can use uncontrolled testing to investigate. We will invite customers to take satisfaction surveys and segment the results based on whether they have been using the website or call center for particular service interactions. We can also calculate the churn rate for each group per period. If these metrics show that the customers using the more expensive channel seem to be doing better over the long term, then we can add a controlled experiment to separate cause from correlation. For example, we can make the more expensive channel more readily available to customers in a particular city to see how satisfaction and churn rates will improve here over time.

These measurements should be further refined by customer segment. For example, low value customers may rarely buy that renter's insurance policy on the phone while changing their address. Yet, higher value customers may be more likely. Similarly, your 80-year-old customers may be more dissatisfied with the website over the long term whereas your teenage customers may be upset if they are not offered the option to handle their tasks themselves via their mobile phone's web browser.

Ultimately, you will reach an opinion on which channel you would like to encourage per customer segment and interaction type. This defines the right-channeling strategy that you wish to implement as part of your strategic communications plan. The rest is plain vanilla direct marketing. The principles from Chapter 4 will help you lobby the right customers, at the right time, and in the right manner to come on board with your right-channel proposal.

Rallying Customers to the Right Channel

A campaign execution plan for right-channeling will probably consist of the following or similar steps:

Segment Customers by Right Channel

- The first step is to pair up each customer with their predicted, right channel based on your right-channeling strategy.

Segmentation by Actual Channel Used

- The next step is to divide each segment into those who are already making preferred used of their designated "right channel" and those who are not yet doing so. These are the ones that we want to target.

Offer Selection

- Determine the offer to present to each targeted customer as an incentive for switching to the right channel.
  - For example, it might be worth it to give a few dollars to customers who agree to stop using paper bills in favor of electronic billing.
  - You might send a store coupon to customers to encourage them to visit your brick and mortar outlets.
  - The higher the lifetime value score of these customers, the higher the face amount of that gift could be.

Reduce Target List

- By calculating a lift curve, you can reduce the target customer list to those most likely to act on your proposal to switch channels.
  - For example, based on demographic information, you may decide that certain customers are not likely to adopt your online channel.
  - Or, by calculating customers' geographic distances to their nearest brick and mortar outlets, you may save the costs of mailing coupons to people who simply live too far away to care.

Channel Selection

- You can further refine the communications by the channel through which you will deliver the right-channeling offer.
  - For example, on the self-service website, switching to electronic billing may be as easy as clicking a highlighted icon and confirming the selection.
  - In your paper bills, it may take more to entice customers to act so that you could offer a financial incentive here.

Optimize Conversions with Multichannel Funnels

- After executing the campaign, be sure to create multichannel funnel reports to monitor your success with channel migration.
  - For instance, monitor the trend of self-service website registrations. Work with your colleagues in the website team to keep improving the self-registration process so that drop-offs are reduced.
  - Also experiment with different offers to see which ones are the most persuasive.

Repeat

- Measure who has and who has not responded to your campaign. Repeat the proposal to those customers who have not yet switched to the new channel.

Avoid Fatigue

- Don't overdo it though. If a few proposals have not born fruit, you may want to just leave the customer alone to use whichever channel they prefer.

Keep Measuring

- Continuously monitor customer satisfaction, churn rates, and lifetime values to make sure your efforts have been moving these needles in the right direction.

Automating Customer Relevancy

The mainstay of a normal customer life cycle is the time following the initial acquisition phase, and after on-boarding (if applicable), but before the day when the risk of attrition arises on the horizon. During this core period, marketers seek to keep their customers engaged with the brand and coming back for more business. So, if your business is somewhat like Coca-Cola's, you will probably get in front of your customers regularly with brand advertising. (We discussed a reach versus frequency strategy for scheduling these ads in Chapter 8.) On the other hand, if your business is more relationship oriented, then this is typically the time that calls for ongoing customer-centric marketing.

Yet, customer-centric marketing is practiced with varying degrees of maturity at different companies. My colleagues at Unica use the quadrant chart in Figure 11.1 to describe the degree of sophistication that customer centricity may reach in a marketing organization. In Figure 11.1, the vertical dimension along which maturity grows is that of marketing insights—i.e., various types of analytics for fueling customer centricity. Some companies stop at basic, ad hoc analytics for pulling together target lists for communications. More mature marketing organizations however leverage analytics of much greater depth. They use many or all of the techniques that we discussed for direct marketing, namely, segmentation, predictive modeling, pattern detection, and contact optimization.

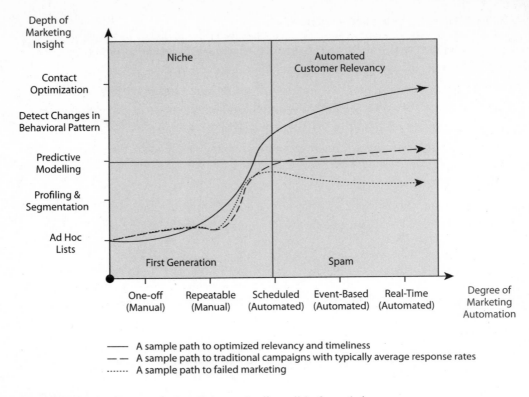

------ A sample path to optimized relevancy and timeliness
— — A sample path to traditional campaigns with typically average response rates
.... A sample path to failed marketing

Figure 11.1 Maturity of customer-centric marketing practices (Source: Unica Corporation)

In Figure 11.1, marketing automation is the horizontal dimension along which maturity grows. Some companies stop at manually or regularly scheduled communications. Others use many or all of the campaign types that we discussed—i.e., rule-based and event-based, as well as real-time campaigns on the occasion of inbound inquiries.

Depending on the levels of marketing insights and marketing automation that a company draws on, their customer-centricity most likely falls into one of the following four buckets.

First Generation Customer-Centric Marketing

At most marketing organizations, the first generation of customer marketing consisted of ad hoc or scheduled campaigns that drew on relatively basic analytics and segmentation. The observation today is that these campaigns usually bring relatively low conversion rates and returns, yet take a long time to design, develop, and execute.

Spam

If the latter problem is addressed by investing in marketing automation technology without deeper insights into understanding each customer's needs, we end up with spam.

You probably don't want your organization to be in the Spam quadrant. It may be profitable in the short term, but it is not customer centric and it does not build loyalty. Negative ROC would likely be the result despite positive, short term cash flows.

Niche Marketing

On the other hand, if you employ more sophisticated analysts without accelerating the degree of marketing automation, you are in the upper-left quadrant, or niche marketing. In other words, you identify a niche opportunity in the data, design a campaign for the niche, and execute the campaign. Then you go looking for the next niche to address. You will, hopefully, experience relatively higher conversion rates compared to generic campaigns. However, the cost and time to develop these niche campaigns remains high. The number of customer communications that can be launched per time period stays low and as a result, so do the total returns that are achieved.

Automated Customer Relevancy

The promised land of customer-centric marketing is found in the upper-right quadrant. My colleagues refer to this stage as *automated customer relevancy*. The term expresses a vision for the long-term direction into which a marketing organization can advance by improving their customer-centric practice. The further the marketing organization's practice develops into the upper-right quadrant, the more customer-centric we would say it has become.

It would be advisable to take a "walk before you run" approach when you chart your course across the quadrants towards automating customer relevancy. Have your desired destination clearly in sight so that you don't waste effort on detours. But don't aim to build out the full 360-degree customer-data warehouse on day one either. As mentioned in Chapter 7, take a bootstrapping approach where you add additional customer insights, leverage them for marketing programs, prove ROI, and then expand from there.

Don't forget that a customer-centric business has to implement many additional dimensions beyond the two outlined in Figure 11.1 related to marketing relevancy. For a good customer experience, a business also has to hire and train employees who take care of their customers. Products and services have to be built with customer satisfaction in mind, and there are many more requirements along these lines. A great place to get more food for thought is the CustomerThink website (CustomerThink.com).

Attrition Risk Detection

Even a romantic relationship needs a little something every now and then to keep it current. Strangely similar, customer relations also come to a point in the life cycle where attrition to a competitor is likely but may be prevented through the right gesture at the right time. Just as with the romantic relationship, it is better to detect the risk long before it is too late instead of having to wield a win-back campaign after the fact.

That is the realm of event-based marketing (EBM) that we discussed earlier in the context of cross-sales and on-boarding. Instead of looking for cross-sales opportunities signaled by a change in customers' behavior, EBM can also be about looking for early signals of a coming attrition. These signals may fall into three different buckets.

Service Failures

As discussed earlier with on-boarding, companies may want to keep a watchful eye on service failures online and offline. A rapid response can be warranted if experience shows that a certain service failure raises a customer's probability for dissatisfaction and attrition.

The data for these failures will come through web analytics or through customer complaints via the call center and stores. For instance, one company implemented a program where service failures at the top 1 percent of their customers would be answered with an outbound phone call by a services representative to apologize.

Specific Telltale Events

Even with everything running smoothly, there can be events that typically suggest trouble ahead. For example, a bank customer may stop their payroll deposit and also their mortgage auto payment. A credit card balance may be paid to zero and stay there. A mortgage customer may go online to check the loan pay-off amount. A retail customer may return a product shipment in its entirety without making a replacement purchase.

The data for most of these events would likely be streaming in from a company's transactional systems. The events could also be flagged in customers' accounts in a CRM system so that the marketing management system can access the data there.

Change of Behavior Pattern

Oftentimes, the only harbinger of a coming attrition may be a change in customers' behavior patterns.

Reduction in Frequency A number of customers may be shopping with a particular retailer twice per month. For most customers, this would be a great sign that the retailer probably enjoys a large portion of these customers' wallet share. But behavior pattern analysis can show that some of these customers may have previously been shopping five times per month with this retailer. Knowing this would be good because these high-value customers might stop coming altogether.

Reduction in Categories Similarly, a customer may continue to be a frequent buyer but instead of buying from multiple product categories as before they may narrow their purchases to products from only a single category. Next thing you know, they may have replaced the retailer altogether with an alternative vendor.

It is critical to know whether these customers have really been reducing their business with the retailer or whether they have simply migrated from one channel to another. For example, a customer who used to frequent the brick and mortar outlets may now be buying online. Or they may be using different channels for specific product categories now. Therefore, customers' transaction history will need to be consolidated into a multichannel marketing profile before you can make any call. Otherwise, a change of customer behavior on one channel would not be sufficient justification for taking action.

Industries other than retail (e.g., news, entertainment, or social networking sites) also have website customers whose behavior can be monitored. Despite continuing frequency, some customers' session durations may have become shorter than earlier patterns indicate. Similar to the retail example, the website visitor may also narrow their interest down from multiple categories of content to just one. Soon they may go elsewhere for their news or networking.

For a credit card customer, it could be a telltale sign if the card is being used less frequently than before or if certain spending categories, such as grocery shopping, cease showing up in the transaction history.

Once a change is detected, the next step for the marketer would be to formulate a response to try to save the customer. As discussed before, direct marketing principles suggest that each customer's segment and value scores should be taken into account when deciding which treatments make economic sense.

Save and Win-Back

Most people already have a bank account, car insurance, and a mobile phone. In saturated markets, companies can gain new customers only by winning them away from the competition. That is usually an expensive endeavor due to the shouting match between competitors. Therefore, it makes sense for businesses to work on their existing customer relationships as diligently as possible to prevent customers from slipping away. For those customers who do decide to leave, companies invest in programs to save the customers and win them back even after they have left.

In some ill-advised cases, this goal had been translated into a nagging experience on the phone when you called to cancel your account. But luckily there are other companies that demonstrate how to do this right. Let's see a shining example from mobile phone carrier Vodafone in the Netherlands who pursue the goal with a genuine effort that starts with the interest of the customer at heart.

Case Study: Customer-Centric Retention Marketing at Vodafone

Marketers at Vodafone Netherlands came up with the idea of asking customers who cancel their mobile phone service what it would take to keep their business. They wanted to enable customers to put together their own retention package that would convince them to stay by picking from available options. This would essentially allow them to match the experience of starting a new service. But given the many options that there are in mobile service plans, how should this idea be translated into practice cost efficiently? How can it be accomplished without spending an hour on the phone with each cancelling customer, which is something that would not be desirable for either party?

The marketers designed a multichannel campaign for saving customers as follows. As you read the following steps, count the number of channels that are integrated in this program.

- A customer who cancels their account in writing quickly receives an SMS message confirming the receipt of their notice. The message also alerts the customer that further communication will arrive by mail within two days.

- Once the mail package arrives, the customer can glean from it that the mobile phone carrier would like to offer the customer the opportunity to reconfigure their service plan and options to their liking.

- The company website provides a perfectly interactive environment to do this, and it puts the customer in the driver seat instead of being on the defensive answering to a call center agent. Therefore, the package directs customers to log in to their account on the self-service website where they will be presented with a special area to configure their desired offer.

- Meanwhile, the campaign also monitors whether or not customers examine these offers by logging into the website. A follow up encouragement is mailed to customers who do not visit online.

In this excellent example of an integrated multichannel campaign, we don't just see that each channel is leveraged for what it is best suited. We also see that the marketers have integrated customers' profiles across mail, SMS, and website in order to stand in front of their customers as one integrated, intelligent partner in dialog.

Vodafone's Cretièn Brandsma, Manager of CRM Operations and Capability Development with responsibility for the campaign, says, "Retention marketing is about keeping your customers by really understanding them and being able to deliver a truly end-to-end customer experience." We should see many more customer-centric, multichannel campaigns in the coming years.

Over to You Now

If you make only a single resolution now, namely to break down barriers, cross the road, and become friends with the colleagues in the other marketing disciplines, this author would be happy enough. Just to be talking and coordinating among all marketing disciplines in the company is a low-hanging fruit that is waiting to be plucked off the tree of opportunity.

No Excuse Not to Be Talking

Integrating marketing campaigns and metrics can wait for a phase 2 if it must. But there is no excuse for not talking to or coordinating actions between all marketing disciplines and channels. As stated in *Return on Customer,* "every interaction with a customer— every conceivable point of contact between the customer and the enterprise—should not only maximize ROC but also reinforce the customer's faith that his or her own interests are being considered first." All employees must work together for this purpose and so must, by corollary, all marketers.

No Excuse for Direct Marketers

As direct marketers, we have no excuse for not coordinating with the online colleagues given that a significant amount of the response to direct response campaigns occurs through the website. We can no longer be satisfied with counting conversions completed on the website thanks to our efforts. Instead, we should be asking our web analytics colleagues why the remainder of the online responses did not translate into completed sales. That question will probably help us unearth the biggest jump in our conversion rates.

There is also no excuse for not using the rich lather of behavioral data from the website as a component for informing our targeting efforts, as soon as possible. Behavioral data is our favored input for targeting marketing communications. Nowhere is behavioral data available as cheaply, generously, and accurately as from our very own colleagues in the online channel.

No Excuse for Brand Marketers

As brand marketers, we have no excuse for not talking to online and direct marketing colleagues in order to synchronize the conversion paths following our ad impressions. There is also no excuse for not synchronizing broadcast campaigns with online advertisement campaigns to run in parallel. Measuring the impact of advertising on brand equity using the survey capabilities available online should not be neglected.

The online medium lends itself perfectly for augmenting brand marketing methods with the techniques from web analytics and direct response marketing. For example, combine the use of cookies with controlled testing to measure the effectiveness of increased opportunities to see (OTS) ads.

No Excuse for Online Marketers

As online marketers, we have no excuse for not negotiating hand-offs with colleagues on the offline side of the house. Due to the research shopper phenomenon that we discussed, the offline behavior of our customers, before and after their website sessions, may often be more important to our success than what happens during the interaction on the website itself.

There is also no excuse for neglecting the fact that website visits are only one facet of an ongoing customer relationship. They occur in the context of repeated interactions with our companies and, hopefully, will lead to repeat transactions through whichever channel.

Finally, it is time to stop ignoring the analytics methods that direct and brand marketers can add to our repertoire, namely:

- Response attribution through matchback for crediting online conversions to preceding touch points when neither cookies nor clicks are available to connect the dots.

- The use of controlled testing for separating cause from correlation.

- Predictive modeling for estimating the complete value generated by online marketing efforts beyond just short term conversions or sales.

- Customer-centric marketing for growing customer lifetime value instead of looking at lifetime value solely as a rearview mirror metric for ad optimization.

- Surveys for estimating the impact of marketing efforts on brand equity.

- Panels for investigating the effect of multiple touch points.

Talk Now, Then Coordinate, Then Integrate

If you did not already, you should now appreciate your marketing colleagues' language, methods, and metrics to a better degree. Your company's opportunity to have all facets of its marketing department cooperate with each other is also your personal opportunity to combine the following:

- Online marketer's wealth of customer data

- Direct marketers' sense for customer targeting, relationship building, and lifetime value maximization

- Brand marketers' skills for bridging uncertainties when direct measurement is not possible

To get your feet wet working with your colleagues, the website channel is the most promising testing ground. While direct and brand marketers had found their disciplines to be of very complementary nature in the offline space, the online space brings them back together. Online, almost any ad has both a brand and a direct response aspect to it. Thanks to the greater measurability of the online medium, ads can be targeted and measured from both these angles.

As you walk down the path with your marketing colleagues and you progress from talking to coordinating to integrating your marketing initiatives, share your experiences and success stories. Your success should become a spark fueling an integrated, multichannel marketing revolution.

Rely on Both Staff and Technology

Marketing technologists, of whom this author is one, get excited about the possibilities opened up through analytics-driven marketing automation. So let me close by saying that nothing plays a bigger role for a good customer experience than thoughtful employees who care about customer service and care about their performance in delivering it. But technology's contribution for helping these employees accomplish their goals is truly exciting. Employees cannot be present everywhere, on a 24/7 basis. Many interactions of customers with your company are not with personnel but with marketing communications, promotional materials, website, mobile messaging, ad impressions, and word of mouth. Marketers who know how to use available technology in a smart fashion can push the envelope and apply the customer oriented-mindset to these other interactions as well.

I could not say it any better than Steve Mayberry of Best Buy did during a web presentation in 2007 in conjunction with Unica. Namely, there is great promise in the goal of "extending the authentic dialog of the 'blue shirts' in the [Best Buy] stores to all of our marketing communications."

Index

Note to the reader: Throughout this index **boldfaced** page numbers indicate primary discussions of a topic. *Italicized* page numbers indicate illustrations.

cell phones. *See* mobile phones

Champion - Challenger approach to testing, 102

channels
addressable, 4
in buying cycle stages, 9
cannibalization, 159
combining transaction history from all, for cross-sales offers, 249
consumer use of, 198
cost efficiency of, 215
experimenting with different online, 79
impact of marketing on multiple, **213–217**
incremental contributions, 126, 216
integrating for extending offers, **250–251**
marketing in one impacting on other, **211–213**
selection, 262

churn rates, 261
monitoring, **258–259**

Circuit City, 22

Clarabridge, 121

click-through, 6, **46–51**, 113
campaign cost per, 65
and display ads, 213
study of ad frequency and, 207
tracking codes for, 43

click-to-call technology, 233

ClickPath, 165

clickstream analysis, 41

ClickTracks, 36

clustering, **92**

CMO Council website, 220

CMS Watch, 36

collaborative filtering, 22

Collins, Kimberly L., 191

commercials on TV, audience skipping of, 132

communications
between all marketing disciplines, **269–270**
with customer, 19
rule-based, **256–257**
suppressing remarketing, 245

company news, in media, 120

Compete, 44, 58

competition, for consumer attention, 6

competitive advertising levels, 125

comScore Networks, 44, 212

confidence interval, 190–191

configurator, 161

Conjoint analysis, 133

consistency of message, 16

consumer attention, competition for, 6

Consumer Direct service, 168

consumers
content generated by, 118, 120
as interpreters of marketing messages, 13
value of multichannel, **12–13**

contact fatigue, avoiding, 108

content analysis, 41

Continental Airlines, DoubleClick study for, 56

continuous tracking, 215

control groups, 104, 105, 169, 182–183
improving selection, 174
for postcard campaign, 148

controlled experimentation, **134–135**
channel suitability for, 203

convenience URLs, **152–153**

conversion rate, 113

conversions
in online customer life cycle, 74
statistics, 64, 113

cookies, **37–38**
first-party vs. third-party, 55
to infer ad view-throughs, **51–56**
for linking unauthenticated visit to previous visits, 182
and online registrations, 187
for testing ad viewing, 214

cooperation, between marketers, 28

Coremetrics, 36

CorporatePress, 179

correlation
vs. causal relationship, 54–56
control groups to separate, **158**
for e-mail viewthrough, **57**
for online lift from offline activity, **157–158**
for segmentation, 42

cost efficiency of channel, 215

cost metrics, 114, 136

cost per OTS, 136

cost per rating point, 136

Cost per Thousand (CPM), 136

costs
of cross-channel measurement, 171
of incremental sales, 171
vs. short-term revenue, 260–261

costs per response metric, 114

data collection methods, logs or page tags, **37**
data mart, location of, 195
data-mining software, 94
data overlay, 40
data visualization, 91
    frequency of conversions, *210*
date comparison analysis, for segmentation, 42
David Shephard Associates, *The New Direct Marketing*, 94
De Pelsmacker, Patrick, *Integrated Marketing Communication: A Primer*, 16
decay, 130
delayed conversions, 38
Deleersnyder, Barbara, 160
demand, being attentive to, **226–227**
demographic data, for predictive analysis, 89
descriptive analytics, 103
design and production stage, for offline marketing cycle, 76
destination URLs, with tracking codes, **47–48**
Didit, 49
Digital Envoy, 149
digital video recorders, and audience measurement, 132
DigitalAdvisor, 29, 32–33
diminishing returns, *128*, 130
    correcting for, **128–129**
direct mail, 9
    cross-sell after browsing online, 251
    measuring impact, 235
    offer expiration, 246
direct marketers, 228
    analysis by, 14
    blind spot of offline, **106–107**
    campaign execution, **100–102**
    cause vs. correlation, **104–106**
    communications with other marketers, **269**
    event-based campaigns for on-boarding, **256–259**
    goals, **84**
    need for adjustment by, 96
    predicting individual response, **88–99**
    strategic communications plan, **84–87**
        linking marketing to targeting, **87**
        tactical communications, **85–87**
    success metrics for, **108–116**
        campaign-centric metrics, **111–116**
        customer centric metrics, **108–111**

Direct Marketing Alliance, 179
    microsite for Prudential, 179
direct response channels, 4
direct sales, cross-sell after browsing online, 251
discount codes, 155
discount coupons, 101
display advertising, 33
    and click-through rates, 213
    impact on paid search, **211–213**
    targeting online, 80
    tracking codes for, **50**
dissatisfied customers, events indicating, 266
DME, 179
Dobney Corporation, 133
dollars spent versus budget metric, 114
donotcall.gov, 5
Doshi, Vinit, 125
dot-com, 14
DoubleClick, 50, 52, 56
Dove Consulting, 255
Drilling Down (Novo), 61, 90
drilling, for segmentation, 42
drop-off report, 107
DVRs (digital video recorders), 6
Dynamic Logic, 214

E

e-consultancy, 36
e-mail filters, 6
e-mail marketing
    inferring view-throughs through matchback, **56–57**
    measuring impact, 235
    vs. spam, 33, 264–265
    tracking codes for, **50–51**
"e-mailing a friend" features, 60
E-Metrics (Sterne and Cutler), 74
eBusiness. *See also* online ...
    or offline business, 72
eCommerce analysis, 41
Effective Frequency (Naples), 205
Efficient Frontier, 49
Eisenberg, Bryan, *Waiting for Your Cat to Bark?*, 20, 68
Eisenberg, Jeffrey, *Waiting for Your Cat to Bark?*, 20, 68
eMetrics Marketing Optimization Summit conference, 25

H

halo effect of visitors, 151
halo response attribution, with matchback, 105
handoff from offline to online, tracing, **178–180**
Harrison, Tom, 29, 32–33
Harvey Ball chart, 9
Heath, Melissa, 207
Hillstrom, Kevin, 104
　Multichannel Forensics, 160
hiring decisions, **28–29**
historical behavior
　analysis, 204
　to identify degree of cannibalization, **159**
historical data, for modeling, 92, 94
Hitwise, 44, 135
Homescan panel, 168
"hot zone", 210
household rating point, 135
householding, for matchback, 105
HTTP protocol, 44
hyperlinks, search for, 61

I

IAB (Interactive Advertising Bureau), 214
Ideal Observer, 36
in-market testing, during ad campaign, 130
in-store triggers, 177
Inan, Hurol, *Measuring the Success of Your Website*, 43
inbound real-time customer decisioning, 102
incremental channel conversions, 170
incremental, cross-channel campaign respondents, 169
incremental sales, costs, 171
IndexTools, 36
individualized message, 4
inferred response attribution, 52, 150
InfoScan, 134
Integrated Marketing Communication: A Primer (Kitchen and De Pelsmacker), 16
Integrated Marketing Communications (IMC), **16–18**
　obstacles to adopting, 200
Interaction History behavioral flag, 109
Interactive Advertising Bureau (IAB), 214

intermediary response types
　direct marketing concept of, 107
　measuring drop-off from, 107
International Journal of Research in Marketing, 10
Internet. *See also* online ...; websites
　display advertising impact on search marketing, 211
　impact on views, 6
Internet Retailer, 13
interruption marketers, **5–6**
IP addresses, and website visitor location, 149
iPods, 6
IT department, cooperation with marketing department, 28

J

JavaScript, tags for data collection, 37
J.D. Power and Associates, 120
Jones, John Philip, 207, 208
　The Advertising Business, 205
Journal of Advertising Research, 208
Jupiter Research, 36
　studies on third-party cookies, 55
　US Online Retail Sales Forecast 2006 to 2011, 10

K

Kamarainen, Jukka, 227, 259
Kaushik, Avinash, *Web Analytics, An Hour A Day*, 20, 43, 64
Keller, Kevin Lane, 139, 231
key attributes, lift in, 137
key influencer strategies, 120
key performance indicators (KPIs), 29, **39–40, 88**
　segmentation for actionable insights, 41–42
keyword ad, paid, 33
Kitchen, Philip, *Integrated Marketing Communication: A Primer*, 16
Knowles, Jonathan, 119
Korea, 180
Krugman, Herbert, 205

L

M

web analytics, 14–15
    and ad views impact on search, 212
    choosing solution, **36**
    contribution to insights, **34–36**
    data collection methods, 26
    funnel report, 107, *108*, 155, *155*
    to measure view-throughs, **52–54**
    report on local site searches by offline
        store customers, *250*
    staff for, 29
    visitor retention chart, *157*
Web Analytics, An Hour A Day (Kaushik),
    20, 43, 64
Web Analytics Association, 38, 62
Web Analytics Demystified (Peterson), 43
web channel, for feedback, 226
Web Metrics (Sterne), 43
web pages, optimizing for usability, 34
web resources, Web Analytics Association,
    39
Web Site Measurement Hacks (Peterson), 43,
    46
web visitors, targeting based on behavior, 82
websites
    click data collection, 37
    conversion paths to TV from, 200
    crawling content for location information,
        149
    determining geo location of visitors, 149

evaluating features, 33
    local search engine, customer's
        unsuccessful use of, 257
Webtrends, 36
weighted match attribution, **220–221**
what if analysis, 220
Whiteboard campaign by UPS, 60
WHOIS, 149
Wikipedia, 21
    on logs vs. tags, 37
wish lists, sending to mobile phones, 186
word-of-mouth marketing, inferring viral
    infection, **58–61**

X

XMOS (cross media optimization studies),
    213–216
    branding effects and cost efficiency, 215
    offline ad exposure, 215
    online ad exposure and survey collection,
        214
    sample results, 215–216

Y

Yahoo!, 168
Yahoo! Search Marketing, 49